ROSALIND

ROSALIND

SHAKESPEARE'S IMMORTAL HEROINE

ANGELA THIRLWELL

PEGASUS BOOKS
NEW YORK LONDON

Rosalind

Pegasus Books Ltd
148 West 37th Street, 13th Floor
New York, NY 10018

First Pegasus Books hardcover edition March 2017

ISBN: 978-1-68177-335-3

10 9 8 7 6 5 4 3 2 1

Printed in the United States of America
Distributed by W. W. Norton & Company, Inc.

For Rosa

Whoever has the luck to be born a character
can laugh even at death.

LUIGI PIRANDELLO

Writing Rosalind's Biography

How can you write the biography of an imaginary character? A person who has never lived – and therefore can never die. I like experimenting with biography, and freedom from inevitable death scenes feels liberating. This idea came to me after writing two biographies of multiple subjects who themselves faced the deaths of those closest to them. In *William and Lucy: the other Rossettis* (2003) the persistent tuberculosis of Lucy and her eventual harrowing death had a demoralising effect on an intimate marriage. William's own decline into old age came twenty-five years later. *Into the Frame: the four loves of Ford Madox Brown* (2010) dealt with the deaths of Brown's two wives, Elisabeth and Emma, one in early youth, the other after a long slide into alcoholism. These were key factors in unlocking personality and looking at his art. Brown's own death, witnessed in deathbed accounts and portraits, had a morbid Victorian dimension. Of the two loves who survived him, Mathilde Blind died shortly afterwards. Marie Spartali Stillman looked death in the face much later with her famous grace and spirit. So many deaths, so much death. While being about life, biography is necessarily death infected.

So for a complete change, I've chosen a person who though forever young, learns important truths through her life experience. Shakespeare's Rosalind will never die. She is as humane and complex as any in Shakespeare's parade of characters. Rosalind is a true original, a one-off, as well as a universal individual, but she's never alone. She always behaves in relation to other people, as any subject of a biography does. Although Rosalind dominates the comedy of *As You Like It* and is the emotional focus of the play, we never find her alone on stage, soliloquising. Her only speech that seems at first glance to be a soliloquy is her Epilogue but even that is a dynamic two-way conversation – with her audience.

A fictional character from drama is different from a fictional character in a novel. Theatre is a communal, collaborative act. It depends on the contract with spectators to give life to a play and its characters. It is public and mutable, different with every performance and with every audience. This gives dramatic characters their special unpredictability and contradictoriness, an impression of his or her reality that is tantalisingly human. Shakespeare endows Rosalind with some of his most inventive, muscular language to transport her from stage and page into our very own world. In Pushkin's words, Shakespeare's characters are 'living beings, compacted of many passions and many vices; and circumstances unfold to the spectators their varied, many-sided personalities.' Rosalind herself is mercurial, witty, brave, loving, mischievous and cruel, in varying proportions, at different times throughout the play. In other words, she has all the contradictions of an authentic person.

I wanted to present Rosalind's life within a framework that imitates the biographies of usual real-life subjects. At the end of *As You Like It*, Rosalind delivers an Epilogue. So to balance that I've given her a Prologue, with the stage direction 'Enter Rosalind.' I then begin with Rosalind's literary antecedents, move on to her 'sisters' in other Shakespeare plays, then later to her cousin Celia, and her lover Orlando. The core of the biography explores key turning points in Rosalind's life, such as when she changes identity from female to male in 'Call me Ganymede', her love life as deep as 'the Bay of Portugal', her high-handed dealings with other people, and her powers as an impresario in the 'Epilogue.' Finally, Rosalind's 'Afterlife' asks who are her literary descendants, or 'Rosalind's daughters'?

In the 'Interval' there's time out for the audience to go to the bar, read the Programme, and in this case, engage with the only character in this book, apart from the actors I've interviewed, to have lived in our world. She is Queen Elizabeth I. Exploring the unexpected connections between Rosalind and Gloriana blurs the boundaries between what is real and what is imaginary, and reveals how each impacts on the other. While Rosalind is a creation of Shakespeare's imagination, historians, playwrights and film directors have endlessly recreated and re-cast the Tudor queen. So where does reality begin or end?

Rosalind sashays across a stage, whether in open air or indoor spaces, in large national theatres, in small offbeat venues, in every country in the world where Shakespeare is performed. So, playfully, like Rosalind herself, I charted a way through the book marked by theatrical signposts, called Acts and Scenes instead of chapters. As a trip to the theatre often includes buying a programme, I've supplied one at the back of the book which contains Family Trees, Cast List, Synopsis, famous phrases from *As You Like It* and a 'map' of the Forest of Arden.

This is an unusual biography then – of Shakespeare's immortal Rosalind. Biographers often depend on the memoirs, autobiographies, diaries and letters left by their subject. Rosalind, of course, left me none of these resources. Except her words. This gives me creative freedom like the thrill of independence that Rosalind herself finds in Arden – and beyond.

CONTENTS

Enter Rosalind

W hen I was thirteen my parents gave me Walter de la Mare's anthology of poetry called *Come Hither* 'for the young of all ages.' He made it sound such an enticing invitation. Come hither, gather round, and listen to a story in every season. That now damp-smelling book with its tattered jacket designed by Julia Trevelyan Oman is in my hands. There's a magic blue landscape glimpsed through a forest where a deep dark pool, a snow-capped mountain and a peacock spreading his tail across the book's spine still draw me in. Where the indigo foliage parts, there's a sunlit path through the woods that leads the eye ever onwards to a small comfortable palace beckoning me to *Come Hither.*

> *Under the greenwood tree*
> *Who loves to lie with me*
> *And turn [tune] his merry note*
> *Unto the sweet bird's throat,*
> *Come hither, come hither, come hither!*[1]

Dipping into that anthology was the first time I fell in love with the language of *As You Like It*. My earliest experience of Shakespeare onstage had been three years earlier when I saw Frankie Howerd at the Old Vic as a wonderfully sexplicit Bottom in *A Midsummer Night's Dream*. The cast included Judi Dench as First Fairy.

By 1962 I was a schoolgirl in scratchy net ballerina petticoats. It was a Saturday matinée at the Aldwych Theatre in London. From high up in the circle, I watched transfixed as Vanessa Redgrave, who was twenty-five, played Rosalind in the Royal Shakespeare Company's *As You Like It*. And it was, I found out, as I liked it. Redgrave's unisex Rosalind in knee-length capri pants and denim cap was literally on the cusp between boy and girl. I was on the cusp, too, between child and teenager. It was a pivotal moment for me, a growing-up moment.

At the end of the play, after Rosalind has won Orlando with her love-play of words, there is a surprise. She steps forward to deliver the only epilogue Shakespeare ever entrusted to a female character. To the men in the audience she speaks as a woman – and to the women in the audience she speaks as a man. I've been both baffled and enchanted by Rosalind's remarks about beards and sweet breaths and curtsies. Even today it's not entirely transparent to a modern audience.

You assume the epilogue signals the end of the play, the end of its magic reality. But this time it wasn't the end. Redgrave herself stepped forward, leaving the circle of actors behind her. She told the audience that on that morning, before the show, she'd married the actor-director, Tony Richardson. *As You Like It* was about the triumph of romantic love in an idealised but threatened world – and suddenly the world of the play meshed with the world of reality.

For me it was an idyllic outcome, as well as perfect theatre. Redgrave's announcement gave the play its imprimatur in the modern world, even if it was a marriage that would end in divorce within five years. Rosalind could achieve anything – and more equal love between women and men could exist.

Since that special performance Rosalind has spoken to me, become part of my DNA. During the many courses on Shakespeare I've taught, I've noticed how deeply people engage with the interaction between his women and men, whether in his poetry, tragedies, comedies, political plays or late romances. My recent Pre-Raphaelite biographies focused on the lives of Victorian artists and the women in their orbit who longed to challenge the borders of convention that separated them from men. Like women of today, Rosalind puts on the trousers and permeates those borders. Not a gender-bender, she's more of a gender-buster.

I love Rosalind because she is merry and mischievous, impetuous, empowering and brave. Her play is about love. It's for everyone and anyone who has ever loved, either unrequitedly or to joyous fulfilment. Every kind of love is in this play, from carnal to divine: not only heterosexual love, but also homoerotic love, the love between friends, between women, love across the generations, brotherly love and sibling rivalry, the love between parents and children. Rosalind faces up to love inside out and its spectre of rejection that all lovers fear.

She takes us with her on an escape mission to the Forest of Arden that culminates in healing and compassion for all. She returns the characters in her play and the audience in the theatre to the real world where we feel more enlightened than we were before. Like Prospero, the organizing magus of his play, *The Tempest*, Rosalind speaks out for Shakespeare himself, the great actor-manager of his time and ours, to remind us that love, self-knowledge and forgiveness are keys to the meaning of life.

Rosalind's voice is fizzing, funny and wise. She's an irrepressible chatterbox. She speaks a full quarter of her play, more lines than any other female character in Shakespeare, more than Juliet or Beatrice, more even than Cleopatra. That's why actors of both sexes, from Adrian Lester to Juliet Rylance, love to play her, or like Ellen Terry and Harriet Walter, regret it if they haven't.

Across the years, Rosalind collapses time. Ageless, and forever young, she is for all times, especially our own. Endlessly renewable, she promises 'eternal summer'. This is what I love about her. It's why I choose Rosalind.

ↀↀ

When I saw Sir William Beechey's portrait of Dorothy Jordan in the *First Actresses* show at the National Portrait Gallery, I thought I'd seen Rosalind face to face.[2] Mrs Jordan, as she called herself, first played Rosalind at Drury Lane in 1787 and would reprise the role over nearly three decades. She was as celebrated for comedy as Sarah Siddons was for tragedy. Mrs Siddons failed as Rosalind. Fanny Burney saw her attempt the role in 1789. In spite of her admiration for Siddons' tragic powers, Burney noted she was the wrong shape for Rosalind's *alter ego*, Ganymede, and that 'gaiety sits not naturally upon her, – it seems more like disguised gravity.[3]

Siddons hated displaying herself in male dress and managed to swathe herself in unisex concealing robes. By contrast, voluptuous Dora Jordan's Rosalind was an instant and enduring success even 'though she was neither beautiful, nor handsome, nor even pretty, nor accomplished, nor 'a lady', nor anything conventional or *comme il faut* whatsoever,' recalled Leigh Hunt, autobiographer, literary critic, and famous friend of the Romantic poets.[4] Mrs Jordan's successful career in the role over thirty years proved that Rosalind can grow older. A bewitching actress, she flouted convention and embraced cross-dressing and celebrity. For years she was the mistress of the Duke of Clarence and bore him ten FitzClarences. Later he cast her off and became King William IV.

Beechey's portrait shows Mrs Jordan's shapely legs wrapped in sunshine yellow breeches. A floating cream lace collar plunges to a deep V accentuating her tightly fitted jacket. Neither blonde nor brunette, a froth of auburn curls sets off her intelligent modern face and spills almost to her shoulders. Resting her head on an upturned hand, she reverses the usual male gaze of an artist at a woman but instead surveys her audience, and the generations to come.

This portrait is another performance by Mrs Jordan, as engaging in the gallery as her Rosalind was on-stage. There's nothing passive about being painted. This is an actress in full command of her professional persona – and she knows how to project it. If the audience found it titillating to watch her in her most famous cross-dressed role, the painter sees another version, thoughtful, composed, and even demure. It's her intellect that shines out from this picture, not her fabled physical charms, implied by the artist's play of subtle diagonals across her body.

Eighteenth century playgoers found her entrancing as Ganymede. They gasped at the insouciance of her role-play as a man and her erotic combination of bosom and breeches. For 'the attraction, after all, is purely feminine, and the display of female, not male perfections.'[5] I felt Mrs Jordan's Ganymede could speak out at any moment from Beechey's golden canvas. And apparently when she did at Drury Lane, her voice was harmony itself, with 'certain little breaks and indescribable tones.'[6] Victoria's first Prime Minister, Lord Melbourne, reminisced to the Queen about his fond memories of Mrs Jordan. 'She was beautifully formed', Lord M. said, 'and she used to be fond of acting in men's clothes'. Her Rosalind, in *As You Like It*, 'a lovely play…the prettiest play in the world; and her acting in that was quite beautiful.' He added, 'She had a beautiful enunciation.'[7] Mrs Jordan proved you don't have to be tall to play Rosalind. Though short she was far from insignificant and her figure had 'a certain roundness and embonpoint [plumpness] which is very graceful.'[8] Judi Dench has never played Rosalind but she has been a majestic and moving Cleopatra. Height can be acted. And acting is metamorphosis.

So if Rosalind can be chestnut and little like Mrs Jordan, can she also be tall, male and black? Director Declan Donnellan thought so when he cast Adrian Lester in his all-male Cheek by Jowl production at the Lyric Hammersmith in 1991. 'I am employed to play people,' said Lester in a radio interview, 'I can play Rosalind!'[9] From the opening scenes his rich soft voice and striking appearance in a fluid white gown made an unexpected but entirely new Rosalind, a Rosalind for modern, multi-cultural times. But, as he told me, it was a hugely daunting task. 'There were two reasons I found the prospect of playing the role terrifying: how to come to a reasonably believable portrayal of Rosalind's enormous wit and complicated nature, the second was my fear at having to tackle one of the best classical roles ever written for a woman and act the part in front of a modern audience full of women.' But he made the breakthrough. 'I believe it took me two and a half weeks to get to the point that a female actor would've reached on day two. You see, I began rehearsals trying to play woman. It was the wrong thing to do. I spent the first couple of weeks trying to play a generalised sense of womanhood where gender is a major component of character, when I should have been thinking only about playing Rosalind. She is so much more than her gender or her sexuality. Once I realised that, I think I found the way to unlock her personality.'[10]

The extraordinary thing about Adrian Lester's Rosalind, wrote Jonathan Bate, was that 'one simply gave up trying to work out in one's mind whether one thought he was a woman playing a man playing a woman or a man playing a woman playing a man playing a woman.'[11] Adrian Lester himself observed that paradoxically 'she's *more* Rosalind when she's Ganymede! And yet she has to keep control of her sexual passions. It's a very complex situation for Rosalind.'[12] It must have been a very complex situation for Rosalind's original audience, too. Impersonated by a boy actor, first in female court dress, then in androgynous disguise as Ganymede, did they even see her as a woman at all? Or through transvestite Rosalind, was Shakespeare able to show the ferocity of love which affects both sexes? In a sense, we are cross-gendered by the intensity of love.

Like Virginia Woolf's hero-heroine Orlando, whose fantastic adventures span four centuries and both sexes, Shakespeare's Rosalind has the capacity to experience love across the sexual spectrum. She can encompass the globe, shimmy between genders, look like any human being, be black or white, tall or short, blonde, brunette – or auburn. In Orlando's own words,

> Thus Rosalind of many parts
> By heavenly synod was devised,
> Of many faces, eyes, and hearts...[13]

So can we ever know what Shakespeare's Rosalind looks like or must we just imagine her? Outwardly, she's a dextrous shape-shifter. At the beginning of the play she can appear in a whole range of female costumes from Tudor farthingale to modern designer frock, until in Act 2 she makes her famous costume change into doublet and hose, chinos or jeans. But her face is a blank for us to fill in. This means that Rosalind can look like whatever we, as members of the audience, or in our minds' eyes, want her to look like. Shakespeare knew that if you describe beauty, it dissolves. The latest or best actor who plays Rosalind will embody her mesmeric attractiveness. Her looks are as protean, as fluid as a chameleon's. That's the resonance of her impact, not influenced by local fashion or the times. In cosmic but entirely non-physical terms, Orlando simply calls her 'heavenly Rosalind'. Her impact on him is so overwhelming that he can only equate her with epic women from legend and classical history. In his romantic daze she's composed of the most superlative features of Helen, Cleopatra, Atalanta and Lucretia. These women were celebrated for entirely conflicting qualities: extreme physical beauty; sexual and political majesty; fleetness of foot; and abused marital chastity. None of these hyperbolic lookalikes actually tells us what Rosalind looks like.

The only physical detail Rosalind herself mentions while she's still in skirts is that she's 'more than common tall.' Does that mean she's extremely tall, or simply above average height? And what was 'more than common tall' for a woman in 1599? In his *Time Traveller's Guide to Elizabethan England*, Ian Mortimer gives average heights in the late sixteenth century as 5ft 7in or 172 cm for men, and 5ft 2¼in or 158 cm for women.[14] Orlando doesn't seem to think Rosalind is remarkably tall. Instead he tells Jaques that she's literally and amorously, 'just as high as my heart,'[15] which is probably in line with Ian Mortimer's figures.

Once Rosalind is in Arden, in boy's clothes, in role as Ganymede, some details of her physical presence are specified though not by her lover Orlando. The shepherdess Phebe considers Ganymede 'a pretty youth…The best thing in him/Is his complexion.' She agrees with Orlando's estimate, 'He is not very tall,' though she adds,

> …yet for his years he's tall;
> His leg is but so-so, and yet 'tis well.
> There was a pretty redness in his lip,
> A little riper and more lusty red
> Than that mixed in his cheek. 'Twas just the difference
> Betwixt the constant red and mingled damask.[16]

Phebe is riveted by Ganymede's outside, his height, his lips, his confusing feminine bloom, as later she is smitten by his 'bright eyne' too.[17] By contrast, Ganymede mocks Phebe's physical attributes: her 'inky brows,' her 'black silk hair,' her 'bugle eyeballs,' even her 'cheek of cream.'[18] Phebe's complexion is pasty beside Ganymede's own 'mingled damask.'

လ

As You Like It was entered on the Stationers' Register in London on 4 August 1600 and was probably written in 1599 or early 1600. So it may have been one of the opening productions – or even the very first show – at Shakespeare's new Globe Theatre. On the other hand, his company, the Chamberlain's Men, may have premiered *As You Like It* at the Curtain Theatre in Shoreditch, north of the Thames, before they crossed the river and erected the Globe on London's Bankside.[19] However, after these speculative but unconfirmed first performances and a shadowy sighting of the play in the presence of King James I at Wilton House in December 1603, its performance record mysteriously goes dark throughout the whole seventeenth century. It didn't even surface when the theatres were re-opened and actresses allowed on-stage after the Restoration of the monarchy in 1660.

When Charles Johnson first revived *As You Like It* under a new title of *Love in a Forest* in 1723, it was a travesty of Shakespeare's text, excising Jaques and Touchstone as well as the rustic shepherd classes, and stealing *Pyramus and Thisbe* from *A Midsummer Night's Dream*. The play was more accurately restored at Drury Lane in 1740 when Hannah Pritchard's Rosalind in her daring breeches caused a sensation. Thomas Arne's settings for the songs became an essential factor in *As You Like It*'s fresh and continuing popularity.

Arne not only composed settings for 'Under the Greenwood Tree' but also for 'Blow, blow thou winter wind' whose uncompromising view of human nature and man's ingratitude challenged the pastoral ideal implicit in the earlier lyric. Stoical in the face of many emotional and professional losses, Ford Madox Brown, the Victorian painter, chose 'Blow, blow thou winter wind' as his favourite song. Brown was an avid theatregoer and in 1848 he saw Laura Addison cross-dressing as Viola in *Twelfth Night* at Sadler's Wells. I like to think he may have seen one of the great Rosalinds of the Victorian age, ultra-feminine Helen Faucit, androgynous Ellen Tree, or mannish American, Charlotte Cushman.

In 1872 Thomas Hardy borrowed one of *As You Like It*'s songs for the title of his pastoral tale, *Under the Greenwood Tree*, his only work with a happy ending. J.M. Barrie called it Hardy's 'most perfect' novel. I suspect it appealed to Barrie because its exploration of time passing in an already out-dated rural world paradoxically ensured its very timelessness.

If one of the chief attractions of playing Rosalind is the chance to defeat time and be young forever, I wonder if J.M. Barrie knew about Ellen Terry's longing to play Rosalind, one of the few great Shakespearean roles for women she had missed? Because in 1912 when she was sixty-five and he was fifty-two and both undeniably middle-aged, he wrote *Rosalind* a one-act play about a successful but mature actress called Beatrice Page who has been twenty-nine forever.[20] Barrie's choice of the name Beatrice suggests his homage to Ellen Terry's stage triumph as the heroine of *Much Ado About Nothing*, as well as underlining Beatrice's sisterliness with Shakespeare's Rosalind.

Ninety years later Barrie's play *Rosalind* was broadcast on radio with Judi Dench as Beatrice Page. *'Her voice breaks; no voice can break so naturally as BEATRICE's'*, says Barrie's stage direction, which although he couldn't possibly have known it, is a perfect description of Judi Dench's distinctive vocal register.

In *Rosalind* Barrie unravelled some of his favourite themes: the fantasy nature of acting and the treachery of ageing. Beatrice Page, 'forty and a bittock', has retired to a seaside resort to relax in unstructured clothes and try on middle age for size. She rather likes middle age. So she's disconcerted when a young admirer arrives unannounced. Charles Roche discovers his adored 'Rosalind' is in fact a faded palimpsest of his effervescent stage heroine. The photograph on the mantelpiece that Mrs Page refers to as her daughter, is of herself, made-up and dazzling in her finest role – as Rosalind.

It was the same in 1912 as it is now. There are no parts for middle-aged actresses. 'There is nothing for them,' Mrs Page laments, 'between the ages of twenty-nine and sixty…and so, my dear Charles, we have succeeded in keeping middle-age for women off the stage.' But even Father Time occasionally relents. 'The enchanting baggage, I'll give her another year.' 'When you come to write my epitaph, Charles, let it be in these delicious words, 'She had a long twenty-nine.'

Toy-boy Charles is still enchanted by the memory of Mrs Page's Rosalind. 'My dear, I want to be your Orlando to the end.' He plans to whisk her off the stage and accompany her, not into the sunset, but into 'the delicious twilight of middle-age.'

An actress to the bone, Mrs Page is less fired by Charles's passion than by an unexpected call from a London manager to reprise her Rosalind. A subtle but striking change instantly comes over her. In a thrilling reverse of Wilde's *Dorian Gray*, Barrie's Beatrice Page actually grows young by being Rosalind. Rising from her sofa she is already packing her theatrical carpetbag, a double for the one Ellen Terry always took to rehearsals and dropped as a diversion when she forgot her lines in older age.[21] Dressed in *'bravery hot from Mdme. Make-the-woman, tackle by Monsieur, a Rosalind cap jaunty on her head,'* she becomes again *'a tall, slim young creature.'* 'Good God! Is there nothing real in life?' asks Charles as Mrs Page steps out of the shell of middle age. She replies: 'Heaps of things. Rosalind is real, and I am Rosalind; and the forest of Arden is real, and I am going back to it…Everything is real except middle-age…I am Rosalind and I am going back…The stage is waiting, the audience is calling, and up goes the curtain.'

Although Charles begs his 'darling girl' to marry him, she can't and she won't. However, she will let him accompany her on the train back to London:

MRS. PAGE	Middle-age is left behind
CHARLES	For ever young is Rosalind.

The play ends as the train whistle blows and Beatrice Page prepares for a new life. She banishes middle age with the technical skills of her acting and embodies again the eternal summer of being Rosalind.

Like Barrie's Peter Pan, Rosalind can never grow old. But unlike Peter Pan who is embalmed in childhood, Rosalind reaches full and free emotional maturity. She educates her lover Orlando in the university of love to become her rightful equal. True, Rosalind will never age like Wendy Darling who grows up to look ancient in Peter's appalled view. Wendy has to be left behind while he goes on playing, stuck as boy eternal flying back to the Neverland. Rosalind, on the other hand, finally quits the forest of Arden to enter marriage, enlightened and on her own terms, as she's negotiated with Orlando. With her experience of truth telling in the forest, she will take her place in adult society. Her personal life will inform the political. For Rosalind, marriage is not just an end, but a beginning. We can be sure the conversation will continue.

In his own life Barrie married an actress, Mary Ansell, who always dissembled her real age by about a decade and eventually ran off with a much younger lover. Barrie wrote *Rosalind* soon after his marriage fell apart. He tended to fall in love with his leading ladies, although his relationships with women were probably stalled in childhood where he felt most at home, with Peter Pan and the Lost Boys. They had banished growing up. It wasn't altogether surprising that in his eighties Barrie was once more smitten with youth. He fell in love with Elisabeth Bergner who starred as Rosalind – with Laurence Olivier as

Orlando – in her husband Paul Czinner's 1936 film of *As You Like It*. Barrie's long involvement with immortal Rosalind was complete when he suggested the treatment for the film and became adviser to the director.

The movie was technically radical as it was the first full-length film of a Shakespeare play to incorporate sound. But it was also politically radical, as its director and star were among the first to leave Nazi Germany, before even Brecht. They were political campaigners who explored emigration, exile and personal freedom through Shakespeare's play. As they knew, in those years just before the Second World War, Rosalind has the capacity to resonate across time. She is the first fictional character in comedy to animate the emotional depth and complexity of a real woman. She can re-invent herself for every generation. Rosalind claims agency and authority for herself, and in so doing, for us all, men and women equally. Her potential continues to evolve long after the play is over.

ACT ONE

In the Green Room – Rosalind's Ancestors

Ancestors of Shakespeare's Rosalind, though sporting different names, were adventuring far back in classical mythology. Homer's Athene in *The Odyssey* often materialised as a man to rescue her favourite heroes from disaster. This daughter of Zeus, born fully formed from his forehead, apparently bypassed any female involvement in her creation. Champion of wit, reason and purity, Athene exhibits an androgynous, divine intelligence. Her gleaming eyes behind an austere helmet project a masculine beauty down the ages. Like Rosalind, she bears arms, a spear and a cuirass. While protecting Ulysses she crosses borders, nimbly morphs into an old man or a sea-eagle, but also transforms herself into a homoerotic young shepherd lad, 'as are the sons of princes.' This is an early palimpsest of Rosalind, a duke's daughter, who disguises herself as Ganymede, a shepherd boy in the Forest of Arden. Like Athene, the immortal Greek goddess of wisdom and war, Rosalind the character can never die. But unlike Athene, she derives her special authority not through wisdom about war, but through her wit and wisdom about love.

Any Elizabethan with a similar education to Shakespeare's at Stratford Grammar School would have Ovid, the Roman poet, firmly in his cultural landscape. The *Metamorphoses* tells many stories of sensuous transformations like Rosalind's to Ganymede. One of the most touching is the myth of Iphis and Ianthe.[1] Iphis is a girl, brought up as a boy, who falls in love with Ianthe, a girl. To untangle these complications, Hymen the god of marriage allows Iphis to transition to a male in order to marry Ianthe and he presides over their wedding. At the end of *As You Like It*, when in reverse of Iphis, Ganymede appears dressed as Rosalind, Hymen arrives again to celebrate a wedding contract of true love between her and Orlando.

The same Elizabethans brought up on Ovid would have recognised the interchangeable names for Jove, Jupiter or Zeus, supreme ruler of the classical gods. They would also have recognised the gods' erotic bisexuality. Jove was once fired with lust for a beautiful mortal youth, Ganymede, whom he saw tending his sheep on the slopes of Mount Ida. Turning himself into an eagle, Jove swept down and bore the lad off to his home on Mount Olympus.[2] As official boy lover to the deity, Ganymede became the legendary model of erotic ambivalence. Jove appointed him cupbearer to the gods and granted him eternal youth. So Ganymede crossed the border from mortal to immortal, and in a different way, Shakespeare bestowed the gift of immortality on Rosalind. Ganymede is the natural male alias for Rosalind to choose when she flees the court and death sentence pronounced by her wicked uncle, usurper of her father's dukedom. No stage name could have been more apposite for a girl who gets into boy's clothes, and takes on a sheep farm. Ganymede is both Rosalind's ancestor and her *alter ego*, and is also the precursor of Oberon's Puck or Prospero's Ariel. Like Puck and Ariel, Ganymede on an eagle's back can fly to Olympus swifter than wind or thought. In role as Ganymede, Rosalind may not fly physically but she certainly has legs as she strides into Arden. 'Ganymede' with its ambivalent sexual connotations entered the English language in the 1590s. The name would have sounded distinctly edgy to Rosalind's first audience in 1599.

As she first steps into Arden, no longer a Princess but transformed into Ganymede, Jove's own page, Rosalind invokes his lover, Jupiter, sovereign of the gods. 'O Jupiter, how weary are my spirits!'[3] When she overhears Silvius proclaiming his hopeless love for Phebe, Rosalind summons Jove again,

> Jove, Jove, this shepherd's passion
> Is much upon my fashion![4]

And when cousin Celia reports she's improbably found Orlando 'under a tree, like a dropped acorn,' Rosalind blesses Ganymede's protector for the third time, 'It may well be called Jove's tree when it drops forth such fruit.'[5]

Rosalind's classical ancestors cross into native territory with the shadowy source behind the source for Shakespeare's *As You Like It*. The medieval men-only *Tale of Gamelyn* is the forerunner of Thomas Lodge's *Rosalynde* of 1590, and thence of *As You Like It* in

1599. Its hero Gamelyn is an early diagram for Lodge's Rosader and Shakespeare's Orlando. Written in a Middle English dialect from the North East Midlands, this anonymous romance invites us in to 'Litheth and listeneth and herkeneth aright' – that is to list and listen and harken closely.[6] It runs to almost 900 lines of mesmeric rhyming couplets, dating from 1340-70, and plays off violence and loyalty, town and country, courts and wild woods, knights and outlaws. The poem is often associated with Chaucer because it was found among his papers, although he's unlikely to have written it.

Gamelyn's father, Sir Iohan of Boundys (Sir John of the Borders) makes the mistake of dividing his property between his three children, violating the long established feudal custom of primogeniture. Over two centuries later, Lodge re-names the father figure, Sir John of Bordeaux, to emphasise the French milieu of his work *Rosalynde* which Shakespeare picks up in *As You Like It,* then re-christening Orlando's father as francophone Sir Rowland de Boys. Gamelyn, like Orlando, is the youngest of three brothers. His elder brother, like Orlando's brother Oliver, plans to cheat Gamelyn out of his father's legacy, treats him violently and plots his death. We first meet Gamelyn, as we later meet Orlando, in his brother's 'yerde', a garden or orchard with echoes of Genesis. As much later in *As You Like It*, the medieval poem includes a wrestling match, a professional fighter hired to kill the young challenger, a poor old man who has already lost two sons to the champion (upped to three in Shakespeare), a victory for the amateur contender against all the odds, and our hero, strong as a 'wylde lyoun,' rejected for his success. As revenge Gamelyn beats up the clerics who fail to defend him, an antipathy reiterated in the whiff of anti-clericalism in *As You Like It*. Shakespeare makes a mockery of the forest priest, Sir Oliver Mar-text, and brings in mythological Hymen rather than a Christian minister to perform the final weddings.

'Gamelyn stood anon allone frend had he noon,' except for one loyal supporter, hoar-headed Adam Spencer, steward of the buttery, who rescues the boy from hunger and imprisonment. Old Adam doesn't transfer into Lodge's *Rosalynde* but is restored as a poignant character by Shakespeare. When the unlikely companions flee to the 'wilde wode' it's Gamelyn's turn to cheer Adam, just as Orlando cherishes his old friend in *As You Like It*. "'Adam,' seide Gamelyn, "dismay thee right nought.'" They could be in Robin Hood's own Sherwood Forest, or in Lodge's Forest of Ardennes, or with Rosalind and Orlando in the Forest of Arden. There are outlaws in this forest who live like 'the old Robin Hood of England,' as does Duke Senior with his exiled court in *As You Like It*. They are as courteous to Gamelyn and Adam as Duke Senior is to Orlando and his Adam. But there is no love interest for Gamelyn, no Rosalind for him to win. Instead, in half a line at the end of his adventures, Gamelyn is briskly awarded 'a wif good and faire'. Yet much of the groundwork for *As You Like It* is already signposted in this folkloric poem that may stretch back in time and oral tradition even earlier than *The Tale of Gamelyn* itself.

The first contemporary Rosalind to foreshadow Shakespeare's heroine is Spenser's Rosalind. She features in his virtuoso debut work, *The Shepheardes Calender*, published in 1579, just twenty years ahead of *As You Like It*. The name Rosalind with its alternatives, such as Rosalyne, Rosalynde and Rosalinda, arrived in England after the Conquest in 1066. It remained unusual in England until the late Elizabethan age. Then Spenser, Lodge and Shakespeare chose it for their heroines and made it as hip as celebrity names today.

Spenser's hero is Colin Clout, a shepherd with real sheep to be tended. Through twelve pastoral scenes or eclogues, each titled after a month of the year, and loosely modelled on Virgil's *Eclogues*, Colin continues to love Rosalind. She has a devastating effect on him, as Shakespeare's Rosalind has on Orlando. But there are significant differences – for Colin's Rosalind fails to return his adoration. Colin and Rosalind are more like Silvius and Phebe in *As You Like It* than they are like Rosalind and Orlando. Moreover, although Spenser's Rosalind is a potent presence and exerts a lifelong effect on Colin, unlike Shakespeare's dynamic voluble heroine, she never utters a word. Spenser's Rosalind is 'a Gentle woman of no meane house,' fundamentally a golden haired 'Country lasse' firmly planted in her sylvan setting. Although Shakespeare's Rosalind operates in Arden which frees and empowers her, she's not native and endued unto the place, and will eventually leave it. Rosalind's impact on Colin is palpable up to the final Eclogue of *December* which brings the sequence to its cyclical and mortal conclusion, reminiscent of the arc of Jaques' Seven Ages of Man speech in *As You Like It*. Colin concludes his poem by sending his shepherd's calendar of love out into the world with a *'free passeporte'* enjoining his readers, *'The better please, the worse despise, I aske no more.'* At the end of her play, Shakespeare's Rosalind reiterates Colin's message, asking us 'to like as much of this play as please you.'

Thomas Lodge may have been inspired by the huge success of Spenser's Rosalind to choose the name for the female lead of his prose fiction, *Rosalynde*, in 1590 just over ten years later. Lodge's romance is the direct source whose form and plot Shakespeare adapted for *As You Like It* in 1599. Connections between the two are intricate and fascinating. By the time Shakespeare gutted Lodge's tale it had become so popular that it had already gone through four editions. While sailing on Captain Clarke's ship to the islands of Terceira and the Canaries, Lodge amused himself by writing *Rosalynde*, a Tudor rom-com. The story is precisely located in France and culminates in Paris, unlike Shakespeare's play which toys with French references and a semi-French ambience. The Forest of Arden is first tramped through in Lodge, then seamlessly absorbed by Shakespeare who enjoyed its link with Mary Arden, his mother and first storyteller. *Rosalynde's* pastoral roots lay far back in writers from Theocritus to Virgil, and in Middle English metrical romances, but Lodge's modernity anticipated the new genre of the novel, not invented until the eighteenth century.

Somewhere deep in cultural consciousness and Lodge's memory during his long hours on the high seas lay the medieval *Tale of Gamelyn*. He took Gamelyn's basic story but he did something radical. He added women. Lodge's new character, Rosalynde who dresses as a boy, Ganymede, is the model for Shakespeare's Rosalind who does the same. Lodge's Alinda becomes Shakespeare's Celia, and they both take the name Aliena when dressing-down in the forest. Lodge invented the new characters of Phoebe and Montanus who become Shakespeare's Phebe and Silvius; Coridon who becomes Corin; Gerismond who becomes Duke Senior, and Torismond who becomes Duke Frederick. Shakespeare in his turn invented the indelible new characters of Jaques, Touchstone, Audrey and his own namesake, William for *As You Like It*.

To stand on the shoulders of previous texts was not an act of plagiarism but accepted sixteenth century practice of adaptations with which we're equally familiar today. A book is re-invented, adapted, expanded, cut, or changed to translate into a feature film or TV series. In a similar way, *Gamelyn*, a long poem, is adapted for *Rosalynde*, a neo-novel, which in turn generates a play, *As You Like It*. Shakespeare leans on the inciting plot of Lodge's *Rosalynde*,[7] which previously has lent on *Gamelyn*.

GAMELYN	LODGE	SHAKESPEARE
Sir Iohan of Boundys	Sir John of Bordeaux	Sir Rowland de Boys
Johan, 1st son	Saladyne, 1st son	Oliver, 1st son
Otho, 2nd son	Fernandyne, 2nd son	Jacques, 2nd son
Gamelyn, 3rd son	Rosader, 3rd son	Orlando, 3rd son
	Norman champion	Charles the wrestler
	Rosalynde/Ganymede	Rosalind/Ganymede
	Alinda/Aliena	Celia/Aliena
	Torismond, King of France	Duke Frederick, usurper
	Gerismond, 'old banished king'	Duke Senior, usurped
		Jacques (7 ages) 2nd character in the play named Jacques
Adam Spencer	Adam Spencer	Old Adam
	Coridon	Corin
		Touchstone
		Audrey
	Montanus	Sylvius
	Phoebe	Phebe

Like Gamelyn's father, Lodge's Sir John of Bordeaux also breeds trouble between his three sons in a King Lear-like scenario by which he leaves their inheritance uneasily distributed. Archetypal fraternal hatred between sets of brothers incites the potentially tragic opening of *As You Like It*. We get the whole of this lengthy back-story in Lodge but Shakespeare decides to kill off the father figure, Sir Rowland de Boys, before the play even begins. Blanche MacIntyre's production at Shakespeare's Globe in 2015 made this strikingly visual by staging an elaborate state funeral before the cast spoke a single word. Shakespeare adapts Lodge and cuts straight to the dramatic opening scene where the two brothers Orlando and Oliver are already fighting over rights.

In Lodge's romance, Sir John advises his three sons, including his youngest and favourite, Rosader, to let 'time be the touchstone of friendship' – a spark for Shakespeare's invented Fool, Touchstone – but he also warns them to beware of love. For 'Venus is a wanton, and though her laws pretend liberty, yet there is nothing but loss and glistering misery…a woman's eye…snareth unto death. Trust not their fawning favours, for their loves are like the breath of a man upon steel, which no sooner lighteth on but it leapeth off.' In Sir John's misogynist view, ideal qualities in a woman are 'to be chaste, obedient, and silent.' Obedience and silence are exactly those constraints of female behaviour that Shakespeare's Rosalind will smash, though she might fulfil the rest of Sir John's instructions to his sons, to 'choose thy wife by wit and living well.'[8]

Lodge's Rosalynde is the loveliest of all the court ladies, for in her golden hair 'it seemed love had laid herself in ambush.'[9] Her lover, Rosader, just like Shakespeare's Orlando later, is overcome by her beauty. He 'fed his looks on the favour of Rosalynde's face; which she perceiving blushed, which was such a doubling of her beauteous excellence, that the bashful red of Aurora at the sight of unacquainted Phaeton, was not half so glorious.'[10]

Before Rosader steps into the ring for the challenge match, he's already exchanging looks with Rosalynde and even during the bout they can't take their eyes off each other. After Rosader kills the hefty champion, all ladies dart their admiring, amorous glances at him, 'especially Rosalynde, whom the beauty and valour of Rosader had already touched: but she accounted love a toy, and fancy a momentary passion, that as it was taken in with a gaze, might be shaken off with a wink, and therefore feared not to dally in the flame.'[11] This is the first semaphore of Rosalind's freethinking on the subject of love in *As You Like It*. Lodge gives his readers no stock heroine but an independent minded woman. She removes the jewel from round her neck and sends a page to deliver it forthwith to Rosader. Shakespeare omits the pageboy and makes his Rosalind award the necklace direct to Orlando. Rosader has no jewel to offer Rosalynde in return. Instead he writes her a sonnet. Unlike Shakespeare who is deliberately vague about Rosalind's physical attributes, Lodge goes into microscopic and embarrassing detail itemising Rosalynde's body parts. Her shape sends Rosader into rhapsody.

> Two suns at once from one fair heaven there shined,
>> Ten branches from two boughs, tipped all with roses,
> Pure locks more golden than is gold refined,
>> Two pearled rows that nature's pride encloses;
> Two mounts fair marble-white, down-soft and dainty,
>> A snow-dyed orb, where love increased by pleasure
> Full woeful makes my heart, and body fainty:
>> Her fair, my woe, exceeds all thought and measure.[12]

This earlier model Rosalynde is undoubtedly a blonde with 'two pearled rows' of Hollywood teeth. But Shakespeare's Rosalind has hair of no colour or any colour we please, simply As We Like It. We see nothing of her teeth but we hear plenty from her tongue.

Rosalynde feels herself 'grow passing passionate' for Rosader. She lingers over his 'rare qualities' and 'the comeliness of his person, the honour of his parents, and the virtues that, excelling both, made him so gracious in the eyes of every one'. Thinking of her own difficult situation she rails against Fortune, the trigger perhaps for Rosalind and Celia's debate about Fortune and Nature in *As You Like It*. Rosalynde examines the idea of Love in an early stream of consciousness internal monologue. 'Tush, desire hath no respect of persons: Cupid is blind and shooteth at random…Thou speakest, poor Rosalynde, by experience; for being every way distressed, surcharged with cares…yet…love hath lodged in thy heart the perfection of young Rosader, a man every way absolute as well for his inward life, as for his outward lineaments, able to content the eye with beauty, and the ear with the report of his virtue.'[13]

This Rosalynde who knows 'lovers cannot live by looks,' is the technical rehearsal for Shakespeare's rational Rosalind who never voices her inner thoughts alone on stage. She's always in dynamic relationships with other people and therefore has neither time, space, nor taste for private monologues. Lodge's Rosalynde is also cool as well as passionate. 'Be not over rash,' she tells herself, 'choose not a fair face with an empty purse.' But in her eyes, 'Rosader is both beautiful and virtuous.'[14] She sings lyrical madrigals and accompanies herself on the lute – unlike Shakespeare's Rosalind who leaves all the music and singing to others. As she expresses herself mostly in prose it might seem out of character for her to burst into song. Perhaps the boy actor who first played Shakespeare's Rosalind wasn't musical and so the songs were given to other members of the company.

Shakespeare poaches most of his plot from Lodge's story: toxic jealousy in two sets of siblings; a fight between two brothers; a lawful ruler usurped by his younger brother; the contrasting female bond of more than sisterly love between two cousins; a deposed leader living in exile in the Forest of Arden like Robin Hood; the usurper ruling illegally in his place; an elder brother bribing a wrestling champion to finish off his younger brother; the champion felling two or three contestants before being beaten or killed by the hero-challenger; and, most significantly, the exchange of glances at the wrestling match between the dispossessed son and the banished duke's daughter.

In Lodge's romance, Torismond who has deposed Rosalynde's father Gerismond, arrives with a posse of French nobles to turn his niece out of court. He's nervous that one of his peers will marry Rosalynde and de-throne him. So he accuses her of treason as Duke Frederick accuses Rosalind in *As You Like It*. Torismond's daughter, Alinda, who loves Rosalynde 'more than herself,' pleads for her cousin, asserting 'we have two bodies and one soul,' a bond echoed by Celia in Shakespeare's play who declares herself 'coupled and inseparable' with Rosalind. Alinda declares she will share Rosalynde's exile. Enraged, Torismond banishes both women, even his own child. Duke Frederick in *As You Like It* doesn't pronounce the same sentence on his daughter Celia but he might as well have done. He could have guessed it would be Celia's choice to share exile with Rosalind. Just as Celia later feels a passionate attachment for Rosalind, Alinda's love for Rosalynde has a lyric, sapphic quality. She accompanies Rosalynde into banishment, vowing 'I will ever be thy Alinda, and thou shalt ever rest to me Rosalynde; so shall the world canonize our friendship, and speak of Rosalynde and Alinda, as they did of Pylades and Orestes.'*

It's Rosalynde's idea not Alinda's, as it is Celia's in *As You Like It*, to flee the court in disguise. 'Of a tall stature,' like Shakespeare's Rosalind,

---

* In Greek mythology, famous for their intense, homoerotic friendship.

Lodge's heroine decides to cross-dress to face the dangers of banishment. Rosalynde will buy a suit, and belt on a rapier. According to Neil MacGregor in *Shakespeare's Restless World*, broadcast on BBC Radio 4 in 2012, a rapier was a heavy sword, not the light darting weapon we now imagine. Lodge's women set off to the Forest of Arden, disguised as Ganymede and Aliena, the same *noms de guerre* that Shakespeare keeps for Rosalind and Celia as refugees in Arden.

Arriving in the forest, Lodge's Ganymede and Aliena buy a farm and a flock of sheep and go about their shepherding duties 'in more pleasant content of mind than ever they were in the court of Torismond.' In their pastoral hideaway they find love odes written by shepherd Montanus (Shakespeare's Silvius in *As You Like It*) in praise of his Phoebe. Ganymede enquires of Montanus, 'Can shepherds love?' raising a class issue of the period.[15] Noble Rosader is in the forest, too, sighing for love and carving love poems to Rosalynde on the bark of trees, as hackneyed as any of Berowne's, Benedick's, Hamlet's or Orlando's efforts. In her boy's disguise Rosalynde feels free to mock Rosader even though in her heart she's as much in love as he is.[16]

Rosalynde tells her readers in a self-reflective interior soliloquy that she's now 'so full of passions' that she can only sleep brokenly at night. The next morning the cousins go in search of Rosader who has also slept fitfully. Ganymede tells him, ''Tis good, forester, to love, but not to overlove…lest thou fold thyself in an endless labyrinth.' S/he teases Rosader by inviting him to transfer his affections to Aliena, a plot detail that Shakespeare omits. Ganymede teases Rosader for his poetic labours which are all words and no substance. They are conventional enough love poems but they're not quite as ridiculous as Orlando's in *As You Like It*. Shakespeare takes Lodge's basic idea of the lovesick lover writing slushy poetry and ramps it up. He also renovates some of Lodge's tropes. Rosader's awkward thought, 'The sun and our stomachs are shepherds' dials,' becomes Orlando's unforgettable observation, 'There's no clock in the forest.'[17] Lodge dreamed up the absurdly seductive game in which Rosader was to address his love talk by proxy to Ganymede, in the 'absence' of Rosalynde. Shakespeare took over this giddy device as the trigger for the dazzling courtship by conversation between Rosalind and Orlando.

The wooing between Ganymede and Rosader proceeds as a duet of poems, an eclogue, a parrying exchange of pretty verses and lines of poetry – which Shakespeare recasts into the thrilling inventive prose Rosalind uses to educate Orlando about how to love. Aliena performs a mock-marriage between Rosader and Ganymede, the same scene that Shakespeare reprises. But in Lodge, interestingly, Aliena says *she* must carry away the bride afterwards.[18]

For Orlando's story, Shakespeare lifts from Lodge Rosader's rescue of his brother Saladyne, his fight with the lion (a lioness, perhaps alluding to female power in *As You Like It*), and subsequent wounding, leaving Ganymede to lament Rosader's delay in keeping their date. 'For Love measures every minute, and thinks hours to be days, and days to be months, till they feed their eyes with the sight of the desired object.' Shakespeare's Rosalind riffs on this with a whirl of speed in *As You Like It*. 'He that will divide a minute into a thousand parts, and break but a part of the thousand part of a minute in the affairs of love, it may be said of him that Cupid hath clapped him o' th' shoulder, but I'll warrant him heart-whole.'[19]

Shakespeare's variation on the theme of love in his Silvius-Phebe-Ganymede trio is pinched blatantly from Lodge's Montanus-Phoebe-Ganymede threesome, except that Lodge's Phoebe is incredibly beautiful, not mocked by Ganymede, nor told to 'Sell when you can.' Lodge's Phoebe doesn't understand what love means until she falls for Ganymede. Rejected by him, she becomes dangerously ill. Shakespeare treats the boy-girl-girl triangle with a much lighter and more farcical touch than Lodge. Towards the end of the Elizabethan age, perhaps it was safer to read about love between women as you turned the pages of Lodge's novel in your study, than it was for Shakespeare to air the subject openly on the public stage.

At the denouement of *Rosalynde*, exiled Gerismond 'noting well the physnomy of Ganymede, began by his favours to call to mind the face of his Rosalynde' which Shakespeare echoes in Duke Senior's rueful recognition of his daughter Rosalind. These lines always get a laugh,

I do remember in this shepherd boy
Some lively touches of my daughter's favour.[20]

Ganymede/Rosalynde finally dresses as a woman for her wedding and Gerismond recovers his crown in a battle with Torismond. Shakespeare replaces Lodge's violent denouement with Duke Senior's forgiveness and Duke Frederick's repentance, in an ending more like those of his Late Plays which celebrate the healing concept of 'pardon's the world to all.'

Lodge's Rosalynde is gentler and more loyal to Alinda than Shakespeare's Rosalind is to her cousin Celia. Rosalynde deals more gently with Phoebe than Rosalind does with Phebe. Lodge's heroine is more feminine, even in her boy's disguise, than Shakespeare's arousing, erotic Rosalind who discovers an authentic element of her personality in the liberating androgyny of being Ganymede. Both Rosalynde and Rosalind provide forest classes in love for their boyfriends during which they both show determination and self-assertion, both relish their powers of exhilarating language, but ultimately Shakespeare's scintillating Rosalind smashes more glass ceilings and is the wittier and the wiser.

The lineage from Lodge is unmistakeable. But Shakespeare is the great transformer. Lodge's Preface to *Rosalynde* includes the throwaway phrase, 'If you like it, so…' which may have prompted the thought for the disarming title, *As You Like It*. It can be emphasised and unpacked in as many ways, as you like it. No one knows if Shakespeare picked his titles or if they were decided collaboratively with the company. Nevertheless it's much more than a throwaway. Shakespeare did something prescient and revolutionary in *As You Like It*. He changed the balance in the way men and women might think about relations between the sexes. Lodge's Preface explicitly addresses an audience of 'Gentlemen Readers' but, in Rosalind's Epilogue, Shakespeare shatters long-held male expectations by turning first to the opposite sex. 'I'll begin with the women.'

ACT TWO SCENE ONE

Rosalind's Elder Sisters
Two Rosalines, Julia, and Portia

Unlike the goddess Athene sprung fully formed from the forehead of Zeus, fictional characters, like mere mortals, usually stem from their immediate and extended families. But Rosalind is floating free. No nuclear family encircles her. There's no sign of a mother, and her father is lost to her in the Forest of Arden. She only has one loving cousin, Celia, and one hostile uncle, Duke Frederick. However, she has a string of virtual siblings in other Shakespeare plays, mostly sisters. Hamlet could have been her brother if he had found himself in Arden instead of tragic Denmark. Shakespeare tried out two elder sisters, early drafts for Rosalind when he created her namesakes: witty, acerbic Rosaline in *Love's Labour's Lost*; and a second more shadowy Rosaline, the object of Romeo's delirious infatuation before he ever glimpsed Juliet.

Probably written early in the 1590s, *Love's Labour's Lost* was performed at court for Queen Elizabeth in 1597, and published a year later. Its location never moves from court to countryside as the scene shifts dramatically in *As You Like It*. Instead we remain in the park of King Ferdinand of Navarre to watch, as Walter Pater said, 'a series of pictorial groups, in which the same figures reappear, in different combinations but on the same background. It is as if Shakespeare had intended to bind together, by some inventive conceit, the devices of an ancient tapestry, and give voices to its figures.'[1] I could be in Paris, standing in front of the glorious sixteenth century 'Lady and the Unicorn' tapestries, *A mon Seul Désir*, with their inscrutable chivalric romance, heraldic reds and blues, and exquisite natural detail. Here, in tiny stitches, the texture of Shakespeare's *Love's Labour's Lost*, enacted on the pleasure fields of France, is made almost tangible.

On this bucolic background a quartet of couples improvises on the theme of love with variations, just as Shakespeare later composed four different pairings for *As You Like It*. The sharpest and most intelligent voices are those of Rosaline, attendant to the Princess of France, and her suitor, Berowne, follower of King Ferdinand. The King and his three posh-boy friends, Berowne, Dumaine and Longaville, have sworn to found an exclusive college of four. They will devote themselves to study for the next three years, renouncing all female company. But love intervenes when the Princess of France arrives to set up a rival society with her ladies-in-waiting, Maria, Katharine and Rosaline. The young men, 'gallant, amorous, chivalrous,' and their vows of celibacy are soon forsworn.[2] This provocative set-up later inspired Tennyson to write his 1847 poem, *The Princess*, in which the heroine launched an all-female college. Gilbert and Sullivan copied the motif in 1884 for their comic opera, *Princess Ida*, at the same time that university education for women was becoming established. When W.H. Auden lectured on *Love's Labour's Lost* after World War II, he found the play still contemporary. 'You might think of four men meeting in Greenwich Village in 1946.' He found the themes so resonant that later he co-wrote a libretto with Chester Kallman for composer Nicolas Nabokov's 1973 opera, *Love's Labour's Lost*.

There is so much flashy wordplay between Rosaline and Berowne that they threaten to upstage the courtship between the apparent main protagonists, the King of Navarre and the Princess of France. Like Rosalind in *As You Like It*, Rosaline possesses a rapier wit and a 'merry, nimble, stirring spirit,' as her friend Katharine says. Jousting verbally with Berowne, Rosaline spikes the conventions of romantic love, as Rosalind does later in *As You Like It*.

> *Berowne*   Did not I dance with you in Brabant once?
>
> *Rosaline*   Did not I dance with you in Brabant once?
>
> *Berowne*   I know you did.
>
> *Rosaline*   How needless was it then
>
> To ask the question![3]

Rosaline has encountered Berowne before in a shared past – in Brabant. It seems their love failed to prosper and its deferral explains the bright, brittle tone she takes with him now.

Berowne	You must not be so quick.
Rosaline	'Tis long of you that spur me with such questions.
Berowne	Your wit's too hot, it speeds too fast, 'twill tire.
Rosaline	Not till it leave the rider in the mire.[4]

Each sparks off the other like method actors improvising. They seem to have a telepathic instinct about how their opposite will respond. Because Rosaline and Berowne have a history. Will they have a future? In their 'civil war' of words, 'Good wits will be jangling.' Their clashes in verse prefigure the fusillade of prose repartee between Beatrice and Benedick in *Much Ado About Nothing*, another couple who have also met previously. The antagonism and attraction between both pairs is fuelled by unfinished business. First love in *As You Like It* provides a different spur to Rosalind and Orlando's exuberant wit. In the world of Navarre where men apparently hold all the power, language is Rosaline's weapon of choice.

Berowne	I am a fool and full of poverty.
Rosaline	But that you take what doth to you belong,
	It were a fault to snatch words from my tongue
Berowne	O, I am yours, and all that I possess.
Rosaline	All the fool mine?[5]

The vitality of her personality and the sheer agility of her word games inspire Berowne to reject the male-only pact and declare his love for Rosaline. He now understands that the exclusive life of the mind is not enough. The world would be a dry place without the love of women. Heart and head must coexist in Berowne's brave new wisdom.

Berowne	And when Love speaks, the voice of all the gods
	Make heaven drowsy with the harmony…
	From women's eyes this doctrine I derive:
	They sparkle still the right Promethean fire;
	They are the books, the arts, the academes,
	That show, contain and nourish all the world…[6]

Love turns Berowne into a poet. 'By heaven, I do love, and it hath taught me to rhyme,'[7] as it will later teach Orlando. Now he apprehends Rosaline as 'heavenly,' the same epithet that Orlando will bestow on

Rosalind, and feels 'blinded by her majesty,' although he still hankers after his bachelor freedom. 'What? I love, I sue, I seek a wife?'[8]

Rosaline quibbles on the notion that Berowne has become a fool for love – or made a fool of her.

> Rosaline They are worse fools to purchase mocking so.
>   That same Berowne I'll torture ere I go.[9]

Her verbal attack has 'wings/Fleeter than arrows, bullets, wind, thought, swifter things.'[10] Under assault, Berowne has learnt love's lesson. He will forswear 'taffeta phrases' and speak the truth about love in simple, home-spun syllables.

> Berowne Here stand I, lady; dart thy skill at me.
>   Bruise me with scorn, confound me with a flout,
>   Thrust thy sharp wit quite through my ignorance,
>   Cut me to pieces with thy keen conceit...
>   Henceforth my wooing mind shall be expressed
>   In russet yeas and honest kersey* noes.[11]

In spite of Berowne declaring a love '*sans* crack or flaw', the four courtships in *Love's Labour's Lost* do not end, as we expect of comedy, in four weddings and a dance. Frolicking on the tapestry meadows of France must end. On a muted note, the King of France, 'decrepit, sick, and bedrid' since the first scene of the play, is suddenly dead, recalling the Princess to the throne, and all the young lovers to the real world. It's no longer a time for love games and sparring. The joust is over, the mood has changed. There are no weddings but there will be a funeral. This conclusion makes *Love's Labour's Lost* quite different from other Shakespearean comedies. Rosaline, the Princess, Maria and Katharine impose a year's community service on their lovers before undertaking any promise to marry.

> Rosaline To weed this wormwood from your fruitful brain
>   And therewithal to win me, if you please -
>   Without the which I am not to be won -
>   You shall this twelvemonth term from day to day
>   Visit the speechless sick and still converse
>   With groaning wretches; and your task shall be
>   With all the fierce endeavour of your wit
>   To enforce the pained impotent to smile.[12]

---

* Coarse woollen material

In response to Rosaline's challenge, Shakespeare deliberately shifts Berowne outside the play, and makes him speak direct to the audience in a sleight of hand that anticipates Rosalind stepping beyond the apparent end of *As You Like It* to address us in her epilogue. It's a distancing device very familiar to our post-modern taste for unresolved or alternative endings. The actor tells us it's only a play, after all.

> Berowne Our wooing doth not end like an old play;
>   Jack hath not Jill. These ladies' courtesy
>   Might well have made our sport a comedy.
>
> King   Come, sir, it wants a twelvemonth and a day,
>   And then 'twill end.
>
> Berowne   That's too long for a play.[13]

As we leave the theatre we don't know whether the men will pass the tests set by their girlfriends. Extended beyond the close of the play, these trials are similar to the oral exams Rosalind sets Orlando, both inside and no doubt beyond the timeline of *As You Like It*. However, we do enjoy a thoroughly satisfying denouement orchestrated by Rosalind. She delivers us a banquet of four weddings, a dance, and an epilogue, for good measure. The finale of *Love's Labour's Lost* sounds a darker note. In *As You Like It* this structure is reversed so we see the sinister side of life at the beginning. The end of *Love's Labour's Lost* sends the lovers and audience away on uncertain, dividing paths. 'You that way; we this way.'[14] Like Adam and Eve out of Eden, the lovers are turned out of the pleasure park of Navarre.

The RSC set their 2014/15 production of *Love's Labour's Lost* a century earlier in the last carefree summer of 1914 before the outbreak of World War I. It was a perceptive match with the play's ominous ending. In 2000, Kenneth Branagh set his musical film of the play in France during World War II. Shakespeare's witty exploration of relations between the sexes seemed as contemporary as ever. As movie star Alicia Silverstone, playing the Princess of France, asked in an extra feature on the DVD, 'Love, what else is there?'

ɛɔ

Unlike Berowne's voluble Rosaline, Shakespeare's other Rosaline in *Romeo and Juliet*, doesn't say a single word. She is the tease Romeo adores before he catches sight of Juliet at the Capulets' ball. Though we never see Rosaline, she has a devastating effect on Romeo. Rosaline has forsworn Love, seizing the same passive–aggressive position as the men at the beginning of *Love's Labour's Lost*.

> Benvolio   Then she hath sworn that she will still live chaste?
>
> Romeo   She hath, and in that sparing makes huge waste.
>   For beauty starved with her severity
>   Cuts beauty off from all posterity.
>   She is too fair, too wise, wisely too fair,
>   To merit bliss by making me despair.
>   She hath forsworn to love, and in that vow
>   Do I live dead, that live to tell it now.[15]

Romeo is in thrall to Rosaline's compelling physique. Even the sexually ambivalent Mercutio enumerates her 'bright eyes, high forehead, scarlet lip, fine foot, straight leg, and quivering thigh/And the demesnes that there adjacent lie.'[16] Wordlessly, Rosaline's erotic charge lingers in the mind. She's the opposite of Rosalind whose dynamism is powered by her verbal pyrotechnics rather than by any specific details about her physical appearance. We can all inhabit Rosalind.

ço

Rosalind is also related to her other Shakespearean 'sisters', especially the cross-dressers: Julia/Sebastian in *Two Gentlemen of Verona*; Portia/Balthazar in *The Merchant of Venice*; Viola/Cesario in *Twelfth Night*; and Imogen/Fidele in *Cymbeline*. Disguise as a man can prove transformative as well as problematic. In Rosalind's case it enables her to become more herself, to discover the truth about her essential nature. As the boy actor who originally played her, it was probably a relief to be back in male clothes.

Julia in *Two Gentlemen of Verona*, thought to have been written in 1592 or even earlier, is the first of Shakespeare's enterprising transvestite girls, an early rehearsal or elder sister for Rosalind, though not her twin. *Two Gentlemen* may have been Shakespeare's first play. If he wrote it in 1592 he would have been only twenty-eight. It's a young man's play about romantic love in the world of joshing male friendships. Like *As You Like It* at the other end of the 1590s, *Two Gentlemen* is also about young people falling in love for the first time, learning that love can be tough and is never perfect. Julia discovers this through loving a two-timing boyfriend, Proteus. It's the same harsh lesson about relationships that Rosalind teaches head-in-the-clouds Orlando, although she doesn't experience or practise infidelity. She simply warns Orlando that it could lie in their future. 'Say "a day," without the "ever."'

In Verona, best friends Valentine and Proteus find their boyhood lives diverging. Valentine is off to stylish Milan while Proteus stays behind in Verona, near Julia, the girl he loves and who loves him. But Proteus' father soon sends him off to follow Valentine to Milan. At parting, Julia and Proteus exchange rings and vows of faith. When Proteus arrives in Milan, he finds Valentine in love with glamorous Silvia who is engaged to Thurio, her father's choice. Proteus instantly falls for Silvia, too, and forgets Julia. Though 'protean' can suggest embracing and positive attributes, he's as liquid and changeable as the water god from whom his name derives.

> Proteus   Even as one heat another heat expels,
> Or as one nail by strength drives out another,
> So the remembrance of my former love
> Is by a newer object quite forgotten.[17]

Valentine plans to elope with Silvia but Proteus betrays his friend who is consequently banished from Milan, escaping to the forest outside the city.

In *Two Gentlemen* Shakespeare subverts any preconceptions about young men and young women. For it's Julia and Silvia who take action. They exemplify the high ideals of courtly love and generous behaviour that the play's first audience would have associated more naturally with men. Julia and Silvia are far more dynamic and honourable than their fickle boyfriends. To illustrate this transferral, Julia even becomes Sebastian. She's the first Shakespearean woman to get into men's clothes. Simon Godwin, director of the 2014/15 RSC production, observed, 'But more than that, [Shakespeare] has her doing a series of errands to serve the man she loves in order, apparently, to help him win the hand of her rival in love. So the moral complexity of the choices he puts upon his characters, the pressure of the predicaments he makes them face, constantly ups the stakes of the play.'[18]

'Sebastian,' the name Julia chooses, referring to the Christian martyr pierced with arrows and the Church's unwitting gay icon, was as suggestively homoerotic to the Elizabethans as 'Ganymede,' the name Rosalind chooses for her alias in Arden. As her maid, Lucetta, sews Julia into drag, we are voyeurs at a reverse strip tease. Each detail of Julia's new masculine exterior is precisely and erotically described.

Lucetta	What fashion, madam, shall I make your breeches?
Julia	That fits as well as 'Tell me, good my lord,
	What compass will you wear your farthingale?'
	Why, e'en what fashion thou best likes, Lucetta.
Lucetta	You must needs have them with a codpiece, madam.
Julia	Out, out, Lucetta, that will be ill-favoured.
Lucetta	A round hose, madam, now's not worth a pin
	Unless you have a codpiece to stick pins on.[19]

Although Julia fears her male disguise will make her 'scandalized' she's determined to take the necessary action to retrieve her lover, Proteus. But the truth is she doesn't know the man. The perfections she attributes to him are those she needs to believe he possesses. More accurately, she's really describing her own.

Julia	His words are bonds, his oaths are oracles,
	His love sincere, his thoughts immaculate,
	His tears pure messengers sent from his heart,
	His heart as far from fraud as heaven from earth.[20]

Arriving in Milan she's appalled to find Proteus declaring a new passion for Silvia, but she enters his service dressed as a page, Sebastian. Anticipating Orsino's mission to Olivia, entrusted to Viola/Cesario in *Twelfth Night*, Proteus employs Sebastian/Julia to give a love letter to Silvia, together with the very ring she'd given him in Verona. In exchange, he wants Silvia's picture. Julia interrogates her heart and her own motives.

Julia	How many women would do such a message?
	…This ring I gave him when he parted from me
	To bind him to remember my good will.
	And now am I, unhappy messenger,
	To plead for that which I would not obtain…[21]

Julia takes Proteus' letter and her own ring to Silvia who rejects them both. Silvia is faithful to Valentine and sisterly to Julia.

Julia	Madam, he sends your ladyship this ring.
Silvia	The more shame for him that he sends it me,
	For I have heard him say a thousand times
	His Julia gave it him at his departure.
	Though his false finger have profaned the ring,
	Mine shall not do his Julia so much wrong.[22]

Female Julia, played by a boy-actor, cross-dressing back into Sebastian, suddenly remembers himself/herself/himself/herself as s/he once turned out for a pageant dressed as Ariadne, the maiden who in Greek mythology helped Theseus defeat the Minotaur. There are so many dizzying layers of gender to Julia at this moment that prefigure the triple cross-un-dressing of Rosalind at the end of *As You Like It*. Silvia asks 'Sebastian' how tall was Julia?

Julia	About my stature; for at Pentecost,
	When all our pageants of delight were played,
	Our youth got me to play the woman's part,
	And I was trimmed in Madam Julia's gown,
	Which served me as fit, by all men's judgements,
	As if the garment had been made for me;
	Therefore I know she is about my height…
Silvia	She is beholding to thee, gentle youth.
	Alas, poor lady, desolate and left!
	I weep myself to think upon thy words.
	Here, youth, there is my purse. I give thee this
	For thy sweet mistress' sake, because thou lov'st her.
	Farewell. [*Exeunt Silvia and Attendants.*]
Julia	And she shall thank you for't, if e'er you know her.[23]

Julia is left alone to examine the portrait of Silvia, with whom Proteus, her faithless lover, has become obsessed. 'What is in this portrait that I do not have?' she asks herself. 'What is it that makes us fall in love with another human being?'[24] Julia feels her own identity dissolving as she contemplates Proteus's treacherous love for Silvia.

> Julia   Here is her picture. Let me see, I think
>   If I had such a tire,* this face of mine
>   Were full as lovely as is this of hers...[25]

She can only conclude that love is blind. The cast leaves Milan to head for the forest: Silvia to find Valentine; Silvia's father, the Duke of Milan in pursuit with Thurio; and Proteus attended by his 'page' Sebastian. Though it's a convention in Shakespearean comedy that men fail to recognise women when they're in male clothes, yet a clue hides in the tag 'pretty youth' attached to Julia when she's disguised as Sebastian. 'Pretty youth' is also attached to the ambiguous figure of Ganymede/Rosalind in *As You Like It*, once by Orlando, once by Phebe, and once by Jaques. These are the only times Shakespeare depicts a character in these words. He never uses 'pretty youth' to describe a man.

Because *Two Gentlemen* is one of Shakespeare's earliest plays, its denouement feels telescoped like a car crash. Forest outlaws capture Silvia who is rescued by Proteus, who then shockingly threatens to rape her. Valentine confronts Proteus who is forced to confess his guilt. Sebastian faints and is discovered to be Julia. Fickle Proteus re-finds his love for Julia.

In 1850-51, painter Holman Hunt visualised the scene of *Valentine rescuing Silvia from Proteus*.[26] Hunt admired Shakespeare's 'sparkling and brilliant' play. So he matched his own radical Pre-Raphaelite technique of laying colours over a wet, white ground to achieve an equally crystalline effect. On the left-hand side of the picture, leaning for support against a tree, Julia doesn't look masculine at all. She's wearing a baffling costume of Hunt's own devising: a unisex, knee-length, violet-blue tunic and a short crimson cloak. Trousers or breeches were probably a step too far for religious Hunt or for his Victorian times. Julia's face is numb, staring into despair as she witnesses her beloved Proteus foiled in the act of attempting to rape Silvia. Behind her back she twiddles with the ring Proteus had given her in Verona as a token of their everlasting love.

---

*   head-dress

Two Gentlemen is about betrayal but it's also about learning to forgive. Julia as well as Valentine and Silvia all have to forgive Proteus though it's debatable whether erring Proteus will ever re-learn love for his devoted girlfriend. In *As You Like It* Orlando forgives his brother Oliver, as Duke Senior forgives his brother, Duke Frederick. Director Simon Godwin says of *Two Gentlemen*, 'The characters start the journey inexperienced and they leave experienced; and that's probably all we can hope for in life.'[27] Both Julia and Rosalind cross-dress to discover the truth about love. Julia has had practical experience of the dark side of Proteus yet she takes him back with all his faults. Rosalind examines love more theoretically. After the training course in love she's put him through, Rosalind has no need to doubt Orlando but he will always be late for dates. In their two comedies we're left feeling pessimistic for Julia and Proteus but optimistic for Orlando and Rosalind.

⁊

It's hard to like anyone in *The Merchant of Venice*. Distinct from the other so-called romantic comedies, *Two Gentlemen of Verona*, *Love's Labour's Lost, As You Like It* and *Twelfth Night* whose main preoccupation is human love, *The Merchant* of around 1596-8, is about hatred and money. Hard currency makes the world of Venice go round, not passion as in the Forest of Arden.

Portia is the organizing intelligence of her play as Rosalind is the orchestrating director of hers. However, Portia only has to cross-dress for a single scene in order to control events whereas Rosalind exerts her personality and enjoys her intersexual status for 4 of the 5 acts of *As You Like It*. Like Rosalind, Portia has the best mind in her play. But while she's cool, intellectual and astute, Rosalind has a warmer, intuitive wisdom. Portia has a brilliant legal mind whereas Rosalind can playfully impersonate a magician. Rosalind discovers an important part of her nature in her Ganymede persona whereas Portia becomes Balthazar solely for her law court appearance.

Portia, a beautiful heiress of Venice, must take a husband in a transaction far removed from love. Like Rosalind constrained by her father's demotion, Portia is likewise in the shadow of a vanished parent.

As the play unfolds, Portia is revealed as dominant and autocratic but she herself is bound by the even more controlling nature of her father's will. According to its terms, only a lover who chooses correctly between three caskets of worldly value, gold, silver or lead, can win Portia. She will do anything rather than be 'married to a sponge' and favours Lord Bassanio for her hand. 'There's something tells me, but it is not love,/I would not lose you.' Yet she remains suspicious of his motives. 'What treason there is mingled with your love.' Nevertheless, to the accompaniment of a song that rhymes on 'lead', Portia appears to guide him to the right casket.

> *Tell me where is Fancy bred,*
> *Or in the heart, or in the head?*
> *How begot, how nourished?*

Bassanio is a risk-taker so the lead casket with its tab, 'Who chooseth me, must give and hazard all he hath,' speaks to him. He wins the prize, but does Portia?

From infancy my parents labelled me unmusical. I longed for piano lessons and improvised endlessly on my grandparents' baby grand in their suburban garden room. Music lessons were never awarded. Later by way of compensation, aged nine or ten, I was sent to 'elocution' lessons on Saturday mornings. Today I would have gone to drama or performance classes. One of the Shakespeare speeches I had to learn by heart and recite was not Portia's famous 'quality of mercy' lines but her emotional declaration to Bassanio after he's opened the correct lead casket.

> *Portia*   You see me, Lord Bassanio, where I stand,
> Such as I am; though for myself alone
> I would not be ambitious in my wish
> To wish myself much better, yet for you,
> I would be trebled twenty times myself,
> A thousand times more fair, ten thousand times more rich,
> That only to stand high in your account
> I might in virtues, beauties, livings, friends
> Exceed account: but the full sum of me
> Is sum of something: which to term in gross,
> Is an unlessoned girl, unschooled, unpractised,

Happy in this, she is not yet so old
But she may learn; happier than this,
She is not bred so dull but she can learn;
Happiest of all is that her gentle spirit
Commits itself to yours to be directed,
As from her lord, her governor, her king.
Myself, and what is mine, to you and yours
Is now converted. But now, I was the lord
Of this fair mansion, master of my servants,
Queen o'er myself; and even now, but now,
This house, these servants and this same myself,
Are yours, my lord's. I give them with this ring
Which, when you part from, lose, or give away,
Let it presage the ruin of your love,
And be my vantage to exclaim on you.[28]

It's a long speech consisting of only three sentences so the breath control must challenge even a trained actor. I can still see the street in north London and the airless upstairs room with the sunshine pouring in on my sweaty efforts. Apart from the breath control, there was something else about speaking these lines I instinctively baulked at. I couldn't understand why Portia committed her spirit to be directed by a man. Rosalind never does. And why did Portia hand over any of her worldly goods, let alone all of them, to Bassanio who will doubtless squander them away? I had no knowledge of the position of women in sixteenth-century Venice or England but something – which I couldn't even articulate as I struggled with the compulsive beauty of these lines – struck me as unjust.

Justice and mercy are the themes that attach themselves to Portia and are themes the play ought to highlight, instead of leaving us with its indelible shame and bigotry. The eponymous Merchant of Venice is not Shylock but Antonio, 'the bosom lover' of Bassanio, who always counts on Antonio for loans. When he asks for yet another advance, Antonio doesn't have the liquidity so offers to stand guarantor to another lender. When approached, Shylock from the Venetian Ghetto, is reluctant to make any loan to anti-Semitic Antonio.

At that time, the Church opposed money lending at interest, known pejoratively as usury, now undertaken by the banks. Money lending, however, was the only trade allowed to the Jewish community in the sixteenth century throughout most of Europe. Eventually Shylock agrees to lend Antonio 3,000 ducats for three months, without interest, but in exchange for a 'merry bond'. If Antonio fails to repay Shylock by the due date, 'let the forfeit/Be nominated for an equal pound/Of your fair flesh.' Antonio signs the bond and gives the cash to Bassanio to facilitate his courtship of Portia.

By the deadline for repayment, Antonio's fleet, which should have brought him funds to repay the bond, is reported wrecked. Shylock intends to claim his macabre forfeit, in double revenge, not only for a lifetime of abuse he's suffered from Antonio, but also because his daughter Jessica has 'in the lovely garnish of a boy' absconded with her Christian lover, Lorenzo, helping herself to some of her father's wealth at the same time. Shylock's grievance will come to trial in the ducal law courts.

Portia determines to defend Antonio and defeat Shylock in open court. To undertake this, she has no option but to cross-dress as a male lawyer and call herself Balthazar. In real life a sixteenth-century woman would have been allowed neither to study Law nor to practise it. Women were first admitted to the American Bar Association in 1918 but no woman was called to the English bar until Ivy Williams in 1922.[29] By appearing at the bar, Portia was more than three centuries ahead of her times, and Shakespeare a radical in portraying the first professional woman lawyer, even if she did have to disguise herself as a man and was entirely fictional.

Wearing the authority of masculine legal robes, Portia assumes all court functions: barrister, attorney, judge and jury. Her keynote demand of Shylock is mercy. Yet her cross-examination is unremittingly vindictive and she finally exacts a cruel retribution. Only once does she address the plaintiff by name: 'Is your name Shylock?' For the rest of the case she calls him generically 'the Jew' or disparagingly 'Jew' as does everyone else in court. Ignoring the fact that in Christian Venice mercy has never been shown to Shylock, Portia repeatedly invokes its virtue and asks Shylock to dispense it. 'On what compulsion must I?' he asks, 'tell me that.'

Portia launches into her cascading paean to Mercy. 'The quality of mercy is not strain'd,/It droppeth as the gentle rain from heaven,' to arrive at her ultimatum:

Portia	Therefore, Jew,
	Though justice be thy plea, consider this:
	That in the course of justice, none of us
	Should see salvation. We do pray for mercy,
	And that same prayer, doth teach us all to render
	The deeds of mercy.[30]

But Shylock is in a semi-crazed state of mind, beyond mercy. He implores the exact letter of the law, 'the penalty and forfeit of my bond.' Even though Bassanio offers him twice or thrice the original loan of 3,000 ducats, or a new bond of ten times 3,000, he won't budge. Shylock falls straight into the legal trap cleverly prepared by Portia/Balthazar. S/he demands to see the original bond, offers Shylock the chance to tear it up and when he declines, gives judgement that its exact terms must be adhered to.

Portia	Have by some surgeon, Shylock, on your charge,
	To stop his wounds, lest he do bleed to death.
Shylock	Is it so nominated in the bond?
Portia	It is not so expressed, but what of that?
	'Twere good you do so much for charity.
Shylock	I cannot find it; 'tis not in the bond.[31]

Then s/he invites the Merchant, Antonio, to say his final words before facing Shylock's knife. But Portia may hear more than a recently married woman is prepared for in the passionate declaration her new husband Bassanio makes to his gay friend, Antonio.

Bassanio	Antonio, I am married to a wife
	Which is as dear to me as life itself;
	But life itself, my wife and all the world
	Are not with me esteemed above thy life.
	I would lose all, ay sacrifice them all
	Here to this devil, to deliver you.[32]

Portia responds drily to Bassanio's apparent extra-marital love, 'Your wife would give you little thanks for that/If she were by to hear you make the offer.' Then in a dazzling legal manœuvre, Portia swaps the positions of the original defendant, Antonio, with the plaintiff, Shylock. So Shylock suddenly finds himself as defendant in the case he himself brought to court.

Portia	This bond doth give thee here no jot of blood:
	The words expressly are 'a pound of flesh'.
	Take then thy bond: take thou thy pound of flesh.
	But in the cutting it, if thou dost shed
	One drop of Christian blood, thy lands and goods
	Are by the laws of Venice confiscate
	Unto the state of Venice.[33]

'Is that the law?' asks Shylock, realising the effeminate barrister has demolished his case.

Portia	He shall have nothing but the penalty.
	…Therefore, prepare thee to cut off the flesh.
	Shed thou no blood, nor cut thou less nor more
	But just a pound of flesh. If thou tak'st more
	Or less than a just pound, be it but so much
	As makes it light or heavy in the substance
	Or the division of the twentieth part
	Of one poor scruple: nay, if the scale do turn
	But in the estimation of a hair,
	Thou diest, and all thy goods are confiscate.[34]

Shylock tries a desperate plea-bargain, 'Give me my principal, and let me go.' Portia hasn't finished. 'Thou shalt have nothing but the forfeiture/ To be so taken at thy peril Jew.' She stretches him on the rack of her legal genius, and adds a Venetian twist of Christian anti-Semitism.

Portia	Tarry, Jew,
	The law hath yet another hold on you.
	It is enacted in the laws of Venice,
	If it be proved against an alien
	That by direct, or indirect, attempts
	He seek the life of any citizen,
	The party 'gainst the which he doth contrive,
	Shall seize one-half his goods. The other half
	Comes to the privy coffer of the state,
	And the offender's life lies in the mercy
	Of the Duke only, 'gainst all other voice.[35]

It's ironic that Shylock who has been asked to show mercy to Antonio is now dependent on the Duke's mercy to spare his life. Antonio sues for Shylock's property to be split so he can enjoy his share, but at Shylock's death the principal will revert to Jessica and her Christian husband, Lorenzo. Antonio then demands the cruellest penalty. Shylock must convert at once to Christianity. Portia has achieved punitive, recriminatory justice. But she's been left with some difficult personal questions.

As the court disperses, Bassanio asks Balthazar/Portia what fee to pay for such extraordinary legal services. S/he asks for nothing except the ring on Bassanio's finger. It was 'given me by my wife,/And when she put it on, she made me vow/That I should neither sell, nor give, nor lose it.' However, Antonio persuades Bassanio to hand over the ring. Once home at Belmont, Portia torments Bassanio to produce the ring – which of course he can't. Eventually she shows him the very ring, taunting him that she had it from the lawyer Balthazar, with whom she's slept. It's proof that she had been the lawyer in the courtroom. But her revelation is not entirely playful. There's a darker side to this unmasking. Portia finds she has to welcome not only her husband but also Antonio into Belmont. There's a shadow over Portia's union with Bassanio absent from Rosalind's with Orlando. Portia's personal negotiation is complex and modern for Bassanio will bring his past with him. Has Portia allied herself with a fortune hunter, a chancer whose mind is like 'a day in April', and whose heart is elsewhere?

When Herbert Farjeon saw *The Merchant of Venice* at the Old Vic in 1925 he found Portia to be unusually witty and unusually managing – qualities which none of the men in her play possess. Edith Evans' Portia 'was always sure of herself – and how sure of herself Portia always was!...Portia knew that she could bring off a brilliant sally on demand. She knew, too, before she entered the court, that she would emerge victorious.' Though Farjeon found something superb about Portia, he noted she 'fails to capture our sympathy.'[36] We never identify with Portia as we do with Rosalind. Does Portia learn anything? Does she have the makings of a wise and generous woman? She's good at preaching Christian mercy but doesn't show much. Marriage with Bassanio may only harden her further.

The play had a searing effect in 1989 when Dustin Hoffman played Shylock, in Peter Hall's production at the Phoenix Theatre in London. Geraldine James made a serious, intelligent Portia. But the end of the play was, as reviewer John Peter said, 'underscored by melancholy and in a sense almost of fatigue. Everyone has paid dearly for what they have got, and also for what they have lost. The future looks settled but not necessarily benign. That's how modern Shakespeare is.'[37]

Younger Sisters

Viola, Imogen, Beatrice

When I think of the family of Rosalind's cross-dressing 'sisters', almost her coeval is Viola who disguises herself as a boy, Cesario, in *Twelfth Night*. While *As You Like It* is usually dated 1599-1600, *Twelfth Night* is thought to follow in 1600-1601. I have seen an array of Violas from Judi Dench at Stratford in 1969 to Jodie McNee at the rejuvenated Everyman Theatre in Liverpool in 2014. These actors, including Johnny Flynn in an all male production at the Apollo in 2013, have explored a range of gender stereotypes, from girly girls who never even tried to stride like a man, to authentic gasp-inducing lookalikes with Viola's twin brother Sebastian. Jodie McNee worked with choreographer Charlotte Broom to nail the physical aspects of impersonating a man, studying the mannerisms of her co-star Luke Jerdy. 'It was very liberating. You often look at a fella and their bodies are very open. And a woman often closes down her body, crossing her legs or folding her arms over. It's very interesting, the psychology of it.'[1]

Disguise as a man and gender ambiguity are integral to any interpretation of either Rosalind or Viola. But whereas Rosalind is emboldened by her new male authority in Arden, Viola's attitude to her boy's disguise and to her own sex is more rueful and meditative in Illyria.

> *Viola* Disguise, I see thou art a wickedness,
> Wherein the pregnant enemy does much.
> How easy is it for the proper false
> In women's waxen hearts to set their forms!
> Alas, our frailty is the cause, not we,
> For such as we are made of, such we be.[2]

Viola feels trapped in her masculine disguise. Not only does her male identity as Cesario entice Olivia into falling in love with someone she can't have in that time and place, it also prevents Viola from expressing her own love to Orsino. Today Olivia might have an affair with Viola, Phebe might have a fling with Rosalind, and Celia could live as Rosalind's girl friend. In 1599 and ever after, Rosalind finds being Ganymede enables her to speak her mind, and to speak her love to Orlando. Both Rosalind and Viola blur the boundaries between the sexes in their discussion of love. But while Viola, 'poor monster', is an uneasy synthesis of Viola and Cesario, Rosalind finds triumphant liberation by fusing herself with Ganymede.

Rosalind goes further than Viola. She takes on a dizzying extra layer of identity by playing herself, a woman, in her dating games with Orlando. Feste the Fool insinuates that Cesario is really female, 'Now Jove, in his next commodity of hair, send thee a beard,' but Orsino doesn't even half guess the truth. He's too absorbed by self-love, and love of love – which he mistakes for love of Olivia – to notice Viola's passion for him. When he asks Cesario if he's met a woman to love, Orsino remains obstinately dense.

Orsino	My life upon't, young though thou art, thine eye Hath stayed upon some favour that it loves. Hath it not, boy?
Viola	A little, by your favour.
Orsino	What kind of woman is't?
Viola	Of your complexion.
Orsino	She is not worth thee then. What years, i' faith?
Viola	About your years, my lord.[3]

Although both Viola and Rosalind fall in love at first sight, loving seems less complex for Viola than it does for Rosalind who won't be satisfied until she's explored all its inherent risks. More pensive Viola concurs with Orsino that

> women are as roses, whose fair flower
> Being once displayed, doth fall that very hour.[4]

Has Viola less time on her side than Rosalind? Is she slightly older? Director Peter Hall thinks the play itself is 'moving into maturity.'[5] There's a still, calm centre to Viola whereas Rosalind's whirring brain is constantly in motion. I sense a melancholy shade to Viola whereas Rosalind revels in high spirits. Viola knows what longing for love feels like and it's immovable as statuary. In code, as if describing a lost sister, Cesario tells Orsino of the monumental numbness of unspoken, unspeakable love.

Viola	A blank, my lord: she never told her love,
	But let concealment, like a worm i' th' bud
	Feed on her damask cheek: she pined in thought,
	And with a green and yellow melancholy
	She sat like Patience on a monument,
	Smiling at grief. Was not this love indeed?
	We men may say more, swear more, but indeed
	Our shows are more than will: for still we prove
	Much in our vows, but little in our love.[6]

For William Hazlitt, the impassioned sweetness of Viola's confession of her covert love for Orsino, aroused his deepest emotion. Her words 'vibrate on the heart, like the sounds which the passing wind draws from the trembling strings of a harp left on some desert shore!'[7]

Viola/Cesario falls deeply in love with Orsino, at the same time as Orsino continues to profess love for Olivia who has developed a wild crush on Cesario. Through these complications Shakespeare suggests we all contain several degrees of sexual ambiguity. Beneath our binary outsides of feminine and masculine, bubble layers of psychological complexity. This was made visual in Trevor Nunn's sumptuous 1996 film of *Twelfth Night* in which Imogen Stubbs played Viola. Following the wreck, Viola is rescued but believes Sebastian her twin brother drowned. Landing in enemy territory, she disguises herself as Cesario, a boy emigrant. In an unusual interpolation we see Viola physically transform. Her long hair is cut short with a large pair of scissors, her corset unlaced, her breasts bound flat – and suddenly she can pass for a youth. It's a filmic version of the explicit scene in *Two Gentlemen of Verona* when Lucetta lewdly equips Julia with a codpiece. Stubbs's Viola puts on a pencil moustache, practises a male stride and drops her voice. She's sexually ambiguous, rather than the convincing boy Jodie McNee made as Cesario in 2014. In the film we even see Stubbs privately unbind her breasts for a moment's respite as she blames male disguise for proving 'a wickedness'.

But the ambivalence lingers. For Orsino muses that compared with 'dear lad' Cesario,

> Diana's lip
> Is not more smooth and rubious: thy small pipe
> Is as the maiden's organ, shrill and sound,
> And all is semblative a woman's part.[8]

At the finale, when Orsino has decided to fall in love with Viola, now confessedly a woman, he still continues to call her 'Boy' and indeed on the Elizabethan stage in the person of a boy actor, s/he would have been exactly that. W.H. Auden thought it impossible to believe that changeable Orsino could make Viola a good husband. He gives 'the impression of simply having abandoned one dream for another.'[9]

Viola's love for flighty Orsino, whose 'mind is a very opal,' seems far less comprehensible than Rosalind's love for playful and honourable Orlando. But perhaps that's the point about love. It's an expression of the person doing the loving rather than an accurate valuation of the object of that love. It's just as hard to understand why Julia retains her love for fickle Proteus in *Two Gentlemen*. Both Orsino and Proteus are giddy and unreliable while Viola and Julia remain staunchly but perplexingly loyal. By delving into the real intentions of Orlando, challenging and testing him, Rosalind finds her true and equal contemporary. Examining Orlando's love, Rosalind finds out about her own. She has ecstatic epiphanies about the scope of her love, 'as boundless as the sea,' as deep as 'the unknown bottom' of the Bay of Portugal. It's entirely appropriate that argumentative, passionate Rosalind mostly speaks in sinewy prose, whereas Viola's natural element is blank verse. Her rarefied, poetic vision of love, 'like Patience on a monument,' is a response to Orsino's misogynistic view of women.

> *Orsino*   There is no woman's sides
> Can bide the beating of so strong a passion
> As love doth give my heart...[10]

In their male disguises, both Ganymede/Rosalind and Cesario/Viola have to reject stereotypes of female loving and are asked to deal humanely with the comedy and the cruelty of attracting inappropriate admirers. Phebe falls irretrievably in love with Ganymede at first sight, as Olivia falls for Cesario. Both women prefer these 'sweet youths' to their allowed suitors, Silvius and Orsino. But Rosalind and Viola deal differently with their would-be lovers. Rosalind is curt, even brutal with Phebe.

Rosalind	Why do you look on me?
	I see no more in you than in the ordinary
	Of Nature's sale-work.
	…I pray you do not fall in love with me,
	For I am falser than vows made in wine.
	Besides, I like you not.[11]

Rosalind is a born educator and just as she lectures Orlando, she wants to teach Phebe the truth about love. Rosalind thinks Phebe should learn to value Silvius and not set her sights on impossible Ganymede.

Viola takes a more empathetic approach to Olivia's misplaced love for 'boy' Cesario. She identifies with Olivia's unlooked-for love and mentally compares it with her own passion for Orsino.

Viola	I am the man: if it be so, as 'tis,
	Poor lady, she were better love a dream.
	…How will this fadge? My master loves her dearly,
	And I, poor monster, fond as much on him,
	And she, mistaken, seems to dote on me:
	What will become of this? As I am man,
	My state is desperate for my master's love:
	As I am woman (now alas the day!)
	What thriftless sighs shall poor Olivia breathe?[12]

Viola feels herself a 'monster' because of her equivocal position between male and female. But, like Rosalind with Phebe, she has to remain firm with the deluded Olivia. Viola tries her best to explain:

Viola	By innocence I swear, and by my youth,
	I have one heart, one bosom, and one truth,
	And that no woman has; nor never none
	Shall mistress be of it, save I alone.[13]

Even in comedies, it takes courage and enterprise to survive as the asylum seekers Rosalind and Viola are in Arden and Illyria, with false identities and as the other sex. They are both intimately acquainted with death and exile. Rosalind has had sentence of death passed on her. Viola has survived shipwreck. Both rise above death and know the only answer is love and desire. Mortality knocks at the door of life and both Rosalind and Viola answer it with their transcendent loves.

ᴄ⁄ɔ

In Shakespeare's early comedies, unmarried young heroines are the centres of interest, symbols of moral value, and conduits of emotional truth. Women rarely fulfil these functions again until his late plays. Here we meet once more young women who embody virtue, freshness and desire: Perdita in *The Winter's Tale*, Marina in *Pericles* and Miranda in *The Tempest*. We also meet married women whose unblemished reputations are first threatened and then vindicated: Hermione in *The Winter's Tale*, and Rosalind's closer relation, Imogen in *Cymbeline*, thought to have been written 1609-10 but certainly by 1611.

Of these heroines, only Imogen imitates Rosalind by getting into male disguise when she is forced by a cruel turn of the plot to cross-dress as Fidele. The pseudonym she chooses, meaning faithful, is an emblem of her undying love for Posthumus, her doubting husband. She retains this shining, selfless love through the many trials life throws at her. 'We have almost as great an affection for Imogen as she had for Posthumus; and she deserves it better,' noted Hazlitt.[14] Imogen's resolute love, as well as her masquerade as a boy, links her with both Rosalind and Viola. However, even as Fidele, Imogen remains innately feminine, like 'the azured harebell', whereas Rosalind's Ganymede exults in her new swashbuckling, laddish persona. Rosalind's gender is interestingly volatile where Imogen's never is.

In one of his notorious attempts to improve Shakespeare, George Bernard Shaw 'refinished' *Cymbeline* in 1936, making Imogen a more up-to-date woman for the twentieth century. In Shaw's version, reconstructed Imogen is reluctant to return to Posthumus, her once suspicious husband, so she decides, a generation before the UK's Divorce Reform Act of 1969, 'I must go home and make the best of it, as other women must.'[15] Her change of gender has not changed her essential self. Yet Posthumus no more recognises the feminine in Fidele than Orsino does in Cesario, or Orlando in Ganymede. In Shakespeare's comedies we accept this convention as a droll comment on the blindness of lovers. But in *Cymbeline*, Posthumus' failure to recognise either his wife's unchangeable fidelity, or the real Imogen disguised as Fidele, speaks of the malign power of men's sexual jealousy. When finally everything is resolved and nearly everyone reconciled in *Cymbeline*, we still feel the intensity of this theme reverberating from

The Rape of Lucrece, through *Othello*, via *The Winter's Tale* and into Shakespeare's other late romances.

Imogen, daughter of King Cymbeline of Britain, has secretly married lower-ranked Posthumus. However, her wicked fairy-tale stepmother is plotting that her own son, the loutish Cloten, should marry Imogen. Banished from Britain, Posthumus gives Imogen a bracelet and receives from her a ring before he sets off for Rome. Once there he boasts about his wife's virtue to Iachimo, an Italian stage villain. Contemporary audiences would have recognised this figure as the devil incarnate from the popular xenophobic proverb, *Inglese Italianato è un diavolo incarnato*! He bets Posthumus that he will be able to seduce immaculate Imogen.

Iachimo fails, but in revenge steals into Imogen's bedchamber stowed in a trunk. He minutely observes her sleeping body, especially the mole under her left breast, and slides off her precious bracelet. Iachimo's description of Imogen's physical beauty flags her inner grace.

> Iachimo   Cytherea,
> How bravely thou becom'st thy bed! fresh lily!
> And whiter than the sheets![16]

Iachimo salivating over Imogen recalls Tarquin in Shakespeare's 1594 poem, *The Rape of Lucrece*, about the assault on a virtuous woman's chastity, sparked by her husband's boasting of her virtue. Both poem and play have a Roman setting, and the rape, or attempted rape in the case of Imogen, are political actions between male enemies.

> Iachimo   On her left breast
> A mole cinque-spotted: like the crimson drops
> I' th' bottom of a cowslip. Here's a voucher,
> Stronger than ever law could make; this secret
> Will force him think I have pick'd the lock, and ta'en
> The treasure of her honour.[17]

Imogen's physical impact must be evoked as the plot turns on it. However, her beauty defies the 'blazon' or catalogue of feminine bodily perfections common in courtly romance, so we only glimpse one exquisite detail about her mole. Its exact position on her body makes us all voyeurs. With this logged in his brain, it's easy for Iachimo to convince Posthumus that he has indeed slept with Imogen. Believing the lie turns Posthumus into a rampant misogynist, recalling the sexual rages of Othello or Leontes.

> Posthumus   Could I find out
> The woman's part in me – for there's no motion
> That tends to vice in man, but I affirm
> It is the woman's part: be it lying, note it,
> The woman's: flattering, hers: deceiving, hers:
> Lust, and rank thoughts, hers, hers…[18]

In his sense of impotence and humiliation, he chooses to forget his wife's flawless purity and hires Pisanio to murder her.

Posthumus's accusation incites Imogen's fury. Her argumentative powers, sarcastic questioning and outraged tone make her a sister to Rosalind.

> Imogen   False to his bed? What is it to be false?
> To lie in watch there, and to think on him?
> To weep 'twixt clock and clock? If sleep charge Nature,
> To break it with a fearful dream of him,
> And cry myself awake? That's false to's bed, is it?[19]

Rosalind's language is equally forceful and courageous when she repudiates her uncle's accusations with her dignified stand: 'Treason is not inherited, my lord…/My father was no traitor.'[20] Both Rosalind and Imogen suffer from toxic family members. Pisanio reveals her husband's death threat to Imogen and advises her to leave the British court and make for Milford Haven to meet the Roman forces. On his advice she transforms into a boy, foregoes her status as a princess, and exposes her porcelain complexion to the tanning sun. 'I see into thy end, and am almost/A man already.'[21]

In Yukio Ninagawa's dreamlike Japanese production of *Cymbeline* at the Barbican in 2012, a moon hung over Imogen/Fidele as she trundled her suitcase on the way to Milford Haven. All in black, she was not a man, but a generic forsaken refugee as she appeared in front of an eighteenth-century engraving of a cave set in sublime nature.

> Imogen   I see a man's life is a tedious one,
> I have tired myself: and for two nights together
> Have made the ground my bed. I should be sick,
> But that my resolution helps me.[22]

If Shinobu Otake didn't look masculine, this petite Japanese actress was able to assume masculine tones. Aged fifty-four, she looked like a boy of about twelve rather than a man, very touching in her new role as Fidele, constantly loyal to her faithless husband in the face of his betrayal.

> *Imogen*   My dear lord,
> Thou art one o' th' false ones! Now I think on thee,
> My hunger's gone; but even before, I was
> At point to sink, for food.[23]

She still feels total commitment to her husband, even in the grotesque scene when she wakes beside the headless body of Cloten which she mistakes for Posthumus. Believing this to be her husband's dead body, she plans to strew his grave with 'wild wood-leaves' and say 'a century of prayers.' 'Now this is the very religion of love,' said Hazlitt. 'She all along relies little on her personal charms, which she fears may have been eclipsed by some painted jay of Italy; she relies on her merit, and her merit is in the depth of her love, her truth and constancy.'[24] Imogen also inspires her two long-lost kidnapped brothers – unaware of their own true identity and of hers – to sing the most plangent lines in Shakespeare, their dirge for Fidele, the 'boy' fugitive they believe dead.

> *Guiderius*   Fear no more the heat o' th' sun,
>   Nor the furious winter's rages,
> Thou thy worldly task hast done,
>   Home art gone, and ta'en thy wages.
> Golden lads and girls all must,
> As chimney-sweepers, come to dust.[25]

Sir Ian McKellen saw Peggy Ashcroft as Imogen in 1957 and never forgot her impact. 'The beauty and grace of Imogen was so overpowering, that I fancied it was all for my benefit alone. I had seen Dame Peggy up close, when I got her autograph and I knew she was, in life, old enough to be Imogen's mother. But from the back of the stalls, she was essential youth, in voice and gesture: I think I realised that Imogen is a great part – but how did Ashcroft do it? This divinity was beyond what I knew of acting.'[26] There is a kind of divinity about Imogen's fortitude, as she persists in loving her disloyal husband, and enlists in the wars between Rome and Britain.

The play concludes with a labyrinthine round of fairy-tale revelations that lead to reconciliation and forgiveness. Posthumus is eventually restored and reunited with Imogen.

> Imogen   Why did you throw your wedded lady from you?
> Think that you are upon a rock, and now
> Throw me again.   [*Embracing him*]
>
> Posthumus   Hang there like fruit, my soul,
> Till the tree die.[27]

Posthumus absolves Iachimo and tells him to 'Live,/And deal with others better.' Cymbeline forgives banished lord Belarius for abducting his two sons and proclaims, 'Pardon's the word to all'. The war between the Romans and the British is resolved into a peace treaty. Imogen never resumes her female clothes as, depending on the production, Rosalind need never resume hers. Ninagawa's *Cymbeline* concluded with a slow motion dance round a single pine tree, not Shakespeare's lofty cedar, symbolic of regeneration following the devastating tsunami of 2011 in Japan.

Imogen, like Rosalind, is the proper subject and heroine of her play. But unlike Rosalind, it's Imogen's 'conjugal tenderness' that is 'the chief subject of the drama and the pervading charm of her character,' said Victorian critic, Anna Jameson. But she was quick to modify her judgement, 'it is not true, I think, that she is merely interesting from her tenderness and constancy to her husband.' Jameson found some component parts of Shakespeare's earlier heroines in Imogen.

When Harriet Walter played the role a century and a half later for the RSC in Stratford and London, she too found elements of other characters in Imogen: Juliet, Desdemona, Cordelia, Lady Anne, Cleopatra, and of course, Rosalind. Though 'unusually, in Imogen's case, maleness does not bring with it authority... Imogen is forced to reach a more quintessential definition of herself. She has had to slough off 'Imogen' like an old skin, and underneath she finds 'Fidele', the faithful one...With her boy disguise the pressure is somehow off Imogen and off the player of Imogen. The emotional drive relaxes, and there is more opportunity for comedy and lyricism.' Walter compared Imogen's journey with the journey the audience makes. 'The barriers of sex, birth and nation have been broken down. We begin to honour the bonds instead of perpetuating the divisions. Forgiveness is within our range…A society has been purged…and reborn. Glasnost is given a chance…All the principal characters have been through trial of their faith, confrontation with death, resurrection and reconciliation.'[28]

This is also true in *As You Like It* where the main characters triumph over their trials of faith: Orlando's love for Rosalind is proved, and equally Rosalind's love for Orlando; as well as Silvius's love for Phebe. Confrontations with death have been surmounted: Orlando survives Oliver's threat to burn him alive, and against the odds, wins the wrestling match against the champion; Rosalind escapes her uncle's capital sentence; and at great personal risk Orlando rescues his brother from snake and lioness. The play ends in reconciliation with repentance by Oliver and Duke Frederick, Jaques' choice of the contemplative life, Phebe's concession to Silvius, the re-discovered amity between both sets of brothers, and Ganymede's rebirth to a full range of human potential as Rosalind.

Many actresses have played Imogen, from Sarah Siddons to Dakota Johnson, the more exposed star of *Fifty Shades of Grey*, in a 2015 film of *Cymbeline*. When Ellen Terry, who always lamented never being cast as Rosalind, played Imogen, people said, 'Oh what a Rosalind she would have made!' Both she and her audience felt her temperament and her genius were the perfect match with Rosalind.

❧

Beatrice doesn't cross-dress like Rosalind but she does repeat three times that she wishes to *be* a man, avid for the freedom of action denied to her sex in 1600.[29] As *Much Ado* was probably written between 1598-9, entered in the Stationer's Register and printed in a quarto edition of 1600, Shakespeare wrote Beatrice and Rosalind's plays almost at the same moment. But Beatrice seems older and worldly-wiser. Like Rosaline who shared a disrupted history with Berowne in *Love's Labour's Lost*, Beatrice is bruised from a previous encounter with Benedick who once 'lent' her his heart awhile.

Rosalind and Beatrice share a temperamental affinity. They delight in verbal fireworks and find themselves in similarly fractured families.

Both are motherless, both conspicuous nieces who live in their uncles' households as cousin-companions. These female cousins love them, though Beatrice's Hero is far less loyal and effective than Rosalind's Celia. But the major difference between Rosalind and Beatrice is that there's no lightning bolt of young love at first sight between Beatrice and Benedick as there is between Rosalind and Orlando. Instead there's a clash of mixed messages in competitive repartee, founded with psychological acuity, on deep mutual attraction. Beatrice and Benedick enjoy 'merry war', wit and sparring. 'You always end with a jade's trick. I know you of old,' she scolds him. Unlike Rosalind, but similar to Kate, the *Shrew*, Beatrice is known through Messina as a 'harpy'. Uncle Leonato tells her, 'By my troth, niece, thou wilt never get thee a husband, if thou be so shrewd of thy tongue.'[30] Dipping an ironic curtsy, early feminism is embedded in her joke:

> Beatrice   It is my cousin's duty to make curtsy and say, 'Father, as
>   it please you': but yet for all that, cousin, let him be a
>   handsome fellow, or else make another curtsy, and say,
>   'Father, as it please *me*.'[31] [my italics]

Like Rosalind, Beatrice has a zipping brain and a merry heart. 'There was a star danced and under that was I born.' The similarity of the Rosalind/Orlando and Beatrice/Benedick courtships is their witty verbal jousting of quips, puns, epigrams, firecrackers, the 'paper bullets of the brain,' and almost total use of prose.

The arc of Beatrice and Benedick's play – because it is their play in spite of strictly being the subplot – is the reverse of *As You Like It* which opens in potential tragedy before moving on to the high ground of comedy and rationality. *Much Ado* begins in comedy but the mood darkens as the male plot against Hero unfolds. The men in *Much Ado* are all professed misogynists. 'Because I will not do them [women] the wrong to mistrust any, I will do myself the right to trust none: and the fine is, for the which I may go the finer, I will live a bachelor,' insists Benedick.[32] Beatrice has an equally acerbic view of marriage as 'wooing, wedding and repenting.'

The rasping tenor of *Much Ado* is more reminiscent of *The Taming of the Shrew* than it is of *As You Like It*. Why do Don Pedro's military men from Aragon returning to Messina hate women so much? Demobbed troops fear women's sexual appetites and being cuckolded, an age-old obsession for soldiers returning from any wars, who suspect their children may not be their own.

> Don Pedro   I think this is your daughter. [of Hero, Leonato's daughter.]
>
> Leonato   Her mother hath many times told me so.[33]

Suspicion or fear of women may be the reason Don Pedro suggests wooing Hero on Claudio's behalf. He's the one with the power and rank, a fixer, a Pandarus, a matchmaker. The bizarre scheme ensures that Hero, heiress and only child of Leonato, has no say in the matter, and that Claudio knows nothing about Hero, other than he likes her looks and her father's money. 'In mine eye, she is the sweetest lady that ever I looked on.' He says he 'dotes' on Hero – not that he loves her. He craves a mute trophy wife, not a person or a partner. She might as well be a doll.

Benedick, too, is a fortune hunter. One of his main conditions, if ever he were to take a wife in Messina, 'rich shall she be, that's certain,' just like the *Shrew's* Petruchio who comes 'to wive it wealthily in Padua.' In Benedick's view, men are both tormented and un-manned by love. Facing up to lippy, foxy Beatrice, 'My dear Lady Disdain,' and 'My Lady Tongue,' Benedick feels, 'like a man at a mark, with a whole army shooting at me.'[34] So Claudio's engagement to Beatrice's cousin, Hero, seems a great betrayal to Benedick. Claudio has translated into 'Monsieur Love.' He used to 'speak plain and to the purpose, like an honest man and a soldier, and now is he turned orthography – his words are a very fantastical banquet, just so many strange dishes.'[35] Love does strange things to fellows and turns their language to jelly. It makes them write the sort of love poems Orlando hangs on trees in Arden.

Yet through their friends' knowing set-up, Beatrice and Benedick, rivals in the sex war, do fall in love and it proves transformative. Though both are cynics outwardly, they are romantics inwardly, and ripe for being 'tricked' into love in the uproarious comic heart of the play.

> Benedick   This can be no trick…it seems her affections have their full bent. Love me? Why it must be requited.
>
> Beatrice   …Against my will I am sent to call you in to dinner.
>
> Benedick   …Ha! 'Against my will I am sent to bid you come in to dinner' – there's a double meaning in that.[36]

However impervious people think they are, they can be knocked sideways by the merest possibility of being loved, and loving in return. From the moment Beatrice is fooled into believing Benedick loves her, a dramatic change comes over her. A new gentleness propels her from her usual prose into verse.

> Beatrice   What fire is in mine ears? Can this be true?
> Stand I condemn'd for pride and scorn so much?
> Contempt, farewell, and maiden pride, adieu!
> No glory lives behind the back of such.
> And, Benedick, love on; I will requite thee...[37]

Verse is the usual medium of choice for lovers but when Benedick admits, still protesting, to loving Beatrice, 'I love you against my will,' his love poetry is just as tacky as Orlando's. He makes a stab at it but 'cannot show it in rhyme; I have tried. I can find out no rhyme to "lady" but "baby"... No, I was not born under a rhyming planet.'[38]

The mood changes as Don John's counterpointing plot against chaste Hero comes to fruition, and like Posthumus in *Cymbeline*, gullible Claudio denounces his bride as a whore, 'a rotten orange', at the altar. Consumed by paternal shame at his daughter's halted wedding, Leonato is quick to endorse Claudio's act of treachery. 'Hath no man's dagger here a point for me?' he cries, even as he wishes his daughter dead, 'Do not live, Hero; do not ope thine eyes...Why ever wast thou lovely in my eyes?' Hero has been a commodity and now that she's disgraced and worthless, she might as well be dead.

'What shocked me was how the men turn like a pack of dogs on an innocent woman,' said Meera Syal who played Beatrice in an Indian take on *Much Ado* for the RSC in 2012. 'Rehearsing that wedding scene was shocking, and it contained echoes of other things I'm involved with. I'm the patron of the Newham Asian Women's Project and we fund refuges for women escaping violent marriages. These are real. Fifty per cent of cases of women being taken to police stations in India are to do with domestic violence. There is a dowry death – where a woman is killed by her husband because she didn't bring enough money with her as a dowry – every day in India. At least one. And it spoke to Shakespeare's own age as it does to ours.'

Friar Francis, who is now dealing with a brutal jilting rather than a wedding, and Hero, the bride, in a dead faint at the altar, comes up with a scheme, the same that Friar Lawrence proposes to Juliet, and Paulina offers Hermione in *The Winter's Tale*. Feign death and 'die to live.' The Friar's stoical message to Hero, the moral more usually of Shakespeare's tragedies than his comedies, is 'Have patience and endure.'

The vicious débâcle between Hero and Claudio triggers Beatrice and Benedick into their avowals of love, voiced entirely in prose, and pitches them into urgent discussion about how to deal with Claudio.

Benedick	I do love nothing in the world so well as you – is not that strange?
Beatrice	…You have stayed me in a happy hour, I was about to protest I loved you.
Benedick	And do it with all thy heart.
Beatrice	I love you with so much of my heart that none is left to protest.
Benedick	Come, bid me do any thing for thee.
Beatrice	Kill Claudio![39]

These last two words are a violent shock after Beatrice and Benedick's love talk. 'It's audacious writing, but it is as life is', says Meera Syal. 'Life turns on a sixpence like that. It's not neat, it's jagged.'[40] What Beatrice demands of Benedick, to murder his friend, is so immense, so outside morality, that he responds in a salvo of monosyllables. 'Ha! Not for the wide world!' For once, talkative Beatrice chokes. 'You kill me to deny it. Farewell.' Three times in quick succession she rages, 'O God, that I were a man! I would eat his heart in the market place!' because 'Sweet Hero! She is wronged, she is slandered, she is undone.' As Benedick tries to interrupt, she explodes – 'O that I were a man for his sake, or that I had any friend would be a man for my sake!…I cannot be a man with wishing, therefore I will die a woman with grieving.'[41]

So when Benedick presses her, 'Think you in your soul the Count Claudio hath wronged Hero?' 'Yea,' she replies, 'as sure as I have a thought, or soul.'[42] Through loving Beatrice, Benedick learns at last to reject the blinkered misogyny of his male peer group and to trust women. Though he recoils from the ultimate demand to 'Kill Claudio', under persuasion he resolves, to Beatrice's satisfaction, to challenge Claudio to a duel.

By the end of her play, Beatrice, like Rosalind at the beginning of hers, has inspired, and been inspired by the miracle of love. Love moves Beatrice the more deeply for its unexpectedness. And Benedick also convinces us that love has changed him. Like Rosalind, he cites Leander and Troilus as models of archetypal lovers with whom he amazedly compares himself, 'why, they were never so truly turned over and over as my poor self in love.'[43] But outwardly Benedick still finds it hard to depart from his hard-to-get script, 'I love thee against my will.' When he asks, 'Do not you love me?' Beatrice replies, 'Why, no; no more than reason.'[44] Then with absolute parity, she lobs the same question back at him. 'Do not you love me?' He duplicates her reply, 'Why, no; no more than reason.'[45]

A century later Millamant and her lover Mirabell enjoyed a similar battle of wits as the caustic couple in Congreve's play *The Way of the World*:

> *Millamant* I won't be called names after I'm married; positively, I won't be called names.
>
> *Mirabell* Names!
>
> *Millamant* Ay, as wife, spouse, my dear, joy, jewel, love, sweetheart, and the rest of that nauseous cant in which men and their wives are so fulsomely familiar. I shall never bear that… Well, if Mirabell should not make a good husband, I am a lost thing, for I find I love him violently.
>
> *Mirabell* …Well, heaven grant I love you not too well, that's all my fear.[46]

Shakespeare and Congreve, both writers of great comedy, knew how violent desire can underlie the outward antagonism between razor sharp lovers like Millamant and Mirabell or Beatrice and Benedick. At the comic climax of *Much Ado*, mutual love is testified by public revelation of Beatrice and Benedick's letters. 'A miracle! Here's our own hands against our hearts,' concedes Benedick, 'Come, I will have thee; but, by this light, I take thee for pity.' Beatrice ripostes, 'I yield upon great persuasion, and partly to save your life, for I was told you were in a consumption'. With a kiss – their first – they proceed to marriage and Benedick saves face by asserting, 'man is a giddy thing, and this is my conclusion.' Their love has been a fight that will continue into marriage and beyond. Rosalind's courtship is about an education in which she learns as much as she teaches, as all thoughtful educators do. It's a class in life-long learning. *Much Ado* ends, as Shakespeare's comedies do, with a dance – but no epilogue. To Rosalind but not to Beatrice, Shakespeare awards the last word.

In 2014/15 the RSC paired *Love's Labour's Lost* with *Much Ado About Nothing* under a credibly alternative title, *Love's Labour's Won*. Michelle Terry played both Rosaline and Beatrice and Edward Bennett was both Berowne and Benedick. He thought, '*Love's Labour's Lost* is like remembering being twenty-one – there is a fizz and energy to express, [while in] *Much Ado* there is a sense of wisdom, and a heaviness.' Michelle Terry gave a star-making performance as Beatrice, navigating 'the character's acerbity, melancholy and romantic insecurity with a mastery far beyond even her accustomed brilliance.'[47] She graduated to play an exhilarating Rosalind in Blanche McIntyre's production at Shakespeare's Globe during the summer of 2015. 'In years to come those who saw her on stage, and saw McIntyre direct, will count themselves lucky. St Crispin's Day for girls.'[48]

Call Me Ganymede – Rosalind Crosses the Border

Rosalind	Were it not better,
	Because that I am more than common tall,
	That I did suit me all points like a man?
	A gallant curtal-axe* upon my thigh,
	A boar-spear in my hand, and in my heart,
	Lie there what hidden woman's fear there will,
	We'll have a swashing and a martial outside,
	As many other mannish cowards have
	That do outface it with their semblances.
Celia	What shall I call thee when thou art a man?
Rosalind	I'll have no worse a name than Jove's own page,
	And therefore look you call me Ganymede.[1]

Rosalind's uncle Duke Frederick, Celia's father, has turned on his niece in an apparently irrational whirlwind of fury. He expels her from court where she's been living in quiet amity with her cousin Celia since Frederick usurped and banished his brother, the rightful Duke Senior. Takeover was a theme that shuddered through Elizabethan society. The Queen's own grandfather, Henry VII, had returned from France to seize the crown for the House of Tudor at the Battle of Bosworth Field in 1485. Shakespeare had dramatised the events in *Richard III*.

Elizabeth was haunted by fears of rebellion or even assassination which escalated after Pope Pius V excommunicated her in 1570. Records do not reveal whether the more distant abdication of the king in Shakespeare's *Richard II* was performed covertly, openly, or not at all during Elizabeth's reign. What's certain is that when the play appeared in its first quarto edition of 1597, this scene was omitted.[2] The Queen was adamantly opposed to giving air to any notions of regime change. 'I am Richard II,' she is supposed to have said, 'know ye not that?'[3] So when Duke Frederick warns Rosalind if she's found within twenty miles of his court within the next ten days, 'thou diest for it,' he's making no

---

*   A cutlass, a short broad-bladed sword.

idle threat. He means it. Events on stage had political reverberations in the real world.

When Rosalind asks of what crime she's being accused, uncle Frederick replies, 'Thou art thy father's daughter, there's enough.'

> *Rosalind* So was I when your highness took his dukedom;
> So was I when your highness banished him.
> Treason is not inherited, my lord,
> Or if we did derive it from our friends,
> What's that to me? My father was no traitor.[4]

Rosalind dares to speak the truth to power, defending herself and her father from Duke Frederick's fury in passionate, rational language that anticipates the trial scenes of Shakespeare's future wronged women, Hermione in *The Winter's Tale* and Queen Katherine in *Henry VIII*. Rebecca Hall who played Rosalind in 2003 when she was twenty-one says, 'these Shakespearean women caught up in male-centric environments are incredibly eloquent and defiant…there's the sense of utter injustice and incredulity.' Rosalind 'says these lucid things about the paranoid nature of tyranny. This is ridiculous behaviour, and she tells him so.'[5] Tyrants are naturally fearful and feel compelled to eliminate any threats against them, as Shakespeare's Richard III disposed of the boy princes in the Tower.

But like Leontes and Henry VIII, Duke Frederick's edict is 'firm and irrevocable'. He sweeps away leaving Rosalind reduced to silence and inaction for the one and only time in the play. It's her habit of reserve that now enrages him, as he hisses to his daughter, Celia, in sibilant language –

> *Duke Frederick* She is too subtle for thee, and her smoothness,
> Her very silence and her patience
> Speak to the people, and they pity her.
> Thou art a fool. She robs thee of thy name,
> And thou wilt show more bright and seem more virtuous
> When she is gone.[6]

At court, Rosalind's withdrawn mood, the eclipse of her natural exuberance, was a direct outcome of losing her father to exile as well as losing her status as Duke Senior's daughter. Actor Sally Scott thinks Rosalind is 'potentially a tragic figure. She's desperately let down by a lot of people, all of whom are men. Her father is banished, he doesn't come back, he doesn't send anyone for her. He's the first person to do that to her. Her uncle then turns on a sixpence and banishes her. She's deeply vulnerable.'[7] The banishment of Rosalind so early in the play seems to herald a tragedy rather than a comedy. The forecast at court is ominous, dark and threatening. Before Chekhov, only Shakespeare had dared to combine genres so radically, inflecting potential tragedy with comedy, mirroring the authentic experience of the human condition.

Celia is the one who turns the mood. She's dynamic and resourceful in crisis when Rosalind is too shocked to think straight. 'Why, whither shall we go?' Rosalind asks hopelessly. 'To seek my uncle in the Forest of Arden.' Escape seems to have the simplicity of all the most dangerous missions. To the perils ahead of them, Celia adds the sparkle of escapade. Let's go in disguise, she says, let's become different people.

> Celia I'll put myself in poor and mean attire,
> And with a kind of umber smirch my face -
> The like do you; so shall we pass along
> And never stir assailants.[8]

'It's Celia at the beginning, she's making the plans, she just takes it on, she books the tickets, she packs the bags,' observes Sally Scott.

Rosalind quickly picks up the baton from Celia and finesses the proposal. And her inventive spirit adds another layer of energy. Not only will the two aristocrats disguise themselves as artisans and leap over class boundaries, but as the leggier of the two, Rosalind proposes to go in drag. An Elizabethan audience was used to actors defying the Sumptuary Laws which decreed you had to dress according to your social class: furs, silks and purple allowed only for the upper classes; woollen academic gowns expected for lawyers, doctors and clerics; fustian for the lower classes. These laws were designed to keep you in your proper place although in reality they were almost impossible to enforce. Upwardly mobile merchants were challenging the old feudal rigidities. They sold gorgeous fabrics to the nobility but were hardly likely to deny them to their own families. Dress codes denoting social status proclaimed the man and woman then, quite different from today's denim for all occasions, all classes, and both sexes.

Inside the freer though risky sphere of the playhouse, the Sumptuary Laws were openly flouted. In England women were banned from appearing as professional actresses, so boys or youths played all the female roles. In spite of this, some women like Mary Frith did tread the boards, and others, in the daring spirit of Viola de Lesseps imagined by Tom Stoppard in the 1998 film *Shakespeare in Love*, just may have done. It was different in Europe, especially in the Latin countries. Spanish Tirso de Molina's fizzing comedy, *Don Gil de las calzas verdes/ Don Gil of the Green Breeches*, written later in the same decade as *As You Like It*, also turns on cross-dressing. But in Spain women played the female roles. Donna Juana as Don Gil or Donna Elvira is equally convincing whether in gown or breeches. 'The very image of deceit,' s/ he's 'counterfeited coinage' and like Ganymede, not what s/he appears.

But for a real Elizabethan woman in sixteenth-century England, dressing as a man could pitch you into more dangerous territory than challenging social etiquette. It set you against God. Preachers constantly invoked the law laid down in Deuteronomy: 'The woman shalt not wear that which pertaineth unto a man, neither shall a man put on a woman's garment: for all that do so are abomination unto the Lord thy God.'[9] The clergy denounced theatre generally but the specific issue of cross-dressing and displaying a fine pair of legs enraged them. In *The Schoole of Abuse* of 1579, Stephen Gosson literally told women to stay at home. In his view, watching or performing plays 'effeminated' the mind. Philip Stubbes felt play-going could erode masculinity itself. When boy actors impersonated women on stage, the church saw it as a flagrant provocation to lust, lechery and wantonness. Sexual temptation horrified Dr John Rainolds, an influential Oxford theologian. 'A woman's garment being put upon a man doth vehemently touch and move him with the remembrance and imagination of a woman; and the imagination of a thing desirable doth stir up the desire.'[10] Even worse, in Rainolds' view, the troubling appeal of a cross-dressed, effeminate boy actor might incite 'unclean affections,' meaning homosexual desire. He ranted against the eroticism of the stage while nobody seemed to remember that back in 1566, during Queen Elizabeth's visit to Oxford, Rainolds himself had played the part of Hippolyta in a production of *Palaemon and Arcyte*.[11] In a modern riposte to the Sumptuary Laws,

Jeanette Winterson's transvestite heroine Villanelle asks: 'If I went to confession, what would I confess? That I cross-dress? So did Our Lord, so do the priests.'[12]

John Lyly's earlier gender-bending play, *Galatea*, first performed by St. Paul's boys' company 'before the Queen's Majesty at Greenwich, on New Year's day [1588] at night,' pulses with these ideas.[13] Two shepherds decide to cross-dress their daughters, Galatea and Phillida – both played by boys – in order to escape the lust of the sea-god Neptune. When Galatea expresses her disgust for going Ganymede, her father argues: 'To gain love the gods have taken shapes of beasts, and to save life art thou coy to take the attire of men?' His daughter answers, punning, 'they were beastly gods, that lust could make them seem as beasts.'[14] However, for her own safety she accepts male disguise, only to chide herself in a soliloquy with the audience, 'Blush, Galatea, that must frame thy affection fit for thy habit…Oh, would the gods had made me as I seem to be.'[15] As a boy actor playing a girl, now cross-dressing back as a man, Galatea meets Phillida, each unknown to the other, though in the same predicament of male disguise. Of course they fall in love.

Echoing Galatea, Phillida, too, torments herself, 'Poor Phillida, curse the time of thy birth and rareness of thy beauty, the unaptness of thy apparel, and the untamedness of thy affections! Art thou no sooner in the habit of a boy but thou must be enamoured of a boy?'[16] This mirage of gender identity, common on the Elizabethan stage, teased the audience with a heady sense of sexual confusion. Only a dizzying vortex of plot complications could unravel the layers of identity represented by Phillida and Galatea in their multiple selves: boy-girl-boy-girl – although boy in the final analysis. At the denouement, the goddess Venus has no option but to change one of the girl-lovers into a boy, magically re-assigning gender without surgery.

Perhaps another factor agitated the church even more than the sexual implications of cross-dressing. For women in drag undermined the accepted social order which kept women firmly in their subservient relationship of Eve to Adam. If they dressed as men they might decide to claim the same rights and independence as men. As soon as Rosalind disguised as Ganymede arrives in Arden, she assumes the masculine role, superior to cousin Celia, posing as Ganymede's sister, Aliena. 'I must comfort the weaker vessel,' Ganymede says, in irony or provocation when Celia is on the point of exhaustion. After Duke Frederick's deportation order, Celia had been the practical one, but in the forest she dwindles, mostly, into the conventional model of female behaviour.

In contrast with Celia's femininity, Rosalind forces herself to step up to her costume change, as 'doublet and hose ought to show itself courageous to petticoat.' When she urges Celia, 'Therefore, courage, good Aliena!' the courage is as much for herself in trying on her new virility. She soon finds that it fits a certain aspect of her personality that had been hidden or sublimated during her life as a woman. There was a hint of this testosterone at the wrestling match when Rosalind offered Orlando 'the little strength that I have, I would it were with you.' Although a female monarch reigned, physical strength was not usually ascribed to women in Elizabethan times, except to the legendary Queen of the Amazons who married Theseus at the end of *A Midsummer Night's Dream*. Queen Elizabeth's strength was symbolic rather than corporeal. Even today we've become acculturated only gradually, or not at all, to the idea of women in the forces, or female Olympic boxers or wrestlers.[17]

Although aristocratic, Rosalind as a dispossessed, unmarried young woman, would have found it almost impossible, if not downright illegal, to accomplish her first autonomous action in Arden. As Ganymede, she buys some real estate. Cash in hand, she employs Corin, a local shepherd, as her property agent, instructing him to negotiate for a small working farm,

> Rosalind I pray thee, if it stand with honesty,
>   Buy thou the cottage, pasture and the flock,
>   And thou shalt have to pay for it of us.[18]

The deal is closed 'right suddenly' and Rosalind has changed her life and Celia's. For the foreseeable future they will own 'The soil, the profit, and this kind of life.' They've become independent, self-sufficient – and green.

Though moving within similar pastoral conventions to Lyly's Galatea and Phillida, Shakespeare's Rosalind challenges society altogether more assertively. A boy actor in girl's clothes at the beginning of the play, then emerging as Ganymede, a triple layered boy/girl/boy, his/her stage presence would have been thrilling and suggestive to both sexes in the Elizabethan audience, as well as to fellow actors onstage. It was exactly this erotic excitement that Dr Rainolds most abhorred.

In our own times, Michael Billington, theatre critic of *The Guardian*, has identified 'an umbilical connection between acting and sex.' Ever since and probably before Ovid advised young men to haunt the theatre in search of love over 2,000 years ago, the stage has been a magnet for sexual adventure.[19] Plays in performance exploit this heightened mood. 'An actor, in a sense, makes love to his audience…The theatre is rooted in sex,' observes Billington. 'This takes many forms. There is the androgynous, bisexual quality that invariably underpins great acting'. He suggests that why boy actors playing girls were so popular was because the theatre 'is a place where we can all admit that our natures are a compound of masculine and feminine….a place where inhibitions can be released by both the performer and the spectator.'[20]

The striking sexual ambiguity of screen and stage stars like Greta Garbo, Marlene Dietrich and Laurence Olivier in the twentieth century fed into the fantasies of audiences worldwide. And as Janet Suzman observes, every performance needs its audience for the chemistry to work. 'Whatever the show is will be made by the audience seeing it. A play doesn't happen without an audience. It's a complicit friendship, if you like, in that afternoon's run. What I find wonderful is that the actor is saying, we don't live without you, you bring us to life.'[21] For the two hours' traffic of the stage, and maybe as we leave elated after the show, Rosalind dressed as Ganymede transcends gender. Whatever our sexuality we can all identify with the universal experience of falling in love.

There is another frontier or rite of passage that Rosalind and Orlando negotiate as they trace their way through those early stages of life listed by Jaques in his Seven Ages of Man speech. The lovers find themselves in the borderland, or no man's land of growing up where everything is fluid and exciting. Androgynous looks among teenagers were standard then and the look is still current today. With his 'little beard' Orlando hovers between boy and man. As the wild, romantic author of his own poems, he should present 'a beard neglected', but that, as Rosalind points out, 'you have not'. Orlando can only muster some fuzzy designer stubble. So fresh faced are both Orlando and Rosalind/Ganymede that, like Viola/Cesario in *Twelfth Night*, they are poised on the tipping point between 'a squash…before 'tis a peascod, or a codling when 'tis almost an apple.' But while Orlando is still an idealistic teenager, Rosalind is slightly more than an adolescent. She's on the cusp: between girl and boy, between girl and woman. She's intellectually mature but still revels in the mischief and the truth telling of a teenager.

Once established in Arden as 'Master Ganymede', running a small-holding, the fantasy of so many urbanites, Rosalind feels safe and carefree even though she secretly longs for Orlando whom she'd seen once and fallen in love with at the wrestling match. It seems unlikely she'll ever see him again. But to her amazement, she discovers the greenwood trees of Arden are festooned with love poems, addressed to a girl – coincidentally called Rosalind.

> *From the east to western Inde*
> *No jewel is like Rosalind.*
> *Her worth being mounted on the wind*
> *Through all the world bears Rosalind.*[22]

It's doggerel, but a little frisson shivers through her as she reads the lines. According to Touchstone, the sophisticated Fool the girls have brought with them to Arden, these trees yield nothing but 'bad fruit.' With his talent for improvisation Touchstone shows Rosalind just how glibly, and obscenely, he can reel off more of the same.

> *Touchstone* If a hart do lack a hind,
> Let him seek out Rosalind.
> If the cat will after kind,
> So be sure will Rosalind.
> Winter garments must be lined,
> So must slender Rosalind.
> They that reap must sheaf and bind,
> Then to cart with Rosalind.
> Sweetest nut hath sourest rind,
> Such a nut is Rosalind.
> He that sweetest rose will find
> Must find love's prick – and Rosalind.[23]

'This is the very false gallop of verses: why do you infect yourself with them?' he taunts Rosalind. She defends the lines which bear her name, 'but whether wisely or no, let the forest judge'. Celia, too, has found love poems hanging on trees.

> Celia   But upon the fairest boughs,
> Or at every sentence' end,
> Will I 'Rosalinda' write...[24]

Even Rosalind has to admit that 'some of them had in them more feet than the verses would bear.' Her hopes rise as she finds poems everywhere, 'for look here what I found on a palm tree. I was never so berhymed...' Could they really be addressed to her? And who is the author? 'Is it a man?...I prithee who?...Nay, but who is it?' Celia knows the answer. Perhaps she's spotted Orlando decorating trees, and she enjoys prolonging Rosalind's agony. 'O wonderful, wonderful, and most wonderful wonderful, and yet again wonderful, and after that, out of all hooping!' hoots Celia.

In exasperation, Rosalind plays her inner girl. 'Dost thou think, though I am caparisoned like a man, I have a doublet and hose in my disposition?' The outfit can't conceal her essential nature and now her verbal creativity overflows:

> Rosalind   One inch of delay more is a South Sea of discovery.
> I prithee tell me who is it quickly and speak apace. I
> would thou couldst stammer, that thou mightst pour this
> concealed man out of thy mouth as wine comes out of a
> narrow-mouthed bottle – either too much at once or none
> at all. I prithee take the cork out of thy mouth that I may
> drink thy tidings.[25]

Rosalind is given to spontaneous global comparisons like the South Sea of discovery, or the Bay of Portugal, which reflect not only the scale of her emotions but also the pioneering Age of Exploration in which Shakespeare lived. At last Celia reveals that the poet is indeed 'young Orlando, that tripped up the wrestler's heels and your heart both in an instant.' Rosalind is reduced to a single-word enquiry: 'Orlando?' But almost instantly, her irrepressible verbal stream bubbles up.

Rosalind	Alas the day, what shall I do with my doublet and hose? What did he when thou sawst him? What said he? How looked he? Wherein went he? What makes he here? Did he ask for me? Where remains he? How parted he with thee? And when shalt thou see him again?[26]

Ten questions gush out of her in confusion and excitement. The only person who can stem them, momentarily, is Rosalind herself with the unanswerable, 'Answer me in one word.' The spate overflows again: 'But doth he know that I am in this forest, and in man's apparel? Looks he as freshly as he did the day he wrestled?' Her constant interruptions to Celia's account finally crescendo in yet another question, and the line all audiences savour: 'Do you not know I am a woman? When I think, I must speak.'

What are the choices? To reveal herself as a woman? Meet Orlando as Rosalind? Compromise her safety when Duke Frederick's men may be on her heels, as we know 'dead or living' they are hunting Orlando? End a five-act play in the middle of Act 3? Or maintain her persona as Ganymede with all its complications? Events overtake any decision as Rosalind and Celia catch sight of Orlando nearby, joshing with Jaques. She has no option but to continue as Ganymede.

When Rosalind disguises herself as a man and calls herself 'Ganymede', she's using a word first recorded in English in 1591, less than a decade before the first mooted performance of *As You Like It*. Members of the audience with a classical education would have known the reference to the name of Jove's own page. But Ganymede the 'amorous girl-boy' as Thomas Lodge, author of the prototype *Rosalynde* in 1590, described him, sent another distinct frisson through the groundlings and up into the galleries. Richard Barnfield's poem of 1594 is explicit about *The Tears of an Affectionate Shepherd Sick for Love, or The Complaint of Daphnis for the Love of Ganymede*.

> If it be sin to love a sweet-faced boy,
> (Whose amber locks trussed up in golden trammels
> Dangle adown his lovely cheeks with joy,
> When pearl and flowers his fair hair enamels),
> If it be sin to love a lovely lad,
> Oh then sin I, for whom my soul is sad...'[27]

Only a decade or so later, Rubens will paint a seductive Ganymede, borne away to Olympus by Zeus, disguised as an eagle. From antiquity until the beginning of the nineteenth century, the name Ganymede signalled a gay male lover. Marlowe pictured Ganymede's bisexual appeal in his poem *Hero and Leander*. (The Roman version of Zeus was called Jove or Jupiter.)

> Some swore he was a maid in man's attire,
> For in his lookes were all that men desire,
> ... Jove, slylie stealing from his sister's bed,
> To dallie with Idalian Ganimed.[28]

In spite of natural objections from Juno his wife, Jupiter wooed Ganymede quite openly in Marlowe's play *Dido, Queen of Carthage*.

> *Jupiter* Come gentle Ganymede, and play with me,
> I love thee well, say Juno what she will...
> Sit on my knee...
>
> These linked gems
> My Juno ware upon her marriage-day,
> Put thou about thy neck, my own sweet heart,
> And trick thy arms and shoulders with my theft.[29]

There's no doubt that Ganymede, Jupiter's paramour, was up for sale. Derived from 'catamite,' Ganymede implied a rent boy to the Elizabethan audience. Alexander Cooke, one of the most likely young candidates to have played Rosalind in 1599, was then no more than fifteen.[30] Dramatically trained boys were so adept at impersonating women that audiences accepted the illusion, confident 'the boy will well usurp the grace,/Voice, gait and action of a gentlewoman.'[31] Puritan pamphleteer, William Prynne, denounced the illusions practised on the seventeenth-century stage where 'players and play-haunters in their secret conclaves play the sodomites...some modern examples...have been desperately enamored with players' boys thus clad in women's apparel, so far as to solicit them by words, by letters, even actually to abuse them...This I have heard credibly reported of a scholar of Balliol College, and I doubt not but it may be verified of divers others'.[32]

Rosalind's transvestism has an erotic charge even when she's played, as we usually expect today, by a young woman. Juliet Rylance noticed, 'when I got dressed up as a boy, all the men came up with "Oh God, there's something really sexy about this and we don't know what it is!"'[33]

In 1599, a triply layered cross-dressing boy/girl/boy, probably made the effect even more exciting, as Janet Suzman says, 'It's also a little bit homoerotic, I suppose, because Rosalind is a pretty young boy really – and very natural to the Elizabethans. They weren't ashamed of finding that Greek thing – boys adorable.' So when disguise ambushes Rosalind into approaching Orlando as Ganymede, she decides to turn disaster into opportunity. Out of her predicament she summons an ingenious plan to make herself doubly adorable to Orlando.[34]

Rosalind first approaches Orlando with that age-old chat-up line, 'what is't o'clock?' He shows the merest flicker of doubt that Ganymede is not quite what he seems but his misgivings concerns class, not gender. 'Your accent is something finer than you could purchase in so removed a dwelling.' That's easy for Rosalind to bat away. 'I have been told so of many. But indeed an old religious uncle of mine taught me to speak.' She's swiftly into her new boyish stride, and confident enough to brag to Orlando, 'I thank God I am not a woman, to be touched with so many giddy offences as he hath generally taxed their whole sex withal.' It's a test. Will he see through her disguise? Can she maintain it? No and Yes! Only the audience, Celia and Touchstone are complicit about Rosalind's identity. She presses her advantage, probing, challenging.

> *Rosalind*   There is a man haunts the forest that abuses our young plants with carving 'Rosalind' on their barks; hangs odes upon hawthorns and elegies on brambles; all, forsooth, deifying the name of Rosalind. If I could meet that fancy-monger I would give him some good counsel, for he seems to have the quotidian of love upon him.[35]

Orlando confesses it is indeed he who is so 'love-shaked' and author of the poems dangling from Arden's trees in praise of heavenly Rosalind. 'I am that he, that unfortunate he.' Rosalind is immediately wary. Does Orlando really retain the love that had flared between them after the wrestling match? Speaking is not writing and Orlando in conversation doesn't sound like any pastoral patterns of courtly love. He's so different from the histrionic shepherd, Silvius, whom she's overheard declaring his passion for Phebe to his older friend, Corin.

> *Silvius*   If thou rememb'rest not the slightest folly
> That ever love did make thee run into,
> Thou hast not loved.

Or if thou hast not sat as I do now,
Wearing thy hearer in thy mistress' praise,
Thou hast not loved.
Or if thou hast not broke from company
Abruptly as my passion now makes me,
Thou hast not loved.
O Phebe, Phebe, Phebe![36]

How can Rosalind be confident when Orlando doesn't look the least bit like a lovesick swain, epitomised by Silvius? In her witty, semi-ironic inventory of what a true lover should look like, Orlando doesn't tick any of her boxes. He should have:

Rosalind   A lean cheek, which you have not; a blue eye and sunken, which you have not; an unquestionable spirit, which you have not; a beard neglected, which you have not – but I pardon you for that, for simply your having in beard is a younger brother's revenue. Then your hose should be ungartered, your bonnet unbanded, your sleeve unbuttoned, your shoe untied, and everything about you demonstrating a careless desolation. But you are no such man. You are rather point-device in your accoutrements, as loving yourself than seeming the lover of any other.[37]

Even as a refugee in the forest, Orlando looks as composed and desirable as a luminescent miniature by Nicholas Hilliard or Isaac Oliver. He can only protest to Ganymede, the 'fair youth' who has approached him, 'I would I could make thee believe I love.' Ganymede asks Orlando the crucial question Rosalind might never have dared in farthingale or skirts. 'But are you so much in love as your rhymes speak?' Orlando answers, 'Neither rhyme nor reason can express how much.' Rebecca Hall comments, 'I don't think [Rosalind] is quite comfortable enough with herself to believe that anyone could really be in love with her. I think she wants him to fall in love with her as the boy, oddly, because it *is* her. Yes, she's playing the part, but it's very much her personality. I think what scares her is him falling in love with his image of Rosalind, this fantasy Rosalind that he met for two seconds and has been writing poems about. She wants to be sure that he is falling in love with the real Rosalind…Well, the real Rosalind who's pretending to be a boy.'[38] Orlando's Rosalind, the one who left him tongue-tied after the wrestling match, has spiralled into his fantasy life. He doesn't know her at all. Love, Ganymede tells Orlando, 'is merely a madness.' Rosalind must test his fantasy. Is he the real deal?

Rosalind has a sudden inspiration, an audacious plan for a trial courtship. It will be flirting with a serious undertow. She can exploit her masquerade, charade, pretence, and yes, play-acting, as tools to excavate the emotional truth about Orlando. She can turn her predicament, her doublet and hose, to her own advantage. It's rather like being in the wild, concealed in a naturalist's hide. Not only will the trick keep her close to Orlando, but from the safety of her boy's carapace, she can offer to 'cure' Orlando of his lovesickness by impersonating the very Rosalind he thinks he loves. She's done it once before, she tells him cockily, 'and in this manner.'

> Rosalind He was to imagine me his love, his mistress, and I set him
> every day to woo me. At which time would I – being but
> a moonish youth – grieve, be effeminate, changeable,
> longing and liking, proud, fantastical, apish, shallow,
> inconstant, full of tears, full of smiles; for every passion
> something and for no passion truly anything, as boys and
> women are for the most part cattle of this colour; would
> now like him, now loath him; then entertain him, then
> forswear him; now weep for him, then spit at him...And
> thus I cured him.[39]

Ganymede/Rosalind knowingly brackets together boys and women. There was a blurring of genders during the English Renaissance, especially on the stage. It was a constant problem for acting companies to predict when their best boys would cross the border of puberty. Hamlet refers to this when he greets the boy who is to be the Player Queen.

> Hamlet What, my young lady and mistress! By'r lady, your
> ladyship is nearer to heaven than when I saw you last...
> Pray God your voice, like a piece of uncurrent gold, be
> not cracked...[40]

There were many boy actors to choose from in an age when sexual maturity came later than it does now, sometimes not until 17 or 18. Treble voices could even remain unbroken up till 20.[41] Men admired boys who looked effeminate, like Shakespeare's patron, the startlingly beautiful 3rd Earl of Southampton. And they admired girls who looked flat chested and androgynous, like boys. Nicholas Hilliard's portrait miniature of an exquisite *Young Man Leaning Against a Tree Among Roses*, hand on heart, his slender, balletic limbs in white tights, embodies all that gender fusion. It could be a portrait of Ganymede in Arden.[42] So ambiguous and alluring is the identity of Rosalind's 'pretty youth' that s/he not only sustains the love of Orlando but also inflames the desire of Phebe, a cream cheeked, black-eyed shepherdess, played misleadingly enough by another boy. On the Elizabethan stage, gender was totally jumbled. Not only was Rosalind in disguise but so were Celia, Phebe and Audrey. Perhaps gender became simply irrelevant, as we find today when we watch all-female productions of *Julius Caesar* and *Henry IV*,[43] though these productions do not intend to convey the subversive erotic charge of boy actors cross-dressing on the Elizabethan stage.

After setting their next date, Rosalind languishes because like all teenagers Orlando hasn't turned up on time, 'Never talk to me; I will weep.' Celia warns Rosalind not to harbour unrealistic hopes about her play-lover. She points out that having become a man, Rosalind had better behave like one, 'have the grace to consider that tears do not become a man.' She points out Orlando's many shortcomings. His hair is the wrong colour, it indicates betrayal like Judas's; his kisses have the 'ice of chastity' in them; and besides, Celia doubts whether he's still in love. 'Was' is not 'is', she says tartly. Rosalind interrupts to say she'd met her father, exiled Duke Senior, in the forest yesterday, 'and had much question with him: he asked me of what parentage I was; I told him, of as good as he; so he laughed and let me go.'

In the police state operating during the final dangerous years of Elizabethan England, Rosalind in Arden is a new kind of spy in a man's world, infiltrating preconceptions about what makes a woman, what makes a man, as she eavesdrops on masculinity, accessing knowledge forbidden to women. She's thrilled that her Ganymede disguise fools even her father. 'But what talk we of fathers, when there is such a man as Orlando?' Her focus has changed, she no longer needs her father. Instead, her mind constantly reverts to her lover, though Celia cautions her again. Orlando may write fine words but he hasn't kept his promise to return on time. Corin interrupts the cousins, inviting them to witness 'a pageant truly played,' a love scene between shepherds Silvius and Phebe. Rosalind is more than willing to overhear their dialogue, for as she obsesses to Celia, 'The sight of lovers feedeth those in love.'

Into the drama between Silvius and Phebe, Rosalind can project her own longing for love, enacted by Silvius desperate for love of Phebe, who cannot requite him, nor even pity his pain. Rejecting Silvius, a good man's love, Phebe falls catastrophically in love with Ganymede from the moment s/he steps out from a leafy vantage point. 'Why, what means this? Why do you look on me?' This is one more complication that Rosalind hadn't envisaged when she cross-dressed. 'I think she means to tangle my eyes too!' The Silvius-Phebe courtship vibrates with the main love story between Rosalind and Orlando. It's like watching a play within a play. In Phebe's highhanded refusal of Silvius, 'Now I do frown on thee with all my heart/And if mine eyes can wound, now let them kill thee,' Rosalind sees her own worst fears of rejection by Orlando. That's why she reacts, apparently so callously, to Phebe's sudden infatuation with Ganymede.

> *Rosalind*   No, faith, proud mistress, hope not after it.
> 'Tis not your inky brows, your black silk hair,
> Your bugle eyeballs, nor your cheek of cream,
> That can entame my spirits to your worship.
> You foolish shepherd, wherefore do you follow her
> Like foggy south, puffing with wind and rain?
> You are a thousand times a properer man
> Than she a woman. 'Tis such fools as you
> That makes the world full of ill-favoured children.
> 'Tis not her glass but you that flatters her,
> And out of you she sees herself more proper
> Than any of her lineaments can show her.
> But, mistress, know yourself; down on your knees,
> And thank heaven, fasting, for a good man's love.
> For I must tell you friendly in your ear:
> Sell when you can, you are not for all markets.[44]

That line, 'thank heaven, fasting, for a good man's love,' first dropped into my brain when I was studying English Literature at university. On that line I based a personal decision, and the words have lodged in my memory ever since. During a trip to Stratford in 1968 I heard Janet Suzman's Ganymede deliver it to high-handed Phebe, played by Helen Mirren. Rosalind's exchange with Phebe works in both directions, as Janet Suzman points out. 'Rosalind has looked at Phebe. Phebe has been a big educative thing for her, hasn't she? She's looking a gift horse in the mouth with that lovely little Silvius. She's seen the loyalty of little Silvius and she's seen Phebe looking around. So maybe her Orlando isn't Achilles but that was then and now she's discovered that he's morally a nice chap and he's got fibre and bottom – and he truly loves her and that in itself is something worth treasuring.'[45] But Rosalind quickly slips from her blank verse tutorial mode into a prose aside to the audience. Silvius has fallen in love with Phebe's 'foulness, and she'll fall in love with my anger,' Rosalind says as she interferes in the Silvius/Phebe love plot. It's instinctive revenge for seeing her own predicament in theirs.

Choosing the name 'Ganymede' impels Rosalind over so many borders. From girl to boy; from court to exile; from urban to pastoral; from insider to outsider; from poetry to prose. Her choice also somersaults the play from the tragedy of *realpolitik* at court to the comedy of love in Arden, like the cheeky somersault Elisabeth Bergner actually performed in the 1936 film of *As You Like It*. Bergner's somersault was unforgettable for art critic Brian Sewell. Her appeal as Ganymede was homoerotic, establishing for Sewell 'even at that early age [he was five in 1936] a canon of blond beauty that I was later to apply to boys.'[46] Made visual in Bergner's somersault, Rosalind's transvestite exile in Arden brings deliverance. Sporting doublet and hose, or jeans and trainers, unlaced from corset and farthingale, or prom gown and high heels, Rosalind's new erotic androgyny gives her the freedom to speak her mind. 'Well, it's a mask, isn't it,' said Rebecca Hall. 'I found it a liberation. As soon as she starts being a boy she's much more herself. She feels more at ease with herself, and able to say what she's feeling and what she's thinking...I just played it straight in boy's clothes. In doing that you embrace a certain amount of ambiguity about her. I think there's something genderless about Rosalind. She has aspects of femininity and she has aspects of masculinity.'[47]

When Rosalind is played by an adult male, rather than by an Elizabethan boy or a post-Restoration woman, the effect can be as multi-layered as a *mille-feuille* confection. In a daring all-male production which opened in 1967, the year of Twiggy's boyish fashion modelling and Yves St. Laurent's iconic trouser suits for women, Ronald Pickup played Rosalind at the Old Vic. It was the ideal cultural moment for Pickup's 'willowy and breastless' Rosalind, 'clinically drained of sensuality.'[48] Played by a man, going Ganymede can unexpectedly reveal the universality of Rosalind. 'I was gender-free, I knew the play was about passion, between two men, or a man or a woman – you're not sure which – but you're led to a point where it doesn't matter. It's about people in love and it has an extraordinary purity. You're allowed to love whoever and whatever you want. The joy of it is so liberating,' Pickup told me he'd 'insisted on having bare feet. Bare feet are very liberating. So much of a character starts with the feet. It really does.'[49] He was twenty-seven and gangly. 'Becoming Ganymede was the most natural thing in the world. It felt like a release, like a creature being set free in the forest. Rosalind is Ganymede – and she opens up to everything in the forest.'[50]

In 1991 Declan Donnellan cast Adrian Lester with his 'beautiful voice and grace of movement' as Rosalind for the Cheek by Jowl all-male production.[51] Lester thinks 'you have to lose track of gender in the middle of the play. The production must make you feel as though you are watching two human beings wrapped up in the dizzy rush of being in love. Only then does the play truly work. Because then it will be about the nature of fear, trust and love in whatever form you like it.' I asked him what can be unlocked by an adult male actor playing Rosalind, rather than a female actor? 'No one can play the part of a woman, better than a woman. I believe she will have a more immediate connection to the dilemmas Rosalind has to face in the play.' But his masculine perspective may have enabled Lester to add something different. 'From the mouth of a male actor,' Rosalind's comments on 'the nature of women and what they are like either in life or love...have a playful resonance and irony.'[52]

In productions today an actress cross-dressing as Ganymede can choose to heighten either, or both, of the feminine or masculine facets of Rosalind's temperament. She may be able to embody as many, or even more, multiple selves than a male actor. When Buzz Goodbody directed *As You Like It* in 1973 for the RSC, 'any hint of sexual equivocation [was] knocked on the head by Eileen Atkins's minimal attempt to disguise her femininity as Rosalind. Indeed, with her headband, fringed blouse and crotch-hugging jeans, she seemed even more seductive as Ganymede than before.'[53] This was a pivotal moment for one young spectator. 'I remember the first Shakespeare play I ever saw, a production of *As You Like It* at Stratford with Eileen Atkins as Rosalind. And at the end of the show, I came dancing out of the theatre, and we got in our beige Mini and drove back up to Preston in Lancashire, and I turned to my Mum and said 'That's what I want to do when I grow up.'[54] Gregory Doran grew up to become Artistic Director of the RSC. More than a generation after Eileen Atkins, the real-life partnership of Juliet Rylance and Christian Camargo directed by Sam Mendes at The Old Vic in 2010, illumined the masculine energy in her Rosalind and the feminine resources of his Orlando. They encapsulated Montaigne's opinion in the translation by Florio that Shakespeare would have known. 'I say that both male and female are cast in the same mold; instruction and custom excepted, there is no great difference between them.'[55] Or as Harriet Walter said in 2015, 'What I'm finding is how blurred the edge is between being a woman and a man interiorly.'[56] For me, Rosalind is neither feminine nor masculine but embraces both sexes. She's dual-gendered, universal and inclusive.

As Ganymede, Rosalind can reverse the usual dynamics of courtship, man wooing woman. With the liberty of androgyny, she can grasp the initiative. She has already set this up with her genius plan. He's to 'call me Rosalind and come every day to my cote and woo me.' I'll be you and you'll be me. Her words have the simplicity of the nursery but also the guile of a woman in love. And like lovers anywhere waiting for that phone call, text, or ping from social media, Rosalind cannot endure a single minute's delay to her next date, let alone an hour.

> *Rosalind* Why, how now, Orlando, where have you been all this while? You a lover? An you serve me such another trick, never come in my sight more!
>
> *Orlando* My fair Rosalind, I come within an hour of my promise.
>
> *Rosalind* Break an hour's promise in love? He that will divide a minute into a thousand parts, and break but a part of the thousand part of a minute in the affairs of love, it may be said of him that Cupid hath clapped him o'th' shoulder, but I'll warrant him heart-whole.

Orlando	Pardon me, dear Rosalind.
Rosalind	Nay, an you be so tardy, come no more in my sight. I had as lief be wooed of a snail.[57]

Ganymede demands the same punctuality as if he were indeed Orlando's 'very, very Rosalind.' It's courtship by proxy, conducted with the finesse of chess, for a love sparked in the brute physicality of a wrestling match. But Orlando's not playing by the rules of Ganymede's game which is courtship by conversation. Instead he tries stealing a kiss from the impossibly attractive boy. Even though constrained by a bewilderingly transvestite Ganymede/Rosalind, the 'master-mistress of his passion,'[58] Orlando's love is not all theory. There has been kissing in Arden, 'as full of sanctity as holy bread,' Rosalind fervently reports to Celia. It's a courtship full of implications for homoerotic love as well as for straight sex. Love is love, says Shakespeare in his modern way, wherever it's to be found. 'Love is not love/Which alters when it alteration finds.'[59] Nevertheless, Ganymede parries the kiss, 'Nay, you were better speak first.' 'Am not I your Rosalind?' she asks Orlando who ruefully concedes, 'I take some joy to say you are, because I would be talking of her.'

Rosalind	Well, in her person, I say I will not have you.
Orlando	Then, in mine own person, I die.
Rosalind	No, faith, die by attorney. The poor world is almost six thousand years old, and in all this time there was not any man died in his own person, (videlicit, [that's to say] in a love-cause). Troilus had his brains dashed out with a Grecian club, yet he did what he could to die before, and he is one of the patterns of love. Leander, he would have lived many a fair year, though Hero had turned nun, if it had not been for a hot midsummer night; for, good youth, he went but forth to wash him in the Hellespont and, being taken with the cramp, was drowned and the foolish chroniclers of that age found it was Hero of Sestos. But these are all lies. Men have died from time to time and worms have eaten them, but not for love.[60]

When Orlando turns his passion into melodrama claiming it will kill him, Rosalind is ready to challenge him. As Ganymede, Rosalind can be far more forthright with Orlando, 'man' to man, than she could have been in a frock. Don't be silly, she tells him, no one has actually died from lovesickness. 'Men *have* died from time to time, and worms *have* eaten them, but not for love.' [my italics]

However, though she's ticked him off, Rosalind is in the grip of the same malady. Seizing the upper hand, she decides on a flash proposal. Rosalind's 'supreme moment of high camp is the wooing scene, where she pretends to be what she really is – Rosalind,' observes feminist critic Camille Paglia.[61] Rosalind has already disrupted the social etiquette of wooing, now she goes even further by proposing. In Lyly's earlier play *Galatea*, transvestite Phillida said to Galatea, 'It were a shame, if a maiden should be a suitor (a thing hated in that sex).'[62] But as Ganymede, Rosalind is flying free. Under an alias, she can be her real self. And that self wants the commitment of marriage, and wants it now. She can present the proposal as make-believe for Orlando but it's profoundly real for her. She even has a female celebrant, Celia, on hand, in an age which would have found the very idea beyond blasphemous.

Rosalind	But come, now I will be your Rosalind in a more coming-on disposition, and ask me what you will, I will grant it.
Orlando	Then love me, Rosalind.
Rosalind	Yes, faith, will I, Fridays and Saturdays and all.
Orlando	And wilt thou have me?
Rosalind	Ay, and twenty such.
Orlando	What sayst thou?
Rosalind	Are you not good?
Orlando	I hope so.
Rosalind	Why then, can one desire too much of a good thing? Come, sister, you shall be the priest and marry us. Give me your hand, Orlando. What do you say, sister?
Orlando	Pray thee, marry us.
Celia	I cannot say the words.
Rosalind	You must begin: 'Will you, Orlando – '
Celia	Go to. – Will you, Orlando, have to wife this Rosalind?
Orlando	I will.
Rosalind	Ay, but when?

Orlando	Why now, as fast as she can marry us.
Rosalind	Then you must say: 'I take thee, Rosalind, for wife.'
Orlando	I take thee, Rosalind, for wife.
Rosalind	I might ask you for your commission. But I do take thee, Orlando, for my husband. There's a girl goes before the priest, and certainly a woman's thought runs before her actions.[63]

Even in the language of playschool, 'You must begin…Then you must say..,' Rosalind's mock wedding feels as binding as a formal betrothal ahead of the marriage ceremony was in Shakespeare's day. A pre-wedding betrothal may explain why his and Anne Hathaway's first child, Susanna, born just six months after their wedding, did not imply a shotgun marriage. Susanna would have been seventeen when Shakespeare wrote *As You Like It*, the perfect age to inspire his creation of Rosalind. A few years later Susanna married John Hall.

> Witty above her sex, but that's not all,
> Wise to Salvation was good Mistress Hall,
> Something of Shakespeare was in that
> Wholly of him with who she's now in bliss.

Susanna's epitaph in Holy Trinity Church, Stratford-upon-Avon, could be a description of his model for Rosalind, Shakespeare's portrait of his eldest daughter.

Rosalind and Orlando's spontaneous, unofficial greenwood wedding completely renovates an aborted marriage of two scenes earlier. Jaques overhears Touchstone's rash proposal to earthy goatherd Audrey just as Sir Oliver Mar-text, a dubious cleric, arrives to hitch the pair in a hurry. Not being a marrying man, Jaques can't contain himself. He demands of Touchstone whether he wants to be married 'under a bush like a beggar?' Touchstone replies cynically that 'not being well married, it will be a good excuse for me hereafter to leave my wife.' The wedding is called off.

Unlike Touchstone and Audrey's ditched ceremony, Rosalind's mock wedding with Orlando has the sanctity of holy writ, even though she has no licence for it. The words she forces Celia to recite imitate the marriage service in the Book of Common Prayer. 'Will you, Orlando, have to wife this Rosalind?' instead of the more archaic, 'Wilt thou have this woman to thy wedded wife?'[64] The more idiomatic, 'I take thee, Rosalind, for wife,' in place of 'I take thee [Rosalind] to my wedded wife.' Concluding the impromptu ceremony, Rosalind in her role as Ganymede, must instantly puncture its solemnity. Orlando must not look too long or too deeply into her deceptive eyes. Anyway, a wedding is only a beginning, not a happy-ever-after, and Rosalind needs to teach Orlando what marriage really entails. Looking like a boy, she can ask him a graphic question about sex. 'Now tell me how long you would have her after you have possessed her?' Rapturously imagining making love with the Rosalind of his dreams, Orlando answers her question, 'For ever and a day,' in terms that explode time. His crazy hyperbole invites her bitter mockery:

> Rosalind   Say 'a day,' without the 'ever.' No, no, Orlando, men are April when they woo, December when they wed. Maids are May when they are maids, but the sky changes when they are wives.[65]

Alex Waldmann who played Orlando in the 2013 RSC production, reflects that Rosalind 'warns Orlando, you know, through Ganymede, about how difficult things are going to be. A marriage takes work, and it's not always going to be fun, and there'll be tears and pain.'[66] Illustrating her lesson with a bizarre list of animal comparisons, Rosalind prepares Orlando for how a real woman could behave in the years after the wedding ceremony:

> *Rosalind*   I will be more jealous of thee than a Barbary cock-pigeon over his hen, more clamorous than a parrot against rain, more new-fangled than an ape, more giddy in my desires than a monkey. I will weep for nothing, like Diana in the fountain, and I will do that when you are disposed to be merry. I will laugh like a hyena, and that when thou art inclined to sleep.[67]

Bemused by this litany of female mood swings, Orlando asks, 'will my Rosalind do so?' Ganymede confirms, 'By my life, she will do as I do.' Moreover, there are special extra risks for a man who marries a witty, clever, talkative woman. It's exactly her chatty intelligence that makes Rosalind beloved of bright girls everywhere.

> *Orlando*   O, but she is wise.
>
> *Rosalind*   Or else she could not have the wit to do this – the wiser,

	the waywarder. Make the doors upon a woman's wit and it will out at the casement. Shut that and 'twill out at the key-hole. Stop that, 'twill fly with the smoke out at the chimney.
Orlando	A man that had a wife with such a wit, he might say, 'Wit, whither wilt?'
Rosalind	Nay, you might keep that check for it till you met your wife's wit going to your neighbour's bed.
Orlando	And what wit could wit have to excuse that?
Rosalind	Marry, to say she came to seek you there. You shall never take her without her answer unless you take her without her tongue.[68]

Rosalind's tongue has a rough edge. She's determined to raise all the negatives about women, love and marriage, and deflate Orlando's claims for endless adoration. She sets out an intellectual rather than a financial pre-nup. She's trying to prepare Orlando for the real world, for being a real husband to a real wife. Her wit is arousing for him and comforting for her. He can take it. But her speeding brain immediately recurs to the theme of time that torments all lovers.

Orlando	For these two hours, Rosalind, I will leave thee.
Rosalind	Alas, dear love, I cannot lack thee two hours.
Orlando	I must attend the Duke at dinner. By two o'clock I will be with thee again.
Rosalind	Ay, go your ways, go your ways. I knew what you would prove. My friends told me as much and I thought no less. That flattering tongue of yours won me. 'Tis but one cast away, and so, come, death! Two o'clock is your hour?
Orlando	Ay, sweet Rosalind.
Rosalind	By my troth, and in good earnest, and so God mend me, and by all pretty oaths that are not dangerous, if you break one jot of your promise or come one minute behind your hour, I will think you the most pathetical break-promise and the most hollow lover and the most unworthy of her you call Rosalind that may be chosen out of the gross band of the unfaithful. Therefore beware my censure and keep your promise.
Orlando	With no less religion than if thou wert indeed my Rosalind. So adieu.

> *Rosalind*   Well, Time is the old justice that examines all such offenders, and let Time try. Adieu.[69]

Although Rosalind is in control of her multiple identities, her underlying self contains fragility as well as enduring love. The rejection and betrayal she's witnessed throughout her life, in both private and political spheres, have taught her to be on guard. But inhabiting Ganymede has only intensified her love for Orlando. It's taught her as much as she's trying to teach him. So when Celia berates Rosalind for simply misusing 'our sex in your love prate,' she responds with a piercing epiphany. She realises her 'affection hath an unknown bottom, like the Bay of Portugal.' As many fathoms deep in love now as Orlando, Rosalind cannot bear to be without him for a single second: 'I'll tell thee, Aliena, I cannot be out of the sight of Orlando. I'll go find a shadow, and sigh till he come.'

However, before Orlando's expected return, diversion arises in Arden like a musical refrain. Silvius brings a letter from Phebe addressed to Ganymede, which Rosalind first suspects Silvius has written. But when she reads it, she recognises it to be a love letter to Ganymede from the hand and heart of Phebe. In Rosalind's judgement, Silvius deserves no pity. The Phebe/Silvius sub-plot ripples up to counterpoint the love story of Rosalind and Orlando. Missing his cue, Orlando yet again fails to keep his date but sends wicked brother Oliver instead. Oliver explains that Orlando has been injured saving his brother's life, and as evidence he produces a napkin stained with Orlando's blood. Rescuing Oliver from a lioness, the animal tore Orlando's arm. As Ganymede faints, recovers, and then swears his blackout was all a fake, Oliver realises what Orlando probably has never guessed. Ganymede's male identity is a sham. 'You a man! You lack a man's heart…take good heart and counterfeit to be a man.' Rosalind has been outed by love itself.

Shakespeare now cuts from the sublime to the ridiculous, from noble to plebeian, from love to lust, to a glade where goatherd Audrey is nagging Touchstone for failing to get Sir Oliver Mar-text to marry them. The scene is a farcical recapitulation of Rosalind's own faux wedding ceremony. But Touchstone asserts his genuine intentions by dispatching simple William, Audrey's previous boyfriend, with a dozen witty threats that build into a hilarious crescendo of imperatives.

Touchstone	Therefore, you clown, abandon (which is, in the vulgar, 'leave') the society (which in the boorish is 'company') of this female (which in the common is 'woman'); which together is: 'abandon the society of this female', or, clown, thou perishest! Or to thy better understanding, diest. Or (to wit) I kill thee, make thee away, translate thy life into death, thy liberty into bondage. I will deal in poison with thee, or in bastinado or in steel. I will bandy with thee in faction; I will o'errun thee with policy. I will kill thee a hundred and fifty ways! Therefore tremble and depart.[70]

After Touchstone's fandango of words, Orlando finally arrives, his wounded arm in a sling, late for his tryst with Ganymede. Together they gossip about Oliver and Aliena [Celia] who have fallen in love so suddenly, 'on so little acquaintance', in subconscious parallel with their own love at first sight. Oliver has also told Orlando how Ganymede 'counterfeited to swoon' at the sight of the bloody handkerchief, and indeed 'greater wonders than that.' Alarmed that Orlando may have seen through her Ganymede disguise, Rosalind diverts him by ridiculing the speed of Oliver and Celia's love affair. Her riff matches the escalating architecture of Touchstone's speech a few lines earlier.

Rosalind	For your brother and my sister no sooner met but they looked; no sooner looked but they loved; no sooner loved but they sighed; no sooner sighed but they asked one another the reason; no sooner knew the reason but they sought the remedy; and in these degrees have they made a pair of stairs to marriage, which they will climb incontinent or else be incontinent before marriage.[71]

The thought of his brother's imminent consummation with Aliena inflames Orlando. 'O, how bitter a thing it is to look into happiness through another man's eyes!' Games are no longer any use to him. Bluntly he tells Ganymede that he can live no longer by thinking. 'I will weary you no longer with idle talking,' responds Rosalind, taking the plunge.

Rosalind	Believe then, if you please, that I can do strange things. I have since I was three year old conversed with a magician, most profound in his art and yet not damnable. If you do love Rosalind so near the heart as your gesture cries it out, when your brother marries Aliena shall you marry her. I know into what straits of fortune she is driven and

it is not impossible to me, if it appear not inconvenient to you, to set her before your eyes tomorrow, human as she is, and without any danger.[72]

Ganymede promises Orlando, that as well as Aliena and Oliver, he too will be married tomorrow, 'and to Rosalind, if you will.' Inspired by the duality of being Ganymede, Rosalind now bids an amazed Orlando to attend their official marriage ceremony.

> *Rosalind* Therefore put you in your best array, bid your friends;
> for if you will be married tomorrow you shall, and to
> Rosalind if you will.[73]

She is a woman with agency, the character who makes things happen in her play. She speaks in sober prose for 'sober meanings.' Rosalind has never been more in earnest.

Silvius and Phebe join them to change the tempo and the form. Silvius launches into verse to describe what his passionate version of courtly love feels like. It was an accepted convention of pastoral for chivalric love to be expressed by a shepherd. A quartet of lovers' voices, Silvius, Phebe, Orlando and Rosalind, reiterate the same tune.

> *Phebe* Good shepherd, tell this youth what 'tis to love.
>
> *Silvius* It is to be all made of sighs and tears,
> And so am I for Phebe.
>
> *Phebe* And I for Ganymede.
>
> *Orlando* And I for Rosalind.
>
> *Rosalind* And I for no woman.
>
> *Silvius* It is to be all made of faith and service,
> And so am I for Phebe.
>
> *Phebe* And I for Ganymede.
>
> *Orlando* And I for Rosalind.
>
> *Rosalind* And I for no woman.
>
> *Silvius* It is to be all made of fantasy,
> All made of passion, and all made of wishes,
> All adoration, duty and observance,
> All humbleness, all patience and impatience,
> All purity, all trial, all obedience,
> And so am I for Phebe.
>
> *Phebe* And so am I for Ganymede.
>
> *Orlando* And so am I for Rosalind.

Rosalind	And so am I for no woman.
Phebe	[*to Rosalind*] If this be so, why blame you me to love you?
Silvius	[*to Phebe*] If this be so, why blame you me to love you?
Orlando	If this be so, why blame you me to love you?
Rosalind	Who do you speak to, 'Why blame you me to love you?'
Orlando	To her that is not here nor doth not hear.[74]

Out of sheer exasperation Rosalind/Ganymede breaks the roundel with one of her most bizarre similes, 'Pray you, no more of this; 'tis like the howling of Irish wolves against the moon.' She then launches into her speech of the great 'IFs' that underlie all gender possibilities, and instructs the lovers to meet tomorrow, all to be married, in ways that at that moment can seem only opaque.

Rosalind	[*to Silvius*] I will help you, *if* I can. [*to Phebe*] I would love you, *if* I could. – Tomorrow meet me all together. [*to Phebe*] I will marry you, *if* ever I marry woman, and I'll be married tomorrow. [*to Orlando*] I will satisfy you, *if* ever I satisfied man, and you shall be married tomorrow. [*to Silvius*] I will content you, *if* what pleases you contents you, and you shall be married tomorrow. [*to Orlando*] As you love Rosalind, meet. [*to Silvius*] As you love Phebe, meet. – And as I love no woman, I'll meet. So fare you well. I have left you commands.[75] [my italics for *if*]

As soon as Ganymede signals the final untangling of gender, we hear that the unlikely union of the fourth pair of lovers, Touchstone and Audrey, is also re- scheduled for 'the joyful day' tomorrow.

While awaiting Ganymede's appearance, Duke Senior and Orlando wonder whether he can perform what he's promised. Ganymede, master of ceremonies, checks everyone is ready to fulfil their marriage contracts. S/he and Aliena depart, presumably for a costume change. Duke Senior muses that he's noticed 'some lively touches of my daughter's favour' in Ganymede, and Orlando remarks he's thought so, too. Touchstone picks up Ganymede's recent riff and giving the actors time to don their wedding finery, he first recalls Jaques' catalogue of 'Seven', and then extemporises on that pregnant two-lettered word, IF.

Touchstone	Upon a lie seven times removed – bear your body more seeming, Audrey – as thus, sir. I did dislike the cut of a certain courtier's beard. He sent me word, *if* I said his

beard was not cut well, he was in the mind it was. This
is called the 'retort courteous'. *If* I sent him word again
it was not well cut, he would send me word he cut it to
please himself. This is called the 'quip modest'. *If* again it
was not well cut, he disabled my judgement. This is called
the 'reply churlish'. *If* again it was not well cut, he would
answer I spake not true. This is called the 'reproof valiant'.
If again it was not well cut, he would say I lie. This is
called the 'countercheck quarrelsome' – and so to the 'lie
circumstantial' and the 'lie direct'...All these you may
avoid but the lie direct and you may avoid that too, with
an '*if*'. I knew when seven justices could not take up a
quarrel, but when the parties were met themselves, one of
them thought but of an '*if*': as, '*if* you said so, then I said
so'; and they shook hands and swore brothers. Your '*if*' is
the only peacemaker; much virtue in '*if*'.[76]

And *if* Ganymede is now a woman, as appearance seems to say when
Rosalind returns to marry Orlando, in one small sad couplet Phebe
realises that, at least in 1599, she can't marry the pretty youth of her
infatuation.

Duke Senior	*If* there be truth in sight, you are my daughter.
Orlando	*If* there be truth in sight, you are my Rosalind.
Phebe	*If* sight and shape be true,
	Why then, my love adieu.

And Rosalind's declarations as she divests herself of Ganymede, at least
for the time being, are built on a triple *If*.

Rosalind	I'll have no father, *if* you be not he.
	I'll have no husband, *if* you be not he.
	Nor ne'er wed woman, *if* you be not she.[77] [my italics
	for all the *ifs*]

❧

Jan Kott, the influential Polish theatre critic, who famously called
Shakespeare our Contemporary in his inspirational book of 1964, asked
himself what exactly is Rosalind's gender? 'Rosalind is Ganymede,
and Ganymede is Rosalind. But what is Rosalind's gender? What is
Ganymede's gender?'[78] In the endless possibilities of Rosalind, Kott
found a character who extends our concepts of identity. Who are we

in the final analysis? Through Rosalind, Shakespeare explores the idea that none of us is purely female or purely male. As human beings we are complex, and Rosalind offers us the perfect image to encompass the many nuances of human sexuality.

When boys no longer played Rosalind and the stage was accessible to professional women actors, Shakespeare's cross-dressed heroines could be played with a new piquancy. At Smallhythe Place in Kent I saw a full-length lithograph of Ellen Tree, later Eleanora Kean, in her Ganymede costume playing Rosalind, which she did both in America and England in the early nineteenth century.[79] Victorian ringlets corkscrew down each side of her face and on her head is a toque that looks as if it's made from a feather boa. Her square-necked, softly belted tunic ends well above the knee. Cross lacing over her bosom accentuates her femininity rather than conceals it. One sleeve is folded over her arm, the other droops into a pointed, medieval shape. Tucked into her belt is a small hunting horn, useful in the forest. Her size zero model legs end in cuffed ankle boots. One long tapering hand cradles her boar-spear and she's slung a short cloak round her shoulders. She doesn't really look male at all.

Ellen Tree had stage presence. Though her features were too strong for conventional prettiness, she was nevertheless considered beautiful. 'Her aquiline nose was offset by large flashing eyes, abundant brown hair, full lips, and a dazzling smile. She stood 5 feet 4 inches tall, was slender and graceful, with a resonant, musical, and emotively expressive voice. Her unique laugh could send audiences into gales.'[80] She could do gaiety and it's easy to imagine how erotic her Rosalind must have been.

American Charlotte Cushman, one of the most famous actresses on both sides of the Atlantic during the nineteenth century, made a splash in 1846 when she played Romeo at the Haymarket Theatre. Ellen Tree had also been Romeo, and earlier, Sarah Siddons had played Hamlet. Cross-gender casting existed long before the twenty-first century. Cushman's Rosalind looked 'every inch a man…Her mind became masculine as well as her outward semblance.'[81] 'Airy young gentlemen would have said she was "a deuced good fellow" and so she was!'[82] Cushman's lesbianism informed her acting, although it couldn't be openly acknowledged. *La grande* Charlotte's figure 'might have been that of a robust man; while her amorous endearments were of so erotic a character that no man would have dared to indulge in them *coram publico*.'[83] She made a majestic and 'veritable Ganymede' when she lounged into the Forest of Arden. 'Her comedy was rich and racy. Certain Shakespearian lines, which in this superfine age we have suppressed as indecorous, came lilting off her lips with a sense of enjoyment in which she appeared to relish,' reminisced fellow actor, John Coleman in 1904, once Silvius to the Rosalind of 'La Cushman', as he looked back over fifty years on the stage.[84]

Coleman played Orlando to a completely different Rosalind, the super-feminine, 'divine' and 'incomparable' actress, Helen Faucit. Nevertheless, he expressed equal and undying admiration for both these Victorian women, from opposite ends of the female spectrum. Sexual ambiguity reaches perfection in Rosalind when a boy actor playing a girl, dresses up as a boy who then pretends to be a girl. By the epilogue, the boy actor at the Globe in 1599, or the man or woman playing Rosalind today, has explored many liberating options for human identity.

Gloriana

Elizabeth I of England and Rosalind of Arden

E lizabeth I was the complete performance artist: a great actress, great director, great scriptwriter. The shrewdest political operator of her time, she was also Queen of England when Shakespeare wrote *As You Like It*. Rosalind's speeches could have come fresh from her tongue. Or in another dimension Shakespeare could have written Elizabeth's scripts. The court was her thrust stage. The playhouse was his court. They could have swapped roles. Born 7 Sept 1533, Elizabeth was in her 66th year and had been on the throne for forty of those years when Rosalind first stepped on stage. Immortalised as Gloriana in Edmund Spenser's poem, *The Faerie Queen*, Elizabeth was a generation older than Shakespeare, but when she acceded to the crown in 1558 she had been a young woman of twenty-five, coincidentally the same age as Elizabeth II when she acceded in 1952 nearly four centuries later. Gloriana was a grand paradox. She could embody both youth and age. She could include both genders.

Although Elizabeth existed in fact and Rosalind lives in fiction, they have so much in common, as well as the common touch. Both were aristocrats: Elizabeth the daughter of King Henry VIII; Rosalind the daughter of Duke Senior. Both had been abandoned by their fathers and had no mothers. Henry VIII had beheaded Elizabeth's mother, Anne Boleyn, and bastardised his daughter. She had similarly lost successive stepmothers, Jane Seymour, Anne of Cleves, Katherine Howard and Katherine Parr, and her father King Henry VIII himself had died in 1547. Deposed and vanished into exile, Rosalind's father, Duke Senior is effectively lost to her throughout the greater part of the play. Even when she comes face to face with him in the forest, he doesn't see through her Ganymede disguise to recognise his daughter. Rosalind's mother is never mentioned. These parental chasms in both Elizabeth and Rosalind's lives were emotionally profound. As young women they had to fend for themselves at court against dangerous and unpredictable adversaries. Rosalind has to survive with a brave face, showing 'more mirth' than she is 'mistress of,' while inwardly raging at the court of her usurping, changeable uncle, Duke Frederick. Elizabeth was buffeted by successive regime changes, under new stepmothers, then during the reign of her younger Protestant brother, Edward VI, and subsequently in a complete volte-face under her elder Catholic sister, Mary I. During Mary's reign, Elizabeth's life was perilous; she was imprisoned in the Tower and only survived through her wits, enterprise and courage.

These adverse experiences coloured both their lives. By 1599, the year of *As You Like It*, long reigning Queen Elizabeth dominated her court, whereas Rosalind only attended Duke Frederick's court under sufferance. However, Elizabeth never forgot what it had felt like to be marginalised at court in her youth, even to be declared illegitimate. She was proud of her resourcefulness. 'I thank God I am indeed endued with such qualities that if I were turned out of the realm in my petticoat, I were able to live in any place in Christendom,'[1] she said, imagining a costume almost as transgressive as Rosalind fleeing her uncle's court dressed as a man. Rosalind and Elizabeth share resilient spirits, and both were young when they were most threatened.

Elizabeth and Rosalind were powerful women who in normal sixteenth century circumstances would have been excluded from public life by their gender. But they had the brains and strength to devise a life far beyond the usual boundaries of their sex. They knew how to stage-manage events in their own worlds, whether at court or in Arden. And both were onstage. Elizabeth was in the spotlight of her court and of the state, as Rosalind is the lodestar of Arden and of her play. Sheer magnetism of personality fuelled both Elizabeth and Rosalind. Biographers have called Gloriana, 'this amazing Queen, so keenly intelligent, so effervescing, so intimate, so imperious and regal,'[2] qualities possessed in equal measure by voluble, ingenious, commanding Rosalind.

The very name 'Rosalind' was a coded link with Elizabeth. *Rosa linda* is a beautiful rose, and the rose, whether cultivated or wild, sweet-briar or eglantine, is a potent and repeated symbol in the iconography of Elizabeth. In his 1575 *Pelican Portrait* – so-called because of the pelican jewelled pendant she wears – Nicholas Hilliard painted Elizabeth like a religious icon emblazoned with a riot of roses. But the message was political. Tudor roses uniting the red and white of the once warring houses of York and Lancaster were embroidered on her sleeves, appliquéd on her skirt, suggested in the exotic, swirling fan of ostrich feathers in her hand, and inscribed in the heraldic Tudor rose supporting the crown in the upper left-hand corner of the picture.[3]

In its companion piece, the *Phoenix Portrait*, Elizabeth wears a huge jewelled red and white Tudor rose at the centre of a massive pearl studded collar looping across her breast, which culminates in two more fabulous rose jewels on each shoulder. To point up the emblem still further, her elegant right hand holds a single, natural, red rose of England, perfectly pleated.[4] In the magnificent Ditchley portrait of the early 1590s by Flemish artist, Marcus Gheeraerts the Younger, she's standing on a broad map of England, situated on the great globe itself. She is the symbol of national identity who is also semi-divine; a madonna set between dark heavens and English sunlit skies. Elizabeth always projected herself as a strong unifying ruler, cosmically, dynastically, politically, and religiously, with the pragmatic 1559 Church Settlement the lynchpin of her domestic policy. However, this portrait has another, more alluring, feminine message, which is also a key element of her power. Elizabeth's ruff and collar of exquisite stiffened lace framing her face could be the fairy wings of Gloriana or Titania.[5] Prominently pinned to the left side of her airy ruff is a natural pink rose set on a spray of green leaves.[6]

The Tudor rose referred to the body politic but it also referred to the body private although in Elizabeth's case the two were metaphorically entwined. In sixteenth-century poetry, the rose often denoted the chastity of a marriageable virgin. Hilliard's luminous 1572 miniature showed Elizabeth with maiden white roses in her hair and on her dress, in the same year that she was negotiating a never-to-be fulfilled marriage contract with the Duke of Anjou.[7] Elizabeth continued to dally both politically and personally with a whole procession of suitors throughout her reign. However, she told her long-term favourite, Robert Dudley, Earl of Leicester, 'I will have here but one mistress but no master.'[8]

While all Elizabeth's flirtations led to maintaining her impregnable single status, symbolic perhaps of England's invincibility against foreign enemies, Rosalind's one flirtation, after demanding a tough audition from Orlando, led to her informed choice of marriage. Elizabeth promoted an image of herself as the mother of her people, though she never had a child. Rosalind is similarly childless throughout her play, but from the first moment of falling in love, she excitedly predicts Orlando as her 'child's father,' clearly envisaging their future offspring.

Both Elizabeth and Rosalind were egalitarians of a sort, adept at crossing borders, whether social or sexual. Rosalind becomes a shepherd boy, runs a smallholding, earns her own living and integrates into rural life. She can talk equally to highfalutin courtiers like Jaques, and to modest tenant farmers like Corin. This most talkative of Shakespeare's comic heroines chiefly expresses herself in the people's prose rather than in blank verse. Like Rosalind, Elizabeth was a princess who could identify with ordinary people, and even envy them. The chronicler Holinshed said that when interned at Woodstock, 'fraught full of terror,' during her sister Mary's reign, she heard a milkmaid 'singing pleasantlie' outside in the garden and 'wished hir selfe to be a milkemaid as she was, saieng that hir case was better, and life more merrier than was hirs in that state as she was.'[9] She returned to the evocative milkmaid once she was Queen. Under increasing pressure to marry in 1576, she vowed: 'If I were a milkmaid with a pail on mine arm, whereby my private person might be little set by, I would not forsake that single state to match myself with the greatest monarch.'[10] Vacillating over the fate of her seditious cousin, Mary, Queen of Scots in 1586, Elizabeth lamented that 'if it had pleased God to have made us both milkmaids with pails on our arms,' she could not consent to her execution.[11]

Elizabeth may have longed, impractically, for escape into an idyllic pastoral life. But Rosalind really lived it, crossing the gender border as she chose to become shepherd Ganymede in her flight to Arden. Both women had bitter experience of their worlds of *realpolitik*. Like Elizabeth under her sister Mary Tudor, Rosalind was accused of treason by a near relative, her uncle, Duke Frederick. Yet his mistrust 'cannot make me a traitor,' she answers levelly. The memory of the old charge of treason against her was still vivid in Elizabeth's mind when on 12 November

1586 she confronted a parliamentary delegation at Richmond, begging her to implement the sentence of execution on Mary, Queen of Scots, which she had signed but couldn't bring herself to act on.

> I have had good experience and trial of this world: I know what it is to be a subject, what to be a sovereign; what to have good neighbors, and sometime meet evil willers. I have found treason in trust, seen great benefits little regarded, and instead of gratefulness, courses of purpose to cross.[12]

If Elizabeth knew how it felt to be accused of treason, she also had abundant reason to fear treachery. Her own Tudor dynasty had been established on an arguable act of treason by her grandfather, King Henry VII. Fear of plots and uprisings tormented his granddaughter Elizabeth, as they did Rosalind's uncle, Duke Frederick, who had deposed his elder brother, Duke Senior. Throughout her reign Elizabeth dreaded a violent coup. In March 1585 she told Parliament, 'I know no creature that breatheth whose life standeth hourly in more peril' than her own.[13] Major conspiracies against her included the Ridolfi Plot in 1571, the Throckmorton Plot in 1582, and the Catholic inspired Babington Plot of 1586. A year later, Mary, Queen of Scots was finally executed.

Rosalind and Elizabeth were both shaped by and enmeshed in politics. But the Queen's public persona was different from Rosalind's. Since Elizabeth's accession in 1558, England had suffered no foreign husband, no civil wars, and no heavy taxes – in spite of an extensive maritime defence policy – but instead had enjoyed a pragmatic religious settlement, effective government and the expansionist Age of Discovery. Elizabeth was the symbol of all this, and at its height her popularity ensured she was 'received everywhere with great acclamations' on state progresses through the country, as noted de Silva, the Spanish Ambassador.[14] In the view of John Foxe, author of the widely disseminated and much read *Acts and Monuments*, popularly known as *Foxe's Book of Martyrs*, Elizabeth was

> this so princely a lady and puissant princess…who, a virgin, so mildy ruleth men, governeth her subjects, keepeth all things in order, quieteth foreign nations, recovereth towns, enlargeth her kingdom, nourisheth and concileth amity, uniteth hearts and love with foreign enemies, helpeth neighbors, reformeth religion, quencheth prosecution, redresseth the dross, (and) frameth things out of joint.[15]

But the success of the whole country depended on Elizabeth's health and her life. 1599, the year of *As You Like It*, was a key year for England. Elizabeth was ageing but still powerful – and a power dresser. The drama of who was going to succeed her was forever being enacted in secret. In *As You Like It*, illegal Duke Frederick is vulnerable, unpredictable, and as Le Beau says, 'humorous.' By 1599, Elizabeth, too, was 'humorous,' volatile, unwilling to name a successor, ever conscious that not so long ago her Tudor dynasty had been built on appropriated power. There were more threats from Spain of a second Armada, uprisings in Ireland, and an aborted attempt to dethrone her by the Earl of Essex.

So the healing political denouement of *As You Like It* in which Duke Frederick converts to a life of good works, and the benign rule of Duke Senior is re-established under the joint direction of his daughter Rosalind with her husband Orlando, was equally to be wished by Elizabeth. She could have watched Rosalind achieve public resolution during Act 5 of a royal command performance, perhaps at the Palace of Richmond. Towards the end of *As You Like It*, Rosalind vows, 'I have promised to make all this matter even.' On English victory over the first Spanish Armada in 1588, Elizabeth told the troops at Tilbury: 'I myself will be your general, judge, and rewarder of your virtue in the field.'[16]

Elizabeth was an eloquent speechmaker, a talent probably fostered by her tutor Roger Ascham who was public orator at Cambridge. Elizabeth not only had a natural capacity for unforgettable phrase-making in her English speeches, she also had amazing facility for learning a whole range of foreign languages, what Ascham called 'her perfect readiness' in Latin, Greek, French, Spanish, Italian and Flemish. Only upper-class women such as fictitious Rosalind or real-life Margaret Roper, daughter of Sir Thomas More, or Mary, Queen of Scots, or Lady Jane Grey, or poet Mary Sidney had access to an education like Elizabeth's, taught by the finest of scholars. Ascham had two main teaching principles: kindness, and the practice of double translation which produced remarkable results, later expounded in his ground-breaking book, *The Scholemaster*.[17] Elizabeth was so avid for learning that Ascham considered she read more Greek in a day than a priest read Latin in a whole week. Like Elizabeth, Rosalind is at ease both in her second language, courtly French in which she bids Jaques, 'Farewell, Monsieur Traveller,' and in the classics. When she tells Orlando that no man has ever died for love, a spate of classical allusions pours from her tongue, to Troilus, Leander, Hero of Sestos, and the straits of Hellespont. Orlando's comparisons of Rosalind to Helen, Atalanta and Lucretia overwhelm her because she has the classics at her fingertips. Some modern productions have shown her as a bookworm. But she's not a blue stocking, she has an inspirational mind that races ahead at full speed.

From the beginning of her reign, Elizabeth's councillors were in awe of her intelligence, 'that goodly wit; that goodly knowledge and that great and special grace of understanding and judgment', as Lord William Paget commented to William Cecil, her Secretary of State, in February 1559 a bare month after her coronation.[18] Although women, like Shakespeare's Portia, were debarred from practising law, Elizabeth made the rules and was a legislator, in alliance with her parliament. Rosalind's verbal wit and effervescing intelligence are implicit homage to Elizabeth's subtle and powerful intellect whose 'mind was ofttime like the gentle air that cometh from the westerly point in a summer's morn; 'twas sweet and refreshing to all around her. Her speech did win all affections.'[19] Like Elizabeth, one of Rosalind's main characteristics is her flamboyance with language, her verbal gymnastics. As she tells Jaques, 'I had rather have a fool to make me merry than experience to make me sad.'[20] Juliet Stevenson who played Rosalind in 1985 for the RSC says, 'Rosalind has the most glorious wit – her mind moves like mercury – her mind dances, dances. And when you have her language, her words passing through you physically, you have a sense of having to be on tip-top form to keep up with her, to keep up with the vivacity and the nimbleness of her utterance and her thought patterns.'[21]

In the post-Armada world of Tudor England, Gloriana was the framework over-arching everyone's life. Elizabeth dominated the court as Rosalind dominates the Forest of Arden. Both were women with agency, witty, verbal and brilliantly clever. Like Rosalind in affairs of the heart, the Queen controlled affairs of state by implying she contained both genders. Both Rosalind and the monarch were gender-benders. 'I know something of a woman in a man's profession, yes, by God, I do know about that,' was the update Tom Stoppard gave Gloriana played by Judi Dench in the film *Shakespeare in Love*.[22] In her dashing doublet and hose, Rosalind's Ganymede, re-imagined by Gwyneth Paltrow as boy actor Thomas Kent, presented a male façade, but within beat her distinctly feminine heart. With her axe on thigh and spear in hand Rosalind is determined to hide her natural fear and present 'a swashing and a martial outside.'[23]

She's not quite so swashing and martial once she enters Arden but her Ganymede is imperious and charismatic. S/he cuts a beguiling figure, ambiguous and attractive to both sexes, outwardly male but female within. In her exaggerated farthingales encrusted with jewels and pearls, Elizabeth was Rosalind's reverse image: all female on the exterior, but inside powered, famously, by the heart and stomach of a king. In different ways, both Elizabeth and Rosalind exploited to the full their potential for dramatic androgyny. Roger Ascham reckoned Elizabeth's mind had 'no womanly weakness, her perseverance is equal to that of a man.'

During her spellbinding appearance before the troops at Tilbury in August 1588, in the triumph of English victory over the Spanish Armada, Elizabeth, 'being a Virgin of manly Courage,' paraded up and down, 'sometimes like a woman, sometimes with the countenance and pace of a soldier,' wrote William Camden, her first biographer.[24] Shakespeare had put a charismatic female military leader, Joan of Arc, on stage in *Henry VI*, part 1. 'Chaste and immaculate in very thought', Joan la Pucelle seemed like Elizabeth to derive her mysterious strength from the status of virginity itself. Elizabeth knew exactly how to make her virgin body personal express the national body politic. In her wide skirts, bareheaded but encased in a steel corselet from neck to waist, she rode a prancing white horse, while a page carried her plumed helmet on a cushion beside her.[25] She could have been invoking the mythological figure of the goddess Athene, one of Rosalind's own ancestors, who presided over war but preferred peace, and like Elizabeth with her shining helmet, seemed to contain both genders. Elizabeth had an unerring sense of occasion. For the same reasons that American Presidents take the oath of office outside the Capitol,

Elizabeth understood the importance of appearing on stage in the open air, as well as at court.

> My loving people…I have so behaved myself that under God I have placed my chiefest strength and safeguard in the loyal hearts and goodwill of my subjects. Wherefore I am come among you at this time but for my recreation and pleasure, being resolved in the midst and heat of the battle to live and die amongst you all, to lay down for my God and for my kingdom and for my people mine honor and my blood even in the dust.[26]

Without modern microphones, her stirring words would have carried only to the few soldiers standing around her, but like Rosalind in her theatre, Elizabeth was a natural and consummate actor who could maximise the power of performance. The battle at sea was effectively over but Elizabeth knew exactly how to exploit the victory delivered by Francis Drake, Lord Howard of Effingham, and her navy. Shakespeare chose to allude to Elizabeth's great performance at Tilbury in Henry V's rousing speech before the Battle of Agincourt, written like *As You Like It* in 1599.

> This day is called the Feast of Crispian.
> He that outlives this day and comes safe home
> Will stand a-tiptoe when the day is named,
> And rouse him at the name of Crispian.
> He that shall see this day, and live old age
> Will yearly on the vigil feast his neighbours,
> And say 'Tomorrow is Saint Crispian.'
> Then will he strip his sleeve and show his scars,
> And say 'These wounds I had on Crispin's day.'
> Old men forget, yet all shall be forgot
> But he'll remember, with advantages,
> What feats he did that day.[27]

Shakespeare's Henry V could identify with his troops and get his troops to identify with him, just as Elizabeth could. But she did it by embracing both genders.

I know I have the body but of a weak and feeble woman, but I have the heart and stomach of a king and of a king of England too – and take foul scorn that Parma or any prince of Europe should dare to invade the borders of my realm. To the which rather than any dishonor shall grow by me, I myself will venter my royal blood.[28]

Elizabeth's people always remained conscious of her political inheritance from a King of England, her father Henry VIII. Not only her startling white skinned, red-haired appearance but also her decisive powers of governance proclaimed her paternity. 'Although I may not be a lion, I am a lion's cub, and inherit many of his qualities,' said Elizabeth. 'She gives her orders and has her own way as absolutely as her father did,' ambassador Feria told Philip of Spain.[29] As she aged, she became ever more adept at inhabiting both genders. She seamlessly metamorphosed from queen to king in her famous valedictory speech to parliament of 1601, known as the Golden Speech:

> To be a king and wear a crown is a thing more glorious to them that see it than it is pleasant to them that bear it. For myself, I was never so much enticed with the glorious name of a king or royal authority of a queen as delighted that God had made me His instrument to maintain His truth and glory, and to defend this kingdom from dishonor, damage, tyranny, and oppression.[30]

She might have been speaking her own obituary in her resonant use of the vernacular, permanently consolidating English as the language of monarchs and of the people. After her death, her principal Secretary, Sir Robert Cecil, son of William Cecil, 1st Baron Burghley, who had advised her during most of her reign, said 'she was more than a man, and in troth, sometimes less than a woman.'[31] It was Elizabeth's genius for androgyny that made her Gloriana. And it's Rosalind's virtuoso performance of androgyny that makes Ganymede independent and fast-talking as s/he directs affairs in Arden. Both Rosalind and Elizabeth were more than male – and more than female, too. Sure-footedly they extended gender in a time when it was highly dangerous to do so.

Both Rosalind and Elizabeth were advance-guard feminists although the word was unknown to Elizabeth, Rosalind, or indeed Shakespeare. It didn't enter the language until 1895 with the Suffragettes. And yet all three intuited a subtle change in the status quo, embodied in the successful reign of Queen Elizabeth herself, which would take centuries to be enacted, even partially, for women. The great actress, Ellen Terry, who never played Rosalind, though she said in 1894 she'd 'longed for centuries to make the attempt,' instead inhabited Rosalind continuously in her impassioned lectures about Shakespeare's women which she gave round the world between 1911-1921.[32] 'Wonderful women! Have you ever thought how much we all, and women especially, owe to Shakespeare for his vindication of women in these fearless, high-spirited, resolute and intelligent heroines? Don't believe the anti-feminists if they tell you, as I was once told, that Shakespeare had to endow his women with virile qualities because in his theatre they were always impersonated by men! This may account for the frequency with which they masquerade as boys, but I am convinced that it had little influence on Shakespeare's studies of women. They owe far more to the liberal ideas about the sex which were fermenting in Shakespeare's age. The assumption that "the women's movement" is of very recent date – something peculiarly modern – is not warranted by history. There is evidence of its existence in the fifteenth century. Then as now it excited opposition and ridicule, but still it moved!'[33]

In support of her case for early feminism, Terry cited the Renaissance humanist scholar Erasmus who thought, 'men and women have different functions, but their education and their virtues ought to be equal.'[34] Shakespeare's earlier comedy *Love's Labour's Lost* played at court for Elizabeth at Christmas 1597.[35] The linguistic agility of its heroine Rosaline, an initial draft for Rosalind – and indeed the two names are sometimes interchanged in the First Folio text of *As You Like It* – together with Rosaline's refusal to marry would have resonated with the audience and its most attentive listener.

Nubile virgins like Rosalind and Rosaline who were aristocratic but not royal, but claimed the right to make their own decisions, were rare in the sixteenth century. The Virgin Queen wore the coronation ring on the fourth finger of her left hand, and told a parliamentary delegation sent to sue for her early marriage, 'I am already bound unto an husband, which is the kingdom of England, and that may suffice you.'[36] This was her position from the beginning of her reign, one that she continued to reaffirm. 'And in the end this shall be for me sufficient: that a marble stone shall declare that a queen, having reigned such a time, lived and died a virgin.'[37] Shakespeare evoked the amorous though aloof magic of royal virginity in his Fairy King's moonlit vision of Elizabeth in the persona of 'the imperial votaress' in *A Midsummer Night's Dream*.

Oberon	That very time I saw (but thou couldst not),
	Flying between the cold moon and the earth,
	Cupid all arm'd: a certain aim he took
	At a fair vestal, throned by the west,
	And loos'd his love-shaft smartly from his bow
	As it should pierce a hundred thousand hearts.
	But I might see young Cupid's fiery shaft
	Quench'd in the chaste beams of the watery moon;
	And the imperial votaress passed on,
	In maiden meditation, fancy-free.[38]

By dexterous sleight of hand, Elizabeth conflated two contradictory messages. She was both a vestal Virgin and a Holy Mother. 'And so I assure you all that though after my death you may have many stepdames, yet shall you never have a more natural mother than I mean to be unto you all,' she told parliament.[39] The sculpted shape of her farthingale with its narrow maiden waist and exaggerated wide hips was a visual image of her double message: virginity and fertility. Elizabeth who had hardly known her own mother was determined to prove the ideal parent to her people.

Elizabeth never gave birth to a child of her body but she contrived to seem pregnant with the symbolic potential of both virginity and maternity. For the greater part of her reign she enjoyed and encouraged a parade of suitors, her Orlandos, both domestic and foreign. Her most sustained flirtations were with Robert Dudley, Earl of Leicester whom she called her little dog, and during her late forties with the Duke of Alençon of the French House of Valois, whom she called her 'frog.' He wasn't her usual debonair type but she savoured the dalliance and conversation. Their on-off game of courtship probably popularised the folksong we still know today as 'A Frog He Would a-Wooing Go.' She would never marry any of the foreign contenders. More dangerous was the procession of home-grown lovers, most conspicuously the Earl of Leicester, and later Sir Christopher Hatton, Sir Walter Raleigh, and Robert Devereux, second Earl of Essex. She basked in flattery and the diplomatic gamesmanship of marriage proposals, as ambassador de Silva reported to his Spanish King.

'I do not think anything is more enjoyable to this Queen than treating of marriage, though she herself assures me that nothing annoys her more. She is vain and would like all the world to be running after her, but it will probably end by her remaining as she is, unless she marries Lord Robert who is still doing his best to win her.'[40]

Unlike Rosalind who eagerly looks forward to sex, to putting a man in her belly, as Celia lewdly jokes, Elizabeth hungered only for declarations of love, amorous conversation, and devotion unto death but not the sexual connection itself. 'Apter to raise flames than to quench them,' she desired men to desire her – but not to satisfy them.[41] Her rages were legendary and terrifying if any of her courtiers or ladies announced their intentions to marry. Expert at the dialogue of love, she prized tall, handsome, ardent men, fishing for men's souls as Sir Christopher Hatton said, 'with so sweet a bait, no man could escape her net-work.'[42] Yet after his long pursuit, the Earl of Leicester, her exact contemporary, finally accepted, 'I have known her since she was eight years old, better than any man in the world. From that time she has invariably declared she would remain unmarried.'[43] Elizabeth knew what sex had led to for her seductive and beautiful mother, Anne Boleyn. Her life had ended on the scaffold when her daughter was less than three. In quick succession, Elizabeth's stepmothers had died violently or too young. From her earliest years, insomniac and afraid of the dark, the association of sex with death was clear. In maturity she always wore a curious locket ring containing two miniature portraits, one of Anne Boleyn, and one of herself, clasped together as they barely were in life. The ring never left her hand after it was presented to her in 1575, until it was removed on her death, and taken as proof to her heir, James VI of Scotland.[44] She had always retained Anne Boleyn's motto, *semper eadem*, as her own.[45]

Elizabeth's lifelong passion for words, scholarship, languages, speechmaking, music and the arts were part of her survival strategies, and reflected her fear of abandonment from her earliest years. The safe place for courtship for Elizabeth and Rosalind was the man's role, as if they'd appropriated the male position in dances like the galliard, the lavolta or the gavotte. Wooing as a man was not only piquant and coquettish, it was also empowering and controlling. Rosalind usurps the conventional male role in her courtship of Orlando. She gives him a necklace after she's met him for two minutes at the wrestling match. She accosts him in the forest and from then on she conducts the love match on her terms. Because of her royal position, and her temperament, Elizabeth also occupied the male role in all potential marriage negotiations. Though both women were addicted to the rituals of courtship, there were vastly different outcomes for each. Elizabeth's flirtations with dozens of lovers led to her lifelong virginity. Rosalind's flirtation with just one lover leads to a marriage we feel has every hope of happiness.

Love and how to love is the central axis of Rosalind's play as it was of Elizabeth's political and private life. Like Rosalind whose capacity for love is as deep as the unknown bottom of the Bay of Portugal, Elizabeth had heart on an epic scale. The Queen knew the power of governing not only by authority but through love, 'and her subjects did try to show all love to her commands; for she would say her state did require her to command what she knew her people would willingly do from their own love to her.'[46] She unerringly kept faith with what she saw as the sacrament of her marriage contract with her people, and she fostered their mutual love unto death. 'After such sort do I keep the goodwill of all my husbands, my good people; for if they did not rest assured of some special love towards them, they would not readily yield me such good obedience.'[47] When he was a child, the future Bishop Goodman called out to the Queen as she processed past, 'God save your Majesty,' and Elizabeth replied, 'you may well have a greater prince, but you shall never have a more loving prince.'[48] Until the end of her reign she continued to reiterate her interactive love affair with her people.

> I do assure you there is no prince that loveth his subjects better, or whose love can countervail our love. There is no jewel, be it of never so rich a price, which I set before this jewel – I mean your loves. For I do more esteem it than any treasure or riches, for that we know how to prize. But love and thanks I count [i]unvaluable, and though God hath raised me high, yet this I count the glory of my crown: that I have reigned with your loves.
>
> …And though you have had and may have many princes more mighty and wise sitting in this seat, yet you never had or shall have any that will be more careful and loving.[49]

Elizabeth knew how to hold her audience in an age when the play was the popular art form of its day. 'Princes, you know, stand upon stages, so that their actions are viewed and beheld of all men.'[50] Her political skills were sharpened by the drama of live performance. She needed all these skills when at almost sixty-eight, she became entranced by a new, handsome young favourite, the Earl of Essex. He was also lethally dangerous. She dispatched him to the wars in Ireland but he returned unannounced to London filled with a scheme to un-queen Elizabeth, as her distant ancestor, Henry Bolingbroke, had un-kinged Richard II. Shakespeare's play about deposing a legal monarch could not have been more subversive during the build-up to Essex's planned rebellion in February 1601, when the Earl's cohorts recklessly organised a private performance of *Richard II*. Essex saw himself trailing clouds of glory as Bolingbroke re-born. But Elizabeth's secret service foiled the plot, the rebels were arrested and Essex beheaded. Shakespeare was far too worldly wise and emotionally intelligent in his even-handed portrayals of both Richard and Bolingbroke to invite accusations of offending. The playhouse could be a platform for contemporary events but also their safety valve.

The pastoral world of the Forest of Arden is likewise a political critique of Duke Frederick's regime. In the forest Duke Senior rules his exiled court in 'so quiet and so sweet a style' as he'd previously applied to his city leadership. Mobbs Gqirana, one of Nelson Mandela's co-prisoners of conscience in South Africa during the 1970s, chose to sign his name against this speech in the *Robben Island Shakespeare* that circulated secretly among the detainees.[51]

> *Duke Senior*   Sweet are the uses of adversity,
> Which, like the toad, ugly and venomous,
> Wears yet a precious jewel in his head;
> And this our life, exempt from public haunt,
> Finds tongues in trees, books in the running brooks,
> Sermons in stones, and good in everything.[52]

The restoration of his system of honourable governance through peaceful transfer of power to Rosalind and Orlando is a quiet accolade to Elizabeth the Peacemaker. Even her reluctance to name a successor effected a diplomatic handover to James VI of Scotland and 1st of England in 1603. In the aftermath of the abortive Essex coup, Elizabeth, always sensitive to the theatrical moment, crafted her Golden Speech of 30 November 1601 that would reverberate down the centuries.

Mr. Speaker, we have heard your declaration and perceive your care of our estate… I do assure you there is no prince that loveth his subjects better, or whose love can countervail our love.

What you bestow on me, I will not hoard it up, but receive it to bestow on you again… Therefore render unto them from me, I beseech you, Mr. Speaker, such thanks as you imagine my heart yieldeth but my tongue cannot express.

Mr Speaker, I would wish you and the rest to stand up, for I shall yet trouble you with longer speech.

I know the title of a king is a glorious title, but assure yourself that the shining glory of princely authority hath not so dazzled the eyes of our understanding but that we well know and remember that we also are to yield an account of our actions before the great Judge…

There will never queen sit in my seat with more zeal to my country, care to my subjects, and that will sooner with willingness venture her life for your good and safety than myself.[53]

Elizabeth's androgynous power only increased with her advancing years when her choice of the bravura single life seemed definitive, finally even to court observers. Her androgyny was no longer one of the most intriguing facets of her sexual appeal but part of the ageing process itself. Defiance of time became one of the key factors in the construction of Gloriana. Later portraits of Elizabeth show her fixed like a gorgeous butterfly on a pin, sumptuous and flat against the background. In a Faustian pact to conquer time, her wrinkled face was immobilized under layers of caustic makeup, compounded with noxious lead and vinegar. Artists froze her into a changeless icon, creating an image emblematic of the state of England herself. Elizabeth showed that androgyny is not only about cool youth. She maintained its double gendered authority into old age. Sally Potter made an inspired choice when she cast the elderly Quentin Crisp to play Elizabeth across gender in her 1992 film, *Orlando*. Crisp looked authentically like portraits of the aged Elizabeth, while Tilda Swinton as the male Orlando, with her elegant physique, startling auburn hair and porcelain complexion, eerily reanimated the young Elizabeth. I wonder whether the boy actor who first played Rosalind also had red hair and translucent skin? Young or old, mortal Elizabeth lives on in the cultural and historical imagination. Rosalind lives on too, though she will never fade, never wither, never age.

Records suggest that the Queen was present at an early performance of *As You Like It* on Shrove Tuesday, 20 February 1599, at Richmond Palace. If so, a dazzling, boyish Rosalind may have embodied Shakespeare's tacit tribute to the ageing Elizabeth.[54] As principal playwright and partner in the Lord Chamberlain's Company, Shakespeare had the opportunity to observe Elizabeth close up. His actors presented plays at royal command performances, often transfers from the public playhouses, presented fashionably late at night. The age difference gave Shakespeare, a generation younger, a special perspective on the older woman who was his monarch. Towards the end of his life, long after *As You Like It*, he could look back on her reign in a history play called *Henry VIII*, probably co-written with John Fletcher. Elizabeth had been dead for a decade. But the writers spirited the audience back to 1533, to the day of her christening, performed by Archbishop Thomas Cranmer. Through the magic of theatre the playwrights transcended the years and renewed Elizabeth's young promise. 'This royal infant' shall be 'A pattern to all princes,' prophesies the actor with benefit of hindsight, as he intones with clear biblical imagery, the divinity of England's 'maiden phoenix'.

> Cranmer   This royal infant (heaven still move about her)
> Though in her cradle, yet now promises
> Upon this land a thousand thousand blessings...
> She shall be lov'd and fear'd: her own shall bless her;
> Her foes shake like a field of beaten corn,
> ...In her days every man shall eat in safety
> Under his own vine what he plants, and sing
> The merry songs of peace to all his neighbours.
> God shall be truly known, and those about her
> From her shall read the perfect ways of honour...
> She shall be, to the happiness of England,
> An aged princess...yet a virgin;
> A most unspotted lily shall she pass
> To th'ground, and all the world shall mourn her.[55]

Religious ceremonies like christenings and funerals punctuated key moments in the monarch's public life as they did in the private lives of Elizabeth's subjects. Four marriages mark the end of *As You Like It*. Yet one betrothal at its centre, both playful and profound, is more thrilling than any of these. On the face of things, it seems to be uniting two men, Ganymede and Orlando. But the audience knows what Orlando doesn't. Ganymede is his true love Rosalind. Their pre-wedding in the forest uses almost exactly the same words as the marriage service in the English Book of Common Prayer authorised by the Elizabethan Act of Uniformity of 1559.[56] The play wedding is the real thing. In 1568 at the instigation of Elizabeth, and under the aegis of the recently established Church of England, the Bishops' Bible was published as the state alternative to the Calvinist Genevan Bible of 1560, even though both were in English. Its title page showed the Queen enthroned, being crowned by Justice and Mercy, together with Prudence and Fortitude. These were exactly the religious and imperial virtues associated with the Queen, 'England's Astraea, Albion's shining sun!'[57] Astraea was the classical virgin goddess of justice and purity consistently linked with Elizabeth. She had been determined to make toleration work, if only for Christians. Then in May 1570 came her excommunication by Pope Pius V, heralding in response much stricter anti-Catholic measures in England. But Elizabeth maintained, 'There is one faith and one Jesus Christ. The rest is a dispute about trifles.'[58]

One of Elizabeth's favourite biblical images for herself as guardian of her people was as the metaphorical and actual shepherd of her flock. 'For, what a family is without a steward, a ship without a pilot, a flock without a shepherd, a body without a head, the same, I think, is a kingdom without the health and safety of a good monarch.'[59] She wouldn't have missed the parallel when Rosalind bounds across borders to play the role of a shepherd boy. During the Protestant religious settlement, Elizabeth was not only shepherd to her people but she also became the Virgin Queen implicitly replacing the Virgin Mary of Catholicism. Religious references were part of Elizabethan everyday life as they were embedded in the spiritual landscape of *As You Like It*:

> *Duke Senior* True is it that we have seen better days,
> And have with holy bell been knolled to church,
> And sat at good men's feasts, and wiped our eyes
> Of drops that sacred pity hath engendered;
> And therefore sit you down in gentleness
> And take upon command what help we have
> That to your wanting may be ministered.[60]

Church bells and liturgical music accompanied religion. Music both secular and divine was an intrinsic part of Elizabeth's life. In 1559 the Venetian Ambassador recorded, 'the Queen's daily amusements are musical performances and other entertainments and she takes marvellous pleasure in seeing people dance...Last evening at the Court...at the dance the Queen performed her part, the Duke of Norfolk being her partner, in superb array.' [61]

As You Like It is the most musical of Shakespeare's plays with its five songs, or six to include Hymen's chant, 'Wedding is great Juno's crown.' Hymen's *deus ex machina* appearance to solemnize the four weddings at the end of *As You Like It* is a masque-like event. Elizabeth relished dancing, music, theatre and masques. The play's lyrical interludes could be a direct tribute to the Queen's lifelong love of music. She played the virginals, the lute, and its recently invented cousin, the orpharion. William Byrd, who was to English music what Shakespeare was to drama, composed the haunting six-voice sacred anthem based on the words of Psalm 21, substituting Elizabeth for King David.

> O Lord, make thy servant Elizabeth our Queen to rejoice in thy strength: give her her heart's desire, and deny not the request of her lips; but prevent her with thine everlasting blessing, and give her a long life, even forever and ever. Amen.[62]

Byrd was a Catholic who nevertheless continued to write music for the Elizabethan Protestant liturgy that retained some polyphony in church music throughout the land. Elizabeth called for music on her deathbed in March 1603, just a month after she watched the final performance of her life presented by the Lord Chamberlain's Men, Shakespeare's company.

Both Elizabeth and Shakespeare were outsiders who could cross social borders: Shakespeare the commoner who could put kings on stage; Elizabeth the Queen who empathised with milkmaids, and had been sidelined by her father and imprisoned by her sister. Like Rosalind, Elizabeth had virtual sisters in other plays by Shakespeare. Only two were of the blood royal, steadfast Imogen, Princess of Britain, and Cleopatra, the legendary Empress of Egypt whose Shakespearean tragedy Elizabeth did not live to see performed. Shakespeare put

Cleopatra at the head of her troops as Elizabeth had put herself at Tilbury.

> Cleopatra   A charge we bear i' the war,
> And as the president of my kingdom will
> Appear there for a man.[63]

But even Cleopatra was not as resonant and perfect a tribute to Elizabeth as Rosalind, the *rosa linda* or beautiful Rose, both the Queen's own Tudor emblem and the national flower of England. At the centre of a triumphal 1590s engraving sits Elizabeth enthroned, within a gorgeous profusion of heraldic roses and eglantine, clearly entitled ROSA ELECTA.[64]

Elizabeth I Rosa Electa

by William Rogers

Like the Bay of Portugal – Rosalind's Love Life

Rosalind's first genius is for love. She's the agent and initiator of love in her play, setting the whole whirligig in motion. 'Let me see,' she asks Celia mischievously, 'what think you of falling in love?' She discovers for herself what extreme love feels like, though the extremities to which it drives people like Orlando are absurd in her sane, witty opinion.

Rosalind's second genius is for language. The most passionate and rational female lover in western drama talks in soaring prose cadenzas to express every facet of love. Passion can make people irrational but Rosalind's love is clear sighted – and expressed in prose. Anticipating both the Enlightenment and the Romantics, she is both rational and ardent. This 'virgin who has fun'[1] as Camille Paglia describes her, is a linguistic Houdini who fizzes like a firecracker as she detonates all the clichés about love. She's both comic and serious; a risk taker prepared to shatter romantic myths at the same time as confessing the oceanic depth of her love. Shakespeare was thirty-five and at the height of his virtuoso powers when he brought immortal Rosalind joyously to life. Spanning both sexes, Rosalind sprints into Arden like an envoy from Shakespeare himself. The year of *As You Like It*, 1599, was indeed an *annus mirabilis* for Shakespeare, when he wrote not only Rosalind's comedy but also the English history play, *Henry V*; a Roman play, *Julius Caesar*; and his great tragedy, *Hamlet*.[2]

'Would you believe in a love at first sight?' asked the Beatles. 'Yes, I'm certain that it happens all the time.' But why does Rosalind fall in love at first sight with Orlando, the youngest son of Sir Rowland de Boys? And why is Shakespeare so interested in this human phenomenon? It doesn't affect the heroine of *Rosalynde,* his immediate source in Thomas Lodge's earlier novella of 1590. Nevertheless, Shakespeare chooses to make love at first sight the impetus for Rosalind's progress from green girl to the intensity of sexual desire. What makes Rosalind unusual is that she can observe passion and heartache through irony, ruses, jokes and prose.

'Who ever loved that loved not at first sight?' asked Christopher Marlowe in his poem, *Hero and Leander*, a question so universal that Shakespeare quoted it verbatim in Rosalind's play. It spills from Phebe, the susceptible shepherdess, when she falls in love at first sight with Rosalind dressed as the 'sweet youth' Ganymede. Phebe is quoting Marlowe, murdered in 1593 in a Deptford tavern.

Phebe	Dead shepherd, now I find thy saw of might:
	'Who ever loved, that loved not at first sight?'[3]

As Rosalind discovers, love at first sight strikes like a miracle though it feels like being mugged. That's why Cupid comes armed with bow and arrows. Actor Pippa Nixon who played the role in the RSC production of 2013 asked why this sort of love hits Rosalind. 'How can you fall in love at first sight? Actually, in a world that at the beginning feels quite hopeless, and there's no hope – it's a miracle.'[4] Trapped in a world of no hope, the court of her wicked uncle, it's obvious that Rosalind is primed for love at first sight. Perhaps the miracle is that it hasn't happened sooner.

Shakespeare also examines love at first sight in *A Midsummer Night's Dream*, *Twelfth Night*, and most famously in *Romeo and Juliet*. In Verona, Juliet and Romeo fall in love the moment they meet. Like Rosalind and Orlando, they both come from dysfunctional families. Unlike Orlando, Romeo has been in love before, infatuated with Rosaline a previous girlfriend, before he ever glimpses Juliet. But rather than with Rosaline, he's been in love with love, which he vents in clichés and embroidered similes.

Romeo	Is love a tender thing? It is too rough,
	Too rude, too boisterous, and it pricks like thorn.[5]

However, when he sees Juliet for the first time, he realises he's never really been in love before, nor appreciated true beauty.

Romeo	O, she doth teach the torches to burn bright.
	It seems she hangs upon the cheek of night
	Like a rich jewel in an Ethiop's ear –
	Beauty too rich for use, for earth too dear.
	...
	Did my heart love till now? Forswear it, sight.
	For I ne'er saw true beauty till this night.[6]

As they join first hands and then lips, Juliet tells Romeo 'you kiss by the book'. Though she's less than fourteen years old, she instantly recognises her 'true love's passion'. She's shrewder than Romeo, as Rosalind is wiser about love than Orlando. Like Rosalind, Juliet is deeply suspicious of facile language. She ticks off Romeo for swearing by the moon, the hackneyed and 'inconstant moon'. When he tries to invoke some other cliché to swear by, she repeats impatiently, 'Do not swear at all…Well, do not swear.' Bored by empty oaths, she forges ahead and proposes to Romeo – as Rosalind will, twice, to Orlando. Like Rosalind in the later play, Juliet moves the action.

> Juliet   Three words, dear Romeo, and good night indeed.
> If that thy bent of love be honourable,
> Thy purpose marriage, send me word tomorrow
> By one that I'll procure to come to thee,
> Where and what time thou wilt perform the rite,
> And all my fortunes at thy foot I'll lay,
> And follow thee my lord throughout the world.[7]

Actor Juliet Rylance thinks Rosalind and Juliet are the only two Shakespearean women to take the initiative in love from the outset. 'Juliet runs with the story. And the same willpower that Rosalind has, they both share that incredible willpower: I *will* achieve my goal, or I *will* be a man, or I *will* test his love…I think Juliet's large in the same way as Rosalind.' I asked Rylance whether she thought people can and do fall in love at first sight? 'I think I fell instantly in love with Christian [Camargo]. I actually fell in love with him while I was playing *Romeo and Juliet* at the Middle Temple Hall.'[8]

For Rosalind and Orlando, Juliet and Romeo, love at first sight strikes like a spark on dry tinder in their violent worlds. Gang warfare between the Capulets and Montagues runs wild in Verona. In this setting blooms the unlooked-for flower of love. The worlds surrounding Rosalind and Orlando are also vicious and corrupt. Political order is disrupted and so is family order. In an atmosphere bristling with physical danger, love at first sight is a jewel of great price. Dangerous situations can catapult you into love. By contrast, Shakespeare shows other loves at first sight that can be self-deceptive, such as Phebe's sudden passion for *doppelgänger* Ganymede/Rosalind, or Olivia's for double agent Cesario/Viola in *Twelfth Night*.

Four centuries before Rylance experienced love at first sight, Shakespeare showed the force with which love can rage, either across the genders or between people of the same sex. In Rosalind, he shows love ignited in a hostile environment. When Orlando wrestles with Duke Frederick's brawny champion and wins, against all the odds, it's the catalyst for love. 'Sir,' breathes Rosalind with instant self-knowledge, 'you have wrestled well, and overthrown/More than your enemies.' Orlando, in his turn, falls just as spontaneously in love with 'heavenly Rosalind'.

The only person Rosalind can confide in is cousin Celia who reproves her smartly, 'Come, come, wrestle with thy affections.' Celia is quick to sense the causal link between Orlando's victory in the wrestling – and in Rosalind's heart. Why is Rosalind so silent and withdrawn, asks Celia, 'is all this for your father?' Rosalind flashes back, 'No, some of it is for my child's father. O, how full of briers is this working-day world!' The immediate brier is Uncle Frederick's loathing of Orlando de Boys' family and lineage. The Duke's emotions stem from the same branch of deadly feuding that divides the Montagues and Capulets. Swiftly cutting through the briers of family politics, Rosalind mentally fast-forwards to her future children. The biological imperative may be primitive and unconscious but it's one of the substrata beneath young heterosexual love. Rosalind openly demonstrates this drive. Her desire has compelling fertility purposes, as she frankly celebrates.

Her love for Orlando is based first on physical attraction and romantic longing. But soon she combines body and soul, head and heart. Inspired by finding a fit father for her future children, she unleashes the masculine as well as the feminine sides of her nature to go and get exactly what she wants. In a similar way, masculine Orlando is entirely comfortable with his feminine side. They match with perfect complementarity. Finding each other, they illustrate Plato's theory of love, as a search for the lost other half of oneself.

But before Rosalind can pursue any outcome to love at first sight with Orlando, unforeseen political events intervene. Uncle Frederick, usurper of her father's dukedom, orders her deportation from court. At a stroke, she finds herself cast out of society, and even pitched out of her gender, in flight to the Forest of Arden disguised as Ganymede.

Transvestism is her ingenious scheme to escape the death penalty Duke Frederick has placed on her head. Yet within her new boy's exterior, she carries the thumping heart of first love.

Once in Arden, together with cousin Celia disguised as Ganymede's peasant sister Aliena, and the court fool, Touchstone, they overhear shepherd Silvius proclaiming his hopeless, troubadourish love for Phebe, a shepherdess: 'O Phebe, Phebe, Phebe!' His pain pierces Rosalind's soul, reminding her of her own one-sided love for Orlando. Since she impetuously gave him her necklace at the wrestling match, she hasn't heard a single word from Orlando. Silvius's love for Phebe could be Rosalind's own heart speaking. 'Alas, poor shepherd! Searching of thy wound, I have by hard adventure found mine own.' Not to be outdone, Touchstone interjects, 'And I mine.' He soars into an improvisation on his own previous love, or lust, for dairymaid, Jane Smile.

> *Touchstone*   I remember when I was in love I broke my sword upon a stone and bid him take that for coming a-night to Jane Smile; and I remember the kissing of her batlet, [butter paddle] and the cow's dugs that her pretty chopped hands had milked; and I remember the wooing of a peascod instead of her, from whom I took two cods, and, giving her them again, said with weeping tears: 'Wear these for my sake.' We that are true lovers run into strange capers. But as all is mortal in nature, so is all nature in love mortal in folly.[9]

Touchstone and Jane Smile, as well as all the other couples in the play, constantly refract one another like musical themes, recapitulated and rephrased. As we revolve these differing love pairings, we wonder which has the best chance of enduring. Rosalind instantly recognises Touchstone's experience of the craziness of love, 'Thou speak'st wiser than thou art ware of.' Seeing her own love through the filters of Silvius's poetic, Petrarchan love for Phebe, and Touchstone's raunchy carnal love, soon to be transferred to goatherd Audrey, only intensifies Rosalind's yearning. Literary critic, Anna Jameson, understood this exactly. In her book, *Shakespeare's Heroines*, first published in 1832, she wrote, 'Passion, when we contemplate it through the medium of imagination, is like a ray of light transmitted through a prism: we can calmly, and with undazzled eye, study its complicate [sic] nature and analyse its variety of tints; but passion brought home to us in its reality, through our own feelings and experience, is like the same ray transmitted through a lens, – blinding, burning, consuming where it falls.'[10]

Shakespeare had the brilliance to convey what his heroines felt when falling in love for the first time. And he endowed them with far greater freedom of action than Anna Jameson's contemporary male writers: Dickens, Thackeray and Trollope. Novelist and critic, Rebecca West, noticed this in the mid-twentieth century. 'It would have been astounding to find a Juliet in their pages. None of the three would have respected her passion as Shakespeare respected it, for the double reason that it was beautiful in itself and that it had a right to exist, like her own body…like all sound processes of nature.' Rosalind, like Juliet, is at ease with her body and its desires, as she is with the intensity of her emotions. But, Rebecca West conceded, one among the male Victorian novelists, Anthony Trollope, 'was a feminist.'[11]

Like Shakespeare nearly three centuries ahead of him, Trollope showed special empathy with women and the female experience of falling in love. Trollope's final novel in his Palliser series, *The Duke's Children* of 1880, is sprinkled with references to *As You Like It*.[12] Trollope understood the heart of another duke's daughter, Lady Mary Palliser, whose father, the Duke of Omnium, was the 'brier' opposed to her love match with Mr Francis Tregear. Like Orlando, Tregear was a gentleman of no fortune, though 'as beautiful as Apollo.' Trollope described Mary's boundless love as well as her absolute tenacity in pursuing it. However, she had none of Ganymede's freedom of action, nor would it have occurred to her to jump gender like Rosalind. But Mary was very sure that her first and deepest love for Mr Tregear 'had become a bond almost as holy as matrimony itself.' Mary's first love has the same aura of sanctity as Rosalind's. Kissing Orlando is as 'full of sanctity as the touch of holy bread,' she says. In Mary's case, as in Rosalind's, 'No other man had ever whispered a word of love to her, of no other man had an idea entered her mind that it could be pleasant to join her lot in life with his. With her it had been all new and all sacred. Love with her had that religion which nothing but freshness can give it.'[13] Like Shakespeare, Trollope understood that first love thrills by its very newness.

Rosalind's love has that same elation. I talked recently to Jean Hewison, a chic and elegant octogenarian, who played Rosalind in the open air when she was twenty-one. 'Honestly, I think it's young love. It's got to be fresh, like a sudden blossoming, it's spring, and it's all happening.'[14] Youthful it may be, but Rosalind's love is universal, too, and people of all ages relate to its exuberance.

In her state of heightened consciousness, Rosalind finds Orlando's love poems pinned on Arden's greenwood trees. After wringing the poet's identity out of Celia, Rosalind finds herself initially trapped in the persona of Ganymede. But she makes disguise her best friend. It's her passport to freedom, a carte blanche to tell the truth about love to the man she hopes may become her life's partner. 'It's the old conundrum of truth-telling', observes Janet Suzman. 'You tell the truth when you have a disguise upon you…Truth-telling can only properly be done when you are well disguised. That is the only reason to be an artist: to try to tell the truth.'[15] Rosalind seizes upon playacting as a route to the truth, to examine the sincerity of Orlando's love and verify her own. For as Walter Pater observed, 'Play is often that about which people are most serious.'[16]

'The premise that this person [Ganymede] does not exist, cannot exist gives you more licence to talk about love', says Adrian Lester who played Rosalind in 1991. 'Young love really hurts, you're a slave of your feelings, there's an inner violence to them. She's *more* Rosalind when she's Ganymede – and yet she has to keep control of her sexual passions. It's a very complex situation for Rosalind.'[17] Perhaps it was a complex situation for Rosalind's original audience, too. Played by a boy, first in formal female court dress, then in double-crossing costume as Ganymede, did they even see her as a woman at all? Or was the convention so accepted as to be unremarkable? In the transvestite figure of Rosalind, Shakespeare could embody the ferocity of love, which affects both sexes.

By healing the split between male and female in the actor playing triply cross-dressed Rosalind, Shakespeare captures what love feels like for both sexes, in every time and place. Shortly after the fall of the Berlin Wall, I got talking with a group of Latvian banking delegates during their coffee break at a hotel near Stratford-upon-Avon. I asked, tentatively, if they were going to see any Shakespeare on their first trip to England? The group leader leapt in. 'Of course we're going to see a play! Don't you realise Shakespeare is not for the English? He is for Latvia, he is for all Latvians, he is for the world!' Rosalind's love is comprehensive in this Latvian spirit, cross-cultural, international and, yes, dual gendered. S/he belongs to our collective experience. Harold Bloom observes, 'A great role, like Rosalind's, is a kind of miracle: a universal perspective seems to open out upon us.'[18] 'Miracle' seems to attach itself to Rosalind, the same word actor Pippa Nixon used to describe Rosalind's love.

As Rosalind grows from untouched innocence to the full frankness of sexual desire for Orlando, she becomes aware of her uncharted capacity for love. 'My affection hath an unknown bottom like the Bay of Portugal.'[19] The seas between Oporto and the Cape of Cintra off the coast of Portugal sink to a vast depth of up to 1400 fathoms. It's not just an outlandish simile. It expresses exactly what Rosalind feels – and it would have been topical. Living in the exhilarating Age of Discovery, Shakespeare fired Rosalind's mind with all the latest marine knowledge. On tenterhooks to learn the author of the love poems strewn across Arden, she berates Celia with another metaphor from the new navigation. 'One inch of delay more is a South Sea of discovery'.[20] An extra moment's prevarication seems as endless to Rosalind as an Elizabethan explorer's journey to the South Pacific. Her imagery circumnavigates the known world, as it then was.

How do you understand the power of love if you've never been in love before, especially if you're a motherless girl? 'The absence of mothers always puts women in a state of crisis from the start. They are unprotected, they are always alone in the world, even if the world is a drawing-room', says actor Fiona Shaw who has played both Rosalind and Celia.[21] Pre-Orlando, Rosalind's only experience of intimacy and love has flowed to her from cousin Celia.

The two cousins have never been in love with anyone else. They share a unique bond as they've only known the love of one another. Teenage girls may or may not love each other in a sexual way, and Celias today may choose openly the love of women. Each production makes its own interpretation of the Rosalind-Celia friendship. In Sam

Mendes' version at the Old Vic in 2010, Michelle Beck's Celia played the relationship with Rosalind like best friends who have grown up together, 'until a man shows up and changes everything,' says Juliet Rylance, 'and they go through that, the next stage of development.'[22] Watching Beck, I sensed that Celia felt left behind by Rosalind. When Rosalind fell in love with Orlando, Celia just stood there and suddenly became Aliena, the persona she will take on in Arden. She was literally alienated. Her love for Rosalind had been superseded. But Rosalind grows and takes flight from Celia's selfless love. It's her springboard into love for Orlando. And she doesn't look back. That's the cruelty of love.

Up to the point where the two cousins leave Duke Frederick's court in disguise, it could have been Celia's play. Once Rosalind makes the decision to flee to Arden dressed as a boy, she becomes the main protagonist and the focus of all eyes. She's now a performer with the freedom first to approach Orlando, and later to propose to him, not just once, but twice. Proposing to a man at the end of the sixteenth century was seriously transgressive. Yet Juliet also proposes. Both Rosalind and Juliet mastermind their own courtships in a comedy and a tragedy. But Rosalind isn't just an actor in her own drama. She's director, producer, scriptwriter, and stage manager, too.

The language of theatre infuses *As You Like It*. Duke Senior exiled in the forest, finds comfort in the metaphor of life as theatre, or the playhouse as life.

Duke Senior   Thou seest we are not all alone unhappy:
This wide and universal theatre
Presents more woeful pageants than the scene
Wherein we play in.[23]

The Duke's image and his half-line are immediately picked up by Jaques as he sashays into the most often quoted speech of the play, 'All the world's a stage…' referring to the words possibly flown on the flag-pole at the new Globe Playhouse in 1599: *Totus mundus agit histrionem* – the whole world plays the actor.[24] Theatre is life itself, life is theatre, and Rosalind the star in her own drama. Her only counterpart, later, will be Prospero.

Like Prospero, Rosalind is the impresario and organising spirit of her play. To action her love, Rosalind takes control of events in

Arden, even when her transvestite situation threatens to become fatally embarrassing. 'Alas the day!' she groans when Celia reveals that Orlando is also in the forest, 'What shall I do with my doublet and hose?' It is here in Act III at the very epicentre of Shakespeare's 5-act play that Rosalind and Orlando encounter each other for only the second time. This centrality is significant. For their love is the centre of the play, as poet John Donne's bed is the centre of his room and of his relationship with his lover.[25] Rosalind in role as Ganymede now has the space to test the truthfulness of Orlando's heart whose poems seem to proclaim the depth of his affection.

Once Orlando admits he is indeed the author of poems in praise of someone called Rosalind, Ganymede can ask him direct the consuming question, 'But are you so much in love as your rhymes speak?' She could never have asked this as Rosalind, and it's 'the absolute crux of the scene,' thinks actor Rebecca Hall. Then Orlando 'answers her better than she can possibly imagine: "Neither rhyme nor reason can express how much." And it floors her. And she realises that she's utterly in love too. The whole thing is terrifying. This next speech is so beautiful and I love it. It's almost my favourite,' says Hall.

> *Rosalind*   Love is merely a madness, and, I tell you deserves as well
> a dark house and a whip as madmen do; and the reason
> why they are not so punished and cured is that the lunacy
> is so ordinary that the whippers are in love too.[26]

In Hall's view, Rosalind 'suddenly has this incredible lucidity about love. It's sort of rueful...For every funny thing she says, there's an undercurrent of reality as well, of the slightly frightening nature of it all. And she's not being flippant, she really does think love is completely crazy...It's all crazy. Love is mad. And yet we run our lives by it.'[27]

Love feels like madness for both Rosalind and Orlando, but Rosalind applies her mind as well as her emotions to it. Her love is as profound as Juliet's but she tempers it with her own sardonic voice when she lectures on love to her lover. W.H. Auden clearly heard the rational, civilized voice of Rosalind. 'It's very sophisticated, and only adults can understand what [the play's] about. You have to be acquainted with what it means to be a civilized person...Of all of Shakespeare's plays, *As You Like It* is the greatest paean to civilization and to the nature of a civilized man and woman. It is dominated by Rosalind, a triumph of civilization, who like the play itself, fully embodies man's capacity, in Pascal's words, "to deny, to believe, and to doubt well" – *nier, croire, et douter bien.*'[28]

Rosalind's sophisticated reasoning about love is electrifying. She wants to explore the implications of precipitate, headstrong love. If love is a madness as she warns him, it is also an illness from which Orlando has no wish to be cured. But 'cure' is the word that inspires Rosalind with the germ of her brilliant scheme. Safe in her actor's invented male self, she proposes impersonating the 'real' Rosalind. 'I would cure you,' she lures Orlando, 'if you would but call me Rosalind and come every day to my cote to woo me.' Let's pretend we're lovers by proxy. Let's play a flirting game. Behind the mask of Ganymede, Rosalind is free to speak the truth about love and her heart. Hitherto, a woman in a man's world, constricted by dress and expectation, disguise now awards her the freedom of a spy in action. In her game-changing way, Rosalind plots to get exactly what she wants: Orlando, the object of her loving at first sight.

Rosalind was the breakthrough role in Vanessa Redgrave's career, says her daughter, Joely Richardson. It made Redgrave a star for the RSC in Stratford and London in 1961, and more people saw it when the production was broadcast in 1963. During *Shakespeare's Women*, a BBC TV programme made by Richardson in 2012, Redgrave told her daughter how close the 1961 production had come to disaster. At the end of six weeks in rehearsal, director Michael Elliott told her: 'Vanessa, if you don't give yourself to this play, you are going to ruin this production!'[29] Playing Rosalind is like diving, thinks Redgrave, you have to give yourself to the water, you have to abandon yourself to the part. Abandonment worked. 'The naturalness, the unforced understanding of her playing, the passionate, breathless conviction of it, the depth of feeling and the breadth of reality – this is not acting at all, but living, being, loving,' wrote critic Bernard Levin of Redgrave's performance.[30] Rosalind as Ganymede is acting but, paradoxically, her finest acting is not an act. Redgrave found the scene in which Ganymede offers to cure Orlando of love by pretending to be Rosalind, one of the most heartfelt scenes in Shakespeare.

Rosalind's seesaw adventure takes her from romance to realism and back again. Having issued instructions for a play courtship, she lets Orlando go, only to find her confidence dissolving, like him, into the forest. She demands of herself and of Celia, her confidante and sounding board, 'But why did he swear he would come this morning, and comes not?' It's the question with which all lovers torment themselves. But Celia is cold comfort. She voices Rosalind's worst fears, and all lovers' foreboding of rejection.

Celia	Nay certainly, there is no truth in him.
Rosalind	Do you think so?
Celia	Yes. I think he is not a pick-purse nor a horse-stealer – but for his verity in love I do think him as concave as a covered goblet or a worm-eaten nut.
Rosalind	Not true in love?
Celia	Yes, when he is in, but I think he is not in.
Rosalind	You have heard him swear downright he was.
Celia	'Was' is not 'is.' Besides, the oath of a lover is no stronger than the word of a tapster: they are both the confirmer of false reckonings.[31]

Falling in love is fraught with dangers. Falling out of love is one of them. Love's risks are as great as its rewards. Rosalind sees rejection presented before her very eyes when she watches the next episode in the rolling Silvius-Phebe love story. Rosalind is the pattern of all lovers in her fear of rejection, of the future, and of the confusing nature of time. 'The creeping hours of time,' as Orlando says, seem to pass so slowly, fail to bring the longed for results, or wing by too swiftly. It's all too short a step from love to time, and hence to mortality; sexual climax the little death that foreshadows the great oblivion.

'There's no clock in the forest' but the characters are acutely aware of time in all its phases. Seen from afar, the life of Duke Senior's exiled court glows in an aura of Edenic time, in spite of winter weather and physical hardship. As Charles the wrestler reports:

Charles	They say he is already in the Forest of Arden and a many merry men with him, and there they live like the old Robin Hood of England. They say many young gentlemen flock to him every day and fleet the time carelessly as they did in the golden world.[32]

But like a death-knell, time tolls against Rosalind when her uncle banishes her.

Duke Frederick   If you outstay the time, upon mine honour
                   And in the greatness of my word, you die.[33]

Celia transmutes her father's threat of outstaying time by her great-hearted offer to flee the court with Rosalind.

Celia   Let's away,
                   And get our jewels and our wealth together,
                   Devise the fittest time and safest way
                   To hide us from pursuit that will be made
                   After my flight.[34]

Arriving in Arden safe in their disguises, a new kind of forest time stretches ahead for the cousins. 'I like this place/And willingly could waste my time in it,' Celia announces.[35] It's the spirit of *asolare*, the word Robert Browning defined as 'to disport in the open air, amuse oneself at random,' when almost three hundred years after Arden he found himself happily wasting time in the small Italian town of Asolo.[36]

Everyone in Arden seems obsessed with time. Touchstone, the court fool, impresses Jaques with an aria on clocks counting the hours of life, as he pulls a sun-dial out of his pocket, and,

Jaques   Says very wisely, 'It is ten o'clock.
                   Thus we may see', quoth he, 'how the world wags.
                   'Tis but an hour ago since it was nine,
                   And after one hour more 'twill be eleven.
                   And so from hour to hour we ripe and ripe,
                   And then from hour to hour we rot and rot,
                   And thereby hangs a tale.'[37]

Time's action is not only the preoccupation of lovers but it is also the relentless engine that drives Jaques' famous speech on the stages of human life.

Jaques   All the world's a stage,
                   And all the men and women merely players.
                   They have their exits and their entrances,
                   And one man in his time plays many parts,
                   His acts being seven ages.[38]

Within the play's framework of philosophising about time passing, Ganymede/Rosalind accosts Orlando for the first time in Arden. A time check is as corny as spies asking for a light in old black and white movies.

Rosalind	I pray you, what is't o'clock?
Orlando	You should ask me what time o'day. There's no clock in the forest.
Rosalind	Then there is no true lover in the forest, else sighing every minute and groaning every hour would detect the lazy foot of time as well as a clock.
Orlando	And why not the swift foot of time? Had not that been as proper?
Rosalind	By no means, sir. Time travels in divers paces with divers persons. I'll tell you who Time ambles withal, who Time trots withal, who Time gallops withal and who he stands still withal.
Orlando	I prithee, who doth he trot withal?
Rosalind	Marry, he trots hard with a young maid between the contract of her marriage and the day it is solemnized. If the interim be but a se'nnight, Time's pace is so hard that it seems the length of seven year.
Orlando	Who ambles Time withal?
Rosalind	With a priest that lacks Latin, and a rich man that hath not the gout; for the one sleeps easily because he cannot study, and the other lives merrily because he feels no pain; the one lacking the burden of lean and wasteful learning, the other knowing no burden of heavy tedious penury. These Time ambles withal.
Orlando	Who doth he gallop withal?
Rosalind	With a thief to the gallows; for though he go as softly as foot can fall, he thinks himself too soon there.
Orlando	Who stays it still withal?
Rosalind	With lawyers in the vacation; for they sleep between term and term and then they perceive not how time moves.[39]

Ganymede darts insights at Orlando about the psychological contortions of time. Straight man Orlando feeds Ganymede questions to provoke ever more inventive answers. The conversation escalates into an aria of comic and dazzling images. Rosalind makes a lot out of these similes about Time. Or she could be struggling to complete the comparisons she's set herself, as an in-joke against the script-writer's fanciful word-play.

Reviewers who saw Edith Evans play Rosalind in 1936/7 thought her the only actress 'who *could* think of the things Shakespeare makes her say. She is equal to her wit instead of being nonplussed by it. She might, in short, have written the part.' Rosalind convinces us, of course, that she's making up the words as she goes along. Although Edith Evans was not the obvious physical type to play lissome Rosalind, she created impudence and lightness, proving that conventional notions of feminine beauty are no obstacle to inhabiting the role. 'Does she make you fall in love with her? That is not her business. It is her business to make you fall in love with Orlando, and at the Old Vic in 1936 Edith Evans triumphantly [made] you experience her emotions.' 'She can move like an arrow, she can roll over the ground in a delight of comedy, she can mock and glitter.'[40]

When Orlando avows he is indeed the Arden love poet with the 'quotidian of love upon him,' Rosalind seizes the opportunity to uncover the truth about him. If that's your problem, 'I profess curing it by counsel,' says naughty Ganymede. Come round to mine every day and let's pretend I'm your Rosalind. I'll show you what women are really like and you'll soon desist. It's a therapy that's worked before with a previous lovesick fellow, s/he lies. This way 'will I take upon me to wash your liver as clean as a sound sheep's heart, that there shall not be one spot of love in't.'[41] Though he has no wish to be cured of his love, Orlando is up for the game. So when Ganymede invites him, 'Will you go?' he answers, 'With all my heart, good youth.' But the 'boy' reminds him, 'Nay you must call me Rosalind.'

In the merry war of love that now ensues, themes of play-acting and reality merge in Rosalind's badinage.

Orlando	…and my Rosalind is virtuous.
Rosalind	And I am your Rosalind.
Celia	It pleases him to call you so, but he hath a Rosalind of a better leer than you.
Rosalind	Come, woo me, woo me – for now I am in a holiday humour and like enough to consent. What would you say to me now, an I were your very, very Rosalind?
Orlando	I would kiss before I spoke.
Rosalind	Nay, you were better speak first, and when you were gravelled for lack of matter you might take occasion to kiss.

	Very good orators when they are out, they will spit, and for lovers lacking (God warrant us) matter, the cleanliest shift is to kiss.
Orlando	How if the kiss be denied?
Rosalind	Then she puts you to entreaty and there begins new matter.
Orlando	Who could be out, being before his beloved mistress?
Rosalind	Marry, that should you, if I were your mistress, or I should think my honesty ranker than my wit.
Orlando	What, of my suit?
Rosalind	Not out of your apparel and yet out of your suit. Am not I your Rosalind?
Orlando	I take some joy to say you are because I would be talking of her.
Rosalind	Well, in her person, I say I will not have you.[42]

Rosalind tries to deny her heart at the same time as she challenges his. She distrusts his romantic hyperbole. Her tough blend of reason and ardour makes her an unusually brave human being. She would have approved the song, *Let us all ring Fancy's knell. / I'll begin it. Ding, dong, bell.*[43] Yet, in spite of her suspicions about romantics, she is fervently in love with Orlando. So successful is Rosalind's strategy to examine Orlando's authenticity, so unsuccessful is Ganymede's strategy to wash his liver clean of love, that at only their second forest tryst, he's as eager as s/he is to participate in their faux wedding officiated by Celia. Rosalind's passionate desire for Orlando is the centre about which the whole play moves.

Rosalind	I do take thee, Orlando, for my husband. There's a girl goes before the priest, and certainly a woman's thought runs before her actions.
Orlando	So do all thoughts – they are winged.
Rosalind	Now tell me how long you would have her after you have possessed her?
Orlando	For ever and a day.
Rosalind	Say 'a day' without the 'ever'. No, no, Orlando, men are April when they woo, December when they wed. Maids are May when they are maids, but the sky changes when they are wives.[44]

Rosalind contains apparent opposites. Though impassioned, she's also bleakly realistic. She seems to know instinctively that marriage can curdle romance. Rosalind is this and she is that. She even changes sex mid-speech when she imagines herself 'a Barbary cock-pigeon'. Juliet Stevenson notices how Rosalind 'subverts gender stereotypes [and] notions of love as they have been passed down through literature and through society. The very state of marriage is an unequal state historically. It was created for the patrilineal line. It was created to keep women under. It's quite a patriarchal institution as it exists, though these words are modern words used in modern times. It would be inappropriate to suggest that Shakespeare was questioning patriarchy. But it doesn't matter what words you use. The ideas are the same.'[45]

Even from the depths of her emotional vortex, Rosalind can be cerebral almost to the point of cynicism. Her verbal skirmishes with Orlando are whip sharp. She's determined to raise all the negatives about women, love and marriage, and to deflate Orlando's claims for endless adoration. Adrian Lester thinks 'the play shows us the romantic idea of love and then the reality of it. Rosalind has had her heart broken by members of her own family. She is weak and powerless. Then along comes a man with whom she falls completely in love. But upon meeting him she realises that he is in love with the idea of her, not with who she really is.'[46] In the 1940 movie, *The Philadelphia Story*, Katharine Hepburn's character, Tracy Lord, thought like Rosalind, 'I don't want to be worshipped, I want to be loved…really loved.' Ten years later Hepburn was obvious casting for Rosalind on Broadway.

With her innate wisdom, Rosalind understands that the first delirium of young love will not last, that December will follow May. The seasons constantly murmur an elegiac burden to lovers' time. Immediately after her mock wedding with Orlando, Rosalind's speeding mind recurs to time – which torments all lovers. 'Alas! dear love, I cannot lack thee two hours.' Lovers' time is here and now, ''Tis not hereafter,' as Feste the Clown sings in *Twelfth Night*, the play most often coupled with *As You Like It*. The songs in Shakespeare's comedies were part of popular theatre, like musicals today. Songs punctuate Rosalind's play like mood music, light as bubbles even when they sound a melancholy note. In the Elizabethan world picture, music was an echo of the heavenly spheres. It could lead its listeners towards perfection. Even though love's springtime marches inevitably towards 'winter and rough weather,' the songs in Shakespeare's comedies inspire lovers to transcend time's tragedy.

Amiens, official vocalist to Duke Senior's exiled court, voices this theme in the first of six songs in *As You Like It*.

Under the greenwood tree
  Who loves to lie with me
And turn [tune] his merry note
  Unto the sweet bird's throat,
Come hither, come hither, come hither!
  Here shall he see no enemy
But winter and rough weather...

Who doth ambition shun
  And loves to live i'th' sun,
Seeking the food he eats
  And pleased with what he gets,
Come hither, come hither, come hither!
  Here shall he see no enemy
But winter and rough weather.[47]

And he reiterates the chill of winter weather in his second song:

Blow, blow, thou winter wind,
Thou art not so unkind
  As man's ingratitude.
Thy tooth is not so keen
Because thou art not seen,
  Although thy breath be rude.
Hey-ho, sing hey-ho, unto the green holly.
Most friendship is feigning, most loving mere folly.
  Then hey-ho, the holly!
  This life is most jolly.

Freeze, freeze, thou bitter sky,
That dost not bite so nigh
  As benefits forgot.
Though thou the waters warp,
Thy sting is not so sharp
  As friend remembered not.
Hey-ho, sing hey-ho, unto the green holly.[48]

By the time Amiens sings this, Orlando has already proved that his old servant Adam is far from forgotten. Orlando carries him, fainting from hunger, to Duke Senior's feast in the forest, and man's ingratitude is reversed. In 2013 the RSC made the play's songs freshly contemporary by commissioning singer Laura Marling to compose modern settings for its famous lyrics. The songs easily crossed the four centuries since they were written and found a new resonance with today's audience. Music moves love on to universal and timeless planes.

In the build-up to the joyful conclusion of the play, two young pages sing Thomas Morley's pop song of its day, 'It was a lover and his lass.' Springtime becomes 'ringtime', literally, because four weddings are about to be celebrated. Four couples will jubilantly 'take the present time' and seize the day.

> It was a lover and his lass,
>> With a hey and a ho and a hey nonino,
> That o'er the green cornfield did pass,
>> In spring-time, the only pretty ring-time,
> When birds do sing, hey ding a ding a ding,
> Sweet lovers love the spring.
>
> Between the acres of the rye,
>> With a hey and a ho and a hey nonino,
> These pretty country folks would lie,
>> In spring-time, &c.
>
> This carol they began that hour,
>> With a hey and a ho and a hey nonino,
> How that a life was but a flower,
>> In springtime, &c.
>
> And therefore take the present time,
>> With a hey and a ho and a hey nonino,
> For love is crowned with the prime,
>> In spring-time, &c.[49]

Composer, organist, and probably counter-tenor, Morley set this poem to music in his *First Book of Ayres* in 1600.[50] It's the only contemporary arrangement of one of *As You Like*'s songs to survive. The upbeat melodic line with 'cross-rhythms introduced into the refrain' is a perfect match with the cross-hatched moods of the play.[51] Mortality thrums beneath joy. Life is but a flower. Musical time underscores human time and gives it an eternal dimension. Touchstone teases the boy singers that their 'note was very untuneable,' but the elder page stands firm, 'You are deceived, sir; we kept time, we lost not our time.' Lovers triumph by keeping time through music which persists as long as there are singers to sing. *As You Like It*'s songs seem to float in time. They are not specially associated with individual characters but linger in the mind, subtly reprising the play's deepest themes about human love, both melancholy and jubilant. Though Rosalind thinks romantic love may be evanescent, mere folly, she does believe that human love can survive.

As organising genius of the outcome of the four love pairings in the play, Rosalind keeps the final denouement under her strict control.

> *Rosalind* I have promised to make all this matter even.
> Keep you your word, O Duke, to give your daughter,
> You yours, Orlando, to receive his daughter.
> Keep you your word, Phebe, that you'll marry me,
> Or else, refusing me, to wed this shepherd.
> Keep your word, Silvius, that you'll marry her
> If she refuse me; and from hence I go
> To make these doubts all even.[52]

Abandoning her usual springy, colloquial prose for the formality of blank verse in the buildup to one of life's most ritualistic moments, Rosalind leaves the stage, apparently to step out of role as Ganymede and return in a wedding dress. But Shakespeare makes this deliberately vague. Rosalind could return still dressed as Ganymede, as Rebecca Hall did in 2003. Or she could reappear, not in wedding white which only came in with the Victorians, but as Rosalynde did in Shakespeare's source novelette by Thomas Lodge, in 'a gown of green, with kirtle of rich sandal [light silk], so quaint [elegant], that she seemed like Diana in the forest; upon her head she wore a chaplet of roses, which gave her such a grace that she looked like Flora perked in the pride of all her flowers.'[53] In whatever costume she chooses, Shakespeare's Rosalind is perked in all her pride for her official marriage with Orlando. Picking monosyllables for absolute clarity, she expresses her free choice and profound love.

Rosalind [*to Duke Senior*]	To you I give myself, for I am yours.
[*to Orlando*]	To you I give myself, for I am yours.
Duke Senior	If there be truth in sight, you are my daughter.
Orlando	If there be truth in sight, you are my Rosalind.
Phebe	If sight and shape be true, Why then, my love adieu.
Rosalind [*to Duke Senior*]	I'll have no father, if you be not he.
[*to Orlando*]	I'll have no husband, if you be not he.
[*to Phebe*]	Nor ne'er wed woman, if you be not she.[54]

After the verbal fireworks of cross-gender courtship, Rosalind's simple avowals drop into my mind with emotion too deep for tears. Love is the heartbeat. She chooses 'a good man's love' and needs no father to give her away. Instead, the master-mistress of herself, she says with autonomy, 'To you I give myself for I am yours.' Michelle Terry who played Rosalind at Shakespeare's Globe during summer 2015 observes, 'she can only become a daughter, become a wife because by the end of the play, the patriarchy has been completely dismantled. She's re-negotiated the terms.' At the end of the play, the older ducal generation does not return to government. Instead, Rosalind and Orlando will be the new rulers at court, as well as more equal partners in their enlightened marriage.

What's radical about Rosalind is that in 1599, and in every production since, 'she makes love to the man instead of waiting for the man to make love to her – a piece of natural history,' observed George Bernard Shaw, 'which has kept Shakespeare's heroines alive, whilst generations of properly governessed young ladies, taught to say "No" three times at least, have miserably perished.'[55] Shaw's preferred choice for Rosalind's wedding outfit was the 'rational dress' of unisex cycling culottes of the 1890s, an inspired fashion statement for Shakespeare's most rational and ardent comic heroine.

As You Like It parades a quartet of relationships along the spectrum of human love: Rosalind and Orlando, Silvius and Phebe, Celia and Oliver, and Touchstone and Audrey. They culminate in four unconventional weddings, the most in any of Shakespeare's plays. 'All four couples have gone through their own negotiation,' says Michelle

Terry. The love between Rosalind and Orlando is the most debated and the most tested of the four couples. It's an ideal love because it has no blinkers. It's gloves off love. Celia and Oliver's love is a reflection of Rosalind and Orlando's because, like theirs, it's fired by love at first sight, and their mutual attraction is built on the same complementary bonds of class and temperament. Phebe settles for Silvius when she realises she can't marry the boy Ganymede. If Shakespeare was writing today in the era of same sex marriages, Phebe's story might have a different ending. Silvius's love for Phebe is unrealistic and unrequited but also a testament to true fidelity. Their future happiness depends on his capacity to forgive Phebe for lusting after Ganymede, and her aptitude to learn about 'a good man's love.' Touchstone and Audrey are in lust with each other and will stay together, while physical passion survives – which may be longer than cynics suggest. Michelle Terry says, 'I have hope for all of them.'[56]

There are many demonstrations of human love in *As You Like It*. The ideal of sisterly love that Celia offers cousin Rosalind offsets the fraternal hatred between Oliver and Orlando, and between the two dukes. That hostility between brothers is redeemed by conversion and forgiveness. Orlando's attraction to the erotic boy Ganymede still holds a distinct homoerotic frisson, as it would have done in 1599 when a boy played Rosalind. Phebe's infatuation with Ganymede underlines this. There's no way of knowing whether we see, even remotely, a similar performance of sexuality that *As You Like It*'s first audience saw in 1599. But the love between Orlando and old Adam, master and servant, boss and employee, teenager and senior citizen though rare, is recognizable to modern people. It stands proxy for the almost complete lack of parental or filial love in the play. There are no living or loving mothers and the two Dukes' feelings for their daughters, Rosalind and Celia, appear at best attenuated. Nevertheless, Duke Senior exhibits paternal love and care for his courtiers in the forest who have shown him enough loyalty to share his exile. Perhaps they have become his substitute family. His real paternity is restored when lost daughter Rosalind finally unmasks herself to him.

With her own special wisdom, Rosalind fundamentally prefers reality to romance. Her comic, anarchic view of love is sharpened by

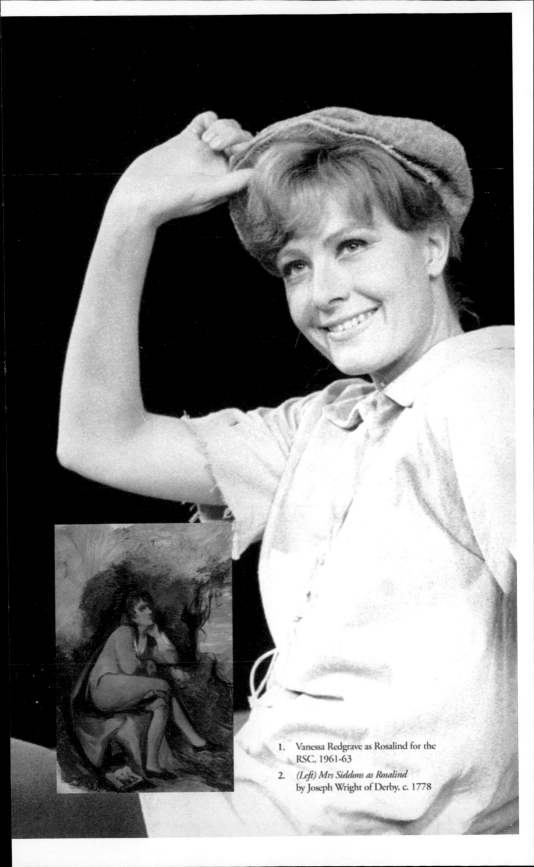

1. Vanessa Redgrave as Rosalind for the RSC, 1961-63

2. *(Left) Mrs Siddons as Rosalind* by Joseph Wright of Derby, c. 1778

3. *(Above) Ganymede with Zeus disguised as an eagle* by Bertel Thorvaldsen, 1817

4. *(Below) Valentine rescuing Silvia from Proteus* by William Holman Hunt, 1850-51, from Shakespeare's play *The Two Gentlemen of Verona*

5. *(Above left)* Rebecca Hall as Rosalind at Theatre Royal Bath and in the USA, 2003; **6.** *(Above right)* Janet Suzman as Rosalind for the RSC, 1968; 7. *(Below)* Sally Scott as Rosalind *(left)* with Kaisa Hammarlund as Celia *(right)* at the Southwark Playhouse, 2014

8. *(Above)* Juliet Rylance as Rosalind with Christian Camargo as Orlando at The Old Vic, 2010; 9. *(Below left)* Adrian Lester *(right)* as Rosalind for Cheek by Jowl, 1991; 10. *(Below right) The Mock Marriage of Orlando and Rosalind* (with Celia looking on) by Walter Deverell, 1853

11. (*Above left*) Pippa Nixon as Rosalind for the RSC, 2013; 12. (*Above right*) Edith Evans (*top*) as Rosalind at The Old Vic, 1936/7; 13. (*Below*) Juliet Stevenson (*left*) as Rosalind with Fiona Shaw (*right*) as Celia for the RSC, 1985

14. *(Above)* Katharine Hepburn as Rosalind with William Prince as Orlando on Broadway, 1950;
15. *(Below left)* Laurence Olivier as Orlando in the 1936 film of *As You Like It*; 16. *(Below right)*
Ronald Pickup as Rosalind at The Old Vic, 1967

17. *(Above)* Helen Faucit, one of the great Victorian Rosalinds

18. *(Below left)* Dorothy Jordan as Rosalind by Sir William Beechey, 1787

19. *(Below right)* Elisabeth Bergner as Rosalind in the 1936 film of *As You Like It*

20. Cush Jumbo as Rosalind at the Royal Exchange Theatre Manchester for which she won the Ian Charleson Award 2012

21. *(Below)* Rosalind in *As You Like It* by Arthur Hughes, 1871-3

her combination of emotional depth with a constant edge of doubt and cynicism. We recognise the authenticity of her love today as they recognised it in 1599. Her approach to love is for our times as well as for hers. Wherever love is to be found is more important than whatever gender one is. Rosalind's aim is more equal love between lovers, a fulfilling emotional life of conversation with Orlando, coupled with the responsibility of principled government over a 'land itself at large, a potent dukedom.' Romantic love is only one of the vital components in Rosalind's life plan. In 1599, the sacred rite of marriage ennobled the play's four couplings, and pre-eminently the union of Rosalind and Orlando. Hymen, a gender-free celebrant, sings the final song.

> Wedding is great Juno's crown,
>   O blessed bond of board and bed.
> 'Tis Hymen peoples every town,
>   High wedlock then be honoured.
> Honour, high honour and renown
> To Hymen, god of every town.[57]

ACT FIVE SCENE ONE

Celia – Juno's Swan

Celia is more than a sister to Rosalind. She's different from the virtual sisters, Julia, the two Rosalines, and Portia in the preceding plays; and Beatrice, Viola and Imogen in contemporaneous and later plays by Shakespeare. Celia is Rosalind's foil and counterpart, and, in Act 1 at least, her equal partner. She's not just Rosalind's sidekick but her own person with strong views and powerful emotions, inflected with her distinctive brand of Celian wit and humour.

Celia is, in fact, not Rosalind's sibling but her first cousin. But as courtier Le Beau says, and everyone else knows, their meshed loves 'are dearer than the natural bond of sisters.'[1] Almost as symbiotic as twins, each is an only child and a motherless girl. Celia accompanies Rosalind throughout almost the whole play, loving, empathising, encouraging, supporting, joking and mocking, step by step in the same actual and liminal space.

The emotional connection between Celia and Rosalind is so intuitive and playful that it's closer to an ideal of sisterhood than to mere cousins. However, when they leave court to enter the Forest of Arden in disguise, it's as a brother and sister partnership: Ganymede and Aliena. By the end of the play, when they marry two brothers, Orlando and Oliver, they become quasi sisters-in-law. From the beginning, in the potential tragedy of the play's first act, Celia is a spirited and enterprising partner for Rosalind. It's Celia who has the energy, takes the initiative, and stands up to her psychopathic father, Duke Frederick, when he banishes Rosalind from court. It's Celia who refuses to be separated from her 'sweet coz', Celia who instantly conceives the plan to seek asylum with Rosalind's father, the rightful Duke in the Forest of Arden, and Celia who has the radical idea of going in disguise.

For Rosalind and Celia, 'coupled and inseparable', this friendship between women is the true rapport of like minds. For Juliet Stevenson who played Rosalind to Fiona Shaw's Celia in 1985 for the RSC, it's 'the greatest female friendship in all of Shakespeare.'[2] It was 'a wonderful relationship…There's no real parallel to their journey anywhere in Shakespeare. I had never seen this friendship fully explored.'[3] Their tie pre-dates Rosalind and Celia's later discovery of heterosexual love. It can be seen as an image of passionate lesbian attraction or of the platonic rapport of female minds – or both.[4] Novelist George Eliot often invoked the love between the cousins, the tender affinity of Juno's swans as Celia calls it, when writing to her women friends. 'I heartily echo your kind wish that we should be "like Juno's swans" coupled together.'[5]

Before we ever meet the two cousins, we're alerted to the unique quality of their bond, as Charles the Wrestler notices.

> Charles   [Celia] the Duke's daughter, her cousin, so loves her,
> [Rosalind] being ever from their cradles bred together,
> that she would have followed her exile or have died to
> stay behind her. She [Rosalind] is at the court and no less
> beloved of her uncle than his own daughter, and never
> two ladies loved as they do.[6]

On Celia's part, it's a love bond deeper than any crush, both yearning and tough. Shakespeare had envisaged same-sex teenage love before when he painted the more than 'sisters' vows' between Hermia and Helena in *A Midsummer Night's Dream*. This aspect of Helena could have been an early draft for Celia, just as there are rehearsals for Rosalind.

> Helena   We, Hermia, like two artificial gods,
> Have with our needles created both one flower,
> Both on one sampler, sitting on one cushion,
> Both warbling of one song, both in one key,
> As if our hands, our sides, voices and minds,
> Had been incorporate. So we grew together,
> Like to a double cherry, seeming parted,
> But yet an union in partition,
> Two lovely berries moulded on one stem;
> So, with two seeming bodies, but one heart…[7]

Helena depicts a powerful and inescapable connection, almost like Siamese twins. But the entrance of men into their lives dramatically severs Helena and Hermia's friendship. Though they are eventually reconciled, we feel it will never be the same again. However, Celia's passion for Rosalind holds firm through and beyond the arrival of romantic heterosexual love.

For it is Celia who does the most loving, the most daring, the most caring, the most forbearing in this relationship. The love flows from her to Rosalind in similar unequal proportions to the love between another pair of Shakespearian cousins, Beatrice and Hero in *Much Ado About Nothing*. Beatrice, like Celia, does most of the cousin-to-cousin loving, fervently supporting Hero when she is wrongly denounced at the altar. Hero appears less loving towards Beatrice, making sure she overhears this personal assassination, albeit for benevolent motives of tricking her cousin into falling in love with Benedick.

> Hero   But Nature never framed a woman's heart
>   Of prouder stuff than that of Beatrice.
>   Disdain and scorn ride sparkling in her eyes,
>   Misprizing what they look on, and her wit
>   Values itself so highly that to her
>   All matter else seems weak. She cannot love,
>   Nor take no shape nor project of affection,
>   She is so self-endeared.[8]

Although Hero utters these words to goad Beatrice into self-examination, they invert the truth about her cousin's character. Beatrice is the female protagonist of her play and she's the active companion in her unswerving loyalty towards Hero. The dynamics switch in *As You Like It* where Rosalind is the female protagonist but does less of the cousin-to-cousin loving.

When we first meet the cousins in *As You Like It*, Celia is taking action to lift Rosalind's lack-lustre mood, 'I pray thee, Rosalind, sweet my coz, be merry.' Rosalind responds flatly, 'Dear Celia, I show more mirth than I am mistress of…Unless you could teach me to forget a banished father you must not learn me how to remember any extraordinary pleasure.'[9]

Celia counters with a breathtakingly complex sentence that attempts to change Rosalind's frame of mind. With one huge lungful of air, and of thought, Celia offers Rosalind an avowal of pure love – and recaps recent politics for the audience. The First Folio of 1623 gives Celia's speech as a single sentence although modern editions break it into three.

Celia	Herein I see thou lov'st me not with the full weight that I love thee. If my uncle, thy banished father, had banished thy uncle, the Duke my father, so thou hadst been still with me I could have taught my love to take thy father for mine. So wouldst thou, if the truth of thy love to me were so righteously tempered as mine is to thee.[10]

Celia longs for reciprocity. Her declaration is made with the same zest for wordplay that can fly like Rosalind's. Fiona Shaw played Celia to Juliet Stevenson's Rosalind in 1985 and knows how demanding this speech is, as she explained in discussion with Adam Phillips at the National Portrait Gallery in 2011. She focused on the commas because they reveal Celia's state of mind. 'You have to learn to *walk* – literally – on the commas – in order to make sense of the speech!' Shaw demonstrated this by performing the speech twice, the first time at top speed. Giving it a second time, Shaw marched from side to side of the stage, pausing to turn on each comma, to show how she physically unlocked the meaning of this difficult, tongue-twisting speech.[11] In performance Shaw explored the subtle intensity of Celia's love for Rosalind. This avowal has a special rhythm to it, noted Shaw. 'It's staccato, it has an incredibly charming formality, all balances and counterbalances and antitheses. It tells you who Celia is: she's a character who has a desire to say things pertinently and yet delicately. She doesn't say, "I love you". Because she is Celia, she says "I love you" in a way which allows for a hint of slight separation from things, the possibility of irony, as though she would like to connect with her feeling, but it is so passionate she dares not.'[12] Shaw's Celia was deeply wounded when Rosalind fell in love with Orlando and she became the loser. Her love for Rosalind had felt symbiotic, 'thou and I am one,' although other Celias may work out a less intense and more humorous, sisterly relationship with their Rosalinds.

Celia reinforces her emotional confession with a wholly practical deed of gift to Rosalind.

Celia	You know my father hath no child but I, nor none is like to have, and truly when he dies thou shalt be his heir, for what he hath taken away from thy father perforce, I will render thee again in affection. By mine honour, I will! And when I break that oath let me turn monster. Therefore, my sweet Rose, my dear Rose, be merry.[13]

At a stroke, Celia appoints Rosalind heir to the dukedom, a promise she will fulfil at the end of the play. She literally gives away what might have been her inheritance. She does this freely for love of Rosalind, disregarding her own interests, to right the wrong performed by her father, Duke Frederick.

Rosalind doesn't comment on the gift of Celia's love. Instead she quickly lightens the tone by suggesting they should 'devise sports.' 'Let me see, what think you of falling in love?' But in the wake of her avowals to Rosalind, Celia can't envisage transferring her affection to any man. 'Marry, I prithee, do, to make sport withal; but love no man in good earnest.' She doesn't want Rosalind falling in love with boys. Instead she tries to divert her from such dangerous pursuits by drawing her into a vigorous debate about the relative merits of Fortune and Nature in their 'gifts to women.'

Celia	Let us sit and mock the good housewife Fortune from her wheel, that her gifts may henceforth be bestowed equally.
Rosalind	I would we could do so, for her benefits are mightily misplaced – and the bountiful blind woman doth most mistake in her gifts to women.
Celia	'Tis true, for those that she makes fair she scarce makes honest, and those that she makes honest she makes very ill-favouredly.
Rosalind	Nay, now thou goest from Fortune's office to Nature's; Fortune reigns in gifts of the world not in the lineaments of Nature.
Enter Touchstone	
Celia	No? When Nature hath made a fair creature may she not by Fortune fall into the fire? Though Nature hath given us wit to flout at Fortune, hath not Fortune sent in this fool to cut off the argument?[14]

Celia definitely prefers the witty semantics of philosophical discussion to any concrete prospect of falling in love. She enjoys colloquial proverbs that remain in the language today, such as 'that was laid on with a trowel.'[15] She's got a light touch, and a talent for friendship as she shows in bantering with Touchstone, the clown or professional entertainer at her father's court.

Touchstone	Stand you both forth now. Stroke your chins and swear by your beards that I am a knave.

> Celia   By our beards – if we had them – thou art.[16]

The cousins' femininity is soon contrasted with the testosterone of a wrestling match. This promises to be an unequal contest between the Duke's brawny champion, Charles, and his amateur challenger, Orlando. 'Alas, he is too young; yet he looks successfully,' reflects Celia. She takes the lead and tries to dissuade Orlando from what seems an impossible task.

> Celia   Young gentleman, your spirits are too bold for your
>   years… We pray you for your own sake to embrace your
>   own safety and give over this attempt.[17]

As soon as the bout begins, she's mentally in the ring with Orlando, so immediate is her empathy for the underdog.

> Celia   I would I were invisible, to catch the strong fellow by the
>   leg.
> *[Orlando and Charles wrestle.]*
>   …If I had a thunderbolt in mine eye I can tell who should
>   down.[18]
> *Shout. [Charles is thrown.]*

Her reaction to Orlando is more practical, less aroused than Rosalind's exclamations, 'Now Hercules be thy speed, young man!…O excellent young man!' But when, unbelievably, Orlando triumphs and Duke Frederick is ungracious to him in victory, Celia becomes both more regal, and more suggestive, as she moves into blank verse.

> Celia   Gentle cousin,
>   Let us go thank him, and encourage him.
>   My father's rough and envious disposition
>   Sticks me at heart. – Sir, you have well deserved.
>   If you do keep your promises in love
>   But justly as you have exceeded all promise,
>   Your mistress shall be happy.[19]

Is there a hint that Celia could have fallen for Orlando first? If so, she's instantly thrust aside by Rosalind as if she's wrestling with her cousin. Rosalind's response is quite different from Celia's, bold, impulsive and reckless. She's completely absorbed in the selfishness of first love. Suddenly no one else exists, not even best friends. In a memory of the ancient Olympic games, Rosalind garlands Orlando, not with laurels, but with a chain from round her own neck. She forces herself to depart from his magnetic aura but immediately invents an excuse for returning, 'Did you call, sir?' Celia has to tear her away, 'Will you go, coz?'[20]

In their tête-à-tête afterwards, Celia tries to bring some logic to bear on Rosalind's sensational *coup de foudre* for Orlando. 'Come, lame me with reasons,' she begs Rosalind, as she emphasises the potency of the wrestling match. 'Come, come, wrestle with thy affections.'

Celia	But turning these jests out of service, let us talk in good earnest. Is it possible on such a sudden you should fall into so strong a liking with old Sir Rowland's youngest son?
Rosalind	The Duke my father loved his father dearly.
Celia	Doth it therefore ensue that you should love his son dearly? By this kind of chase I should hate him for my father hated his father dearly; yet I hate not Orlando.[21]

Humorous and acerbic though her tone is with Rosalind, Celia does understand the predicament of love. Enraptured Rosalind commands her cousin to love Orlando for no better reason than 'because I do.' In her euphoria, Rosalind wants to twine the chain of friendship around their female cousinhood, to embrace her potential male lover.

This playful prose discussion is suddenly interrupted by Duke Frederick who sweeps in to arraign Rosalind on a trumped-up charge of treason. With stern formality he banishes her from his court on ten days' notice. In dignified blank verse to match the severity of his, Rosalind mounts a powerful defence which Celia corroborates with loving testimony. She first interrupts, and then confronts her father, painting a tender picture of more than a sister's bond that has evolved during a youth spent together.

Celia	I was too young that time to value her,
	But now I know her. If she be a traitor,
	Why, so am I. We still have slept together,
	Rose at an instant, learned, played, ate together,
	And whereso'er we went, like Juno's swans,
	Still we went coupled and inseparable.[22]

Juno, queen of the ancient classical gods, was mythic and immortal. Her swans are Celia and Rosalind. Celia probably had in mind that swans mate for life. Or the words of Orlando Gibbons' plaintive madrigal, 'The Silver Swan,' may have already been on the breeze.[23] Mute swans belonged to the Queen, and do so, by default, to this day. In her strong and beautiful image Celia is the real swan. She allies herself completely with Rosalind. Conscious of his shaky hold on power, the Duke counters Celia with a torrent of self-justification and apparent care for his daughter's reputation. 'Thou art a fool. She robs thee of thy name,/And thou wilt show more bright and seem more virtuous/When she is gone.'[24] When he repeats his banishment decree against Rosalind, Celia simply replies,

> Pronounce that sentence, then, on me, my liege;
> I cannot live out of her company.[25]

It's Celia's report on the state of her heart. Yet as the Duke stalks away, it's Celia's brain that immediately begins planning their joint escape. In serious danger, she continues to joke, to brighten Rosalind's spirits, and to reiterate her avowal that 'thou and I am one.'

Celia	O my poor Rosalind, whither wilt thou go? Wilt thou change fathers? I will give thee mine. I charge thee, be not thou more grieved than I am.
Rosalind	I have more cause.
Celia	Thou hast not, cousin. Prithee, be cheerful. Knowst thou not the Duke Hath banished me, his daughter?
Rosalind	That he hath not.
Celia	No? Hath not? Rosalind lacks then the love Which teacheth thee that thou and I am one. Shall we be sundered? Shall we part, sweet girl? No, let my father seek another heir! Therefore devise with me how we may fly, Whither to go and what to bear with us, And do not seek to take your change upon you To bear your griefs yourself and leave me out. For by this heaven, now at our sorrows pale, Say what thou canst, I'll go along with thee.
Rosalind	Why, whither shall we go?
Celia	To seek my uncle in the Forest of Arden.
Rosalind	Alas, what danger will it be to us, Maids as we are, to travel forth so far! Beauty provoketh thieves sooner than gold.[26]

Celia takes command. Thinking on the spot she turns the terrifying prospect of exodus into an exciting adventure. 'I'll put myself in poor and mean attire,' she says, 'And with a kind of umber smirch my face –/The like do you; so shall we pass along/And never stir assailants.'[27] As her creativity soars, a sort of miracle happens. The two cousins start to think as complementary parts of the same whole. Rosalind leaps into the freedom that Celia has outlined and takes off from it. She finesses the plan into a friendship beyond gender.

> Rosalind   Were it not better,
> Because that I am more than common tall,
> That I did suit me all points like a man?[28]

She doesn't waste a moment in choosing 'Ganymede' for her mischievous male incognito while rueful Celia is left behind to pick her own new identity.

> Celia   Something that hath a reference to my state:
> No longer Celia, but Aliena.[29]

Choosing 'Aliena' suggests Celia has not just alienated herself from her royal status at her father's court, but realises she may become estranged and sidelined from Rosalind, too, whose bravado has whirled her into translating her sex. In Celia's self-naming, there's self-knowledge. Her position has shifted from active to reactive. In Act 1, Celia held the power and was heiress apparent. At Uncle Frederick's court, Rosalind had no power. At this point it could have been Celia's play. By Act 2 the power has transferred – and it's all Rosalind's. In the forest Rosalind re-sexes herself and finds the unexpected liberty to say whatever's on her mind. Celia has resigned command, she's handed the energy to Rosalind, and from now on her role will be relegated from equal protagonist to caustic observer, umpire, or shrewd commentator.

Before setting off for Arden, Celia has some practical functions to discharge. When she puts on 'poor and mean attire' to accompany Rosalind in her flight, she has no reservations about stepping down in caste and going as a peasant girl. Rosalind suggests asking Touchstone to accompany them into exile. Celia instantly actions the plan:

> Celia   He'll go along o'er the wide world with me.
> Leave me alone to woo him. Let's away,
> And get our jewels and our wealth together,

Devise the fittest time and safest way
To hide us from pursuit that will be made
After my flight. Now go we in content
To liberty, and not to banishment.[30]

They simply ignore class differences. If they now belong Nowhere, a Fool belongs Everywhere. And Celia belongs with Rosalind. 'That's what I like about Celia,' reflects Janet Suzman who played Celia before she played Rosalind, 'because she says, "I'll come with you." She's wonderful, she could have said, "look darling, I'll give you some clothes and off you go."' Suzman explains, 'My first loyalty was to Celia and it was very difficult in view of the star quality of Rosalind to find what it was about Celia that might be endearing. I found a rather wry humour as she allowed Rosalind to do all these nutty things like dressing up, schlepping her through the forest and falling in love ridiculously with Orlando – and she was a sort of wry counterpoint to that.'[31]

❧

Once in Arden, Celia's new role as Ganymede's sister, Aliena, seems to drain her vitality, perhaps because her main function in the plot is over. Brutal Shakespeare! In resigning her status as the Duke's daughter, Celia becomes more conventionally female. 'I pray you bear with me; I cannot go no further... I faint almost to death.' The first time Rosalind/Ganymede calls Celia by her new name, 'Therefore, courage, good Aliena!' marks the moment when Celia can no longer keep up with her on her journey into her new life and into loving Orlando.

But after meeting the old shepherd Corin who arranges for the brother and sister duo to buy a cottage, smallholding and flock of sheep, Celia revives. They've grasped a new independence they could never have exercised as women at court. In imitation of a subservient male employee, such as a steward, Celia seems to manage the money. 'And we will mend thy wages,' she tells Corin. This assertion reconciles Celia to the forest and she finds it proves a tonic. In their new personae as Aliena and Ganymede, Celia and Rosalind establish themselves as farmers in the Forest of Arden. Is this the ideal life for Celia, making a home with Rosalind, in role as a married couple, not as brother and sister, outside society as they've previously known it? Pastoral life and literature performs a critique of city life and by escaping the court Celia totally re-makes not only her place in society but also her emotional life. She can earn her own living, and spend her free time sauntering and observing.

When Celia overhears rustic Silvius declaring his courtly though surprising love for Phebe the shepherdess, his flowery idiom prepares her for finding Orlando's love poems to Rosalind strewn across Arden. Their feeble rhymes: be-tree, vows-boughs, friend-end, heart-part, provoke Celia's mockery of other people's love. With the poems in her hands and on her lips she spins out Rosalind's suspense about their authorship. Celia reels in Rosalind on a line of tantalizing questions. 'Didst thou hear these verses?… But didst thou hear without wondering how thy name should be hanged and carved upon these trees?… Trow you who hath done this?… Change you colour?' The game erupts in her boisterous exclamation,

> Celia   O wonderful, wonderful, and most wonderful wonderful, and yet again wonderful, and after that out of all whooping![32]

As earthy sheep-farmer, patrician Celia, alias Aliena, can even indulge in sexual innuendo, 'So you may put a man in your belly,' before she finally reveals, 'It is young Orlando, that tripped up the wrestler's heels and your heart both in an instant.'

How much rather would Celia prefer that Orlando had not turned up in Arden, and that Rosalind had not fallen in love with him? She takes a negative view of conventional lovers while her language for Orlando is subtly derogatory.

> Celia   It is as easy to count atomies as to resolve the propositions of a lover; but take a taste of my finding him and relish it with good observance. I found him under a tree, like a dropped acorn – …There lay he stretched along like a wounded knight – [33]

From now on Celia is obliged to witness Rosalind's forest trysts with Orlando. As Rosalind falls deeper and deeper in love with Orlando, she unconsciously sidelines Celia. No wonder Celia grows impatient with Ganymede's continued cross-gender deception.

> Rosalind   Never talk to me, I will weep.
>
> Celia   Do, I prithee, but yet have the grace to consider that tears do not become a man.[34]

Celia snipes to the audience that Rosalind is not a bona-fide male. She's feeling increasingly sour about the Orlando effect on her hitherto exclusive friendship with Rosalind. She plays on Rosalind's qualms about how genuine a lover Orlando will prove. 'Nay, certainly, there is no truth in him…I think he is not a pick-purse nor a horse-stealer, but for his verity in love, I do think him as concave as covered goblet or a worm-eaten nut.' Rosalind asks Celia, 'Not true in love?'

Celia	Yes, when he is in, but I think he is not in.
Rosalind	You have heard him swear downright he was.
Celia	'Was' is not 'is'.[35]

You could say that Celia is being realistic, trying to protect Rosalind from potential rejection, or you could find her tone bitter and jealous – or both. She's fighting Orlando with the best weapon to hand, her witty, satiric language. But she feels victory slipping from her grasp. As Orlando gains the ascendant in Rosalind's heart, Celia's language sadly diminishes. This is her last major, rivalrous attack on Orlando.

| Celia | O, that's a brave man! He writes brave verses, speaks brave words, swears brave oaths and breaks them bravely quite traverse, athwart the heart of his lover, as a puny tilter, that spurs his horse but on one side, breaks his staff like a noble goose. But all's brave that youth mounts, and folly guides.[36] |

On their very next forest date, Ganymede/Rosalind proposes to Orlando and propels him into an immediate play wedding. In a breathtaking act of transgression for 1599, s/he casts a woman, Celia/Aliena, in the role of officiating priest. 'I cannot say the words,' Celia protests. Almost literally, her flow of language is stalled. Rosalind prompts her as if she's a dunce, and goaded, Celia recites: 'Will you, Orlando, have to wife this Rosalind.' 'This Rosalind,' Celia says, as if this isn't the Rosalind she's trusted, supported and loved over a lifetime, but a fake Rosalind, a new alarmingly sexual Rosalind, and perhaps to her, now a lost Rosalind.

When Orlando leaves his 'wife' for two hours to meet Duke Senior for dinner, Celia lets fly a last desperate assault of words against Rosalind.

| Celia | You have simply misused our sex in your love-prate! We must have your doublet and hose plucked over your head and show the world what the bird hath done to her own nest.[37] |

Celia's resentment is spat out in her obscene reference to genitals beneath doublet and hose and the bitter image of Rosalind fouling her own nest. Male disguise has finally polluted Rosalind's femininity in Celia's eyes. Is she very conventional about women's place in the world? Or does Celia secretly envy the way Rosalind has re-sexed herself as Ganymede and been able to flirt openly with Orlando? Or is her thwarted love for Rosalind intensified by all these factors combining to send her into a diversionary fury? When Rosalind declares that her affection for Orlando, 'hath an unknown bottom, like the Bay of Portugal,' Celia retorts sardonically, 'Or rather, bottomless, that as fast as you pour affection in, it runs out.' Not only does Celia ironically accept that Rosalind's new love may be bottomless, but she infers that the old mutual affection between the cousins, always intense on her part, seems to be running away like water through a sieve, obliterated in the flood of Orlando. 'And I'll sleep,' says Celia curtly as she shuts down the scene, together with her most intense emotions. She expresses her loss in three small syllables.

The next two hours pass leadenly for Rosalind as once again Orlando fails to turn up on time. Forest mail provides a distraction when Silvius delivers Phebe's blatant love letter to Ganymede. 'Alas, poor shepherd!' exclaims Celia. She feels for Silvius, as he has to witness Phebe, the object of his love, declaring herself to a rival. His position reflects her own, yet Rosalind dismisses Silvius briskly.

> *Rosalind*   Do you pity him? No, he deserves no pity. – Wilt thou
>   love such a woman? What, to make thee an instrument
>   and play false strains upon thee? Not to be endured! Well,
>   go your way to her, for I see love hath made thee a tame
>   snake...[38]

Celia has no time to wonder whether love for Rosalind has made her a tame snake, too, when a strange man arrives in search of Ganymede and Aliena. He brings a dramatic, if plot-creaking account of brotherly hatred, mortal danger, rescue and redemption. It is Orlando's wicked brother, Oliver, thrown out of Duke Frederick's court, who has been sleeping rough in the forest. Orlando found him, rescued him from snake and lioness, but in the fracas suffered a wounded arm, passed out, 'And cried, in fainting, upon Rosalind.' Oliver brings the evidence, a napkin 'Dyed in his blood,' and Orlando's message for Ganymede to excuse his broken date. Celia physically supports Rosalind who mirrors

Orlando's blackout by losing consciousness herself at the sight of her lover's blood. Celia is back in role as pillar and comforter to Rosalind. 'Why, how now, Ganymede! sweet Ganymede!' For a moment reality breaks in as Celia forgets her mask as Ganymede's sister, Aliena, and automatically calls him 'Cousin Ganymede!' She enlists Oliver to help her rouse Ganymede, 'We'll lead you thither. I pray you, will you take him by the arm?...Come, you look paler and paler; pray you draw homewards. Good sir, go with us.'

☙

After her sparkling parity with Rosalind early in the play, it's a let-down that Celia has no lines at all by Act V. Shakespeare pushes her into love at first sight with Oliver for no apparent reason, as in the best fairy tales, though this reiterates the *coup de foudre* experienced by Rosalind and Orlando at the wrestling match. We learn of Celia and Oliver's impetuous love from Rosalind who knows all about the urgency of physical desire. Her account of their sexual discovery is really about her own, too. And as every romantic knows, falling in love at first sight really does happen, sometimes.

> Rosalind   Nay, 'tis true. There was never anything so sudden but
> the fight of two rams, and Caesar's thrasonical* brag of 'I
> came, saw and overcame.'...They are in the very wrath of
> love and they will together. Clubs cannot part them.[39]

But the ultimate success of Celia and Oliver's union depends upon conversion. Will Oliver's transformation from wickedness to virtue hold? Converts are often staunch to new allegiances so it's not impossible. However, unlike Rosalind and Orlando, Celia and Oliver have had no time to get to know each other, so we are left with a lingering whisper of doubt. Celia has lost Rosalind to Orlando so there's an emotional logic in settling for his brother. Her marriage will keep her close to Rosalind and now they will be related twice over.

When that notorious, cross-dressing, cigar smoking cavalier, George Sand, adapted *As You Like It* as *Comme il vous plaira* for the Comédie Française in 1856, she deliberately wrote up the part of Celia. Instead of giving Celia a formulaic marriage to Orlando's elder brother

---

*   Boastful – from Thraso the bragging soldier in a comedy by the Roman playwright Terence.

Oliver, Sand awarded Celia an eccentric but perhaps more meaningful marriage of like-minded souls with Jaques, the mordant reporter on the seven ages of human life. Both he and Celia have been caustic commentators who function in something of the same way in the play. Dickens saw Sand's version in Paris in 1856 in what sounds like a wooden production. He walked out after only two acts. He got bored watching 'Jacques seat himself on 17 roots of trees, and 25 grey stones,' so no one knows what his reaction might have been to Sand's drastic revision of Celia's story.[40]

Over a century later, Maggie Smith made an indelible impression as Celia to Barbara Jefford's Rosalind at the Old Vic. Her biographer, Michael Coveney, said, 'Her extraordinary inflections have always both highlighted unexpected phrases and declared her own idiosyncrasy. Alec McCowen [who played Touchstone] can still hear today the sonic imprint Maggie left on Celia in phrases such as 'lame me with reason' ('lame' given syllabic extension and a mocking viperish tincture); 'like a dropped acorn', said of Orlando found lolling under a tree; 'I like this place and willingly would waste my time in it' on arrival in Arden; and 'Alas, poor shepherd', a poignantly heartfelt ejaculation. McCowen, no technical slouch himself, says that this colouring of the words, the unexpected highlighting of phrases that normally pass unnoticed, put her, for him, in the same class as Edith Evans. "We knew she was a very special actress, even in that company; we were all pretty good. But to do this with Celia! Barbara Jefford was a bloody good Rosalind, but she must have been quite surprised."'[41]

Victorian writer, Mary Cowden Clarke, captured what she called Celia's 'perfection of feminine attachment' in her *Girlhood of Shakespeare's Heroines*.[42] In this creative experiment, Cowden Clarke invented prequels or backstories for some of Shakespeare's female characters. Her Celia and Rosalind were 'sisters in heart…kindred in spirit…in mind, in soul.' Celia avows to Rosalind, 'I shall never love lover with any love half so worth having, as that with which I love thee, coz.' Even allowing for the heightened register that Victorian women frequently used to express affection for one another, this is an impassioned declaration. How erotically entangled Celia's relationship with Rosalind must have seemed when it was first played by males in 1599, two boy actors dressed as girls, imagining adolescent female friendships. Men have played Celia in all-male modern productions, Charles Kay to Ronald Pickup's Rosalind in 1967, and Simon Coates to Adrian Lester's Rosalind in 1991, a fascinating complication to the intensity of first love between women.

Rosalind and Celia

by John Everett Millais, 1867

Orlando – So Much in the Heart of the World

Fratricide! Shockingly, this play advertised as a Comedy in Shakespeare's First Folio opens like a Tragedy with attempted murder between a pair of brothers, Oliver and Orlando, eldest and youngest sons of Sir Rowland de Boys. The laws of primogeniture being what they were and the will of their father clearly inadequate, Oliver inherited the estate to the huge disadvantage of Orlando. When we hear Orlando raging in an apparently Eden-like orchard, it is because of this snake of bitter resentment. 'I, his brother, gain nothing under him but growth, for the which his animals on his dunghills are as much bound to him as I.' The same visceral fraternal loathing divides the two Dukes, Frederick and Senior who belong to the other family in *As You Like It*. So emotive a theme is fratricide that Shakespeare treats it often, and notably in his History plays. In the tragedies, Claudius the killer of his brother, the rightful King Hamlet, knows that like the archetypal story of Cain and Abel, 'It hath the primal eldest curse upon't – /A brother's murder.' Forgiveness is impossible while he remains 'possessed/Of those effects for which I did the murder.'[1] Shakespeare returns to the theme in *King Lear* to explore Edmund's compulsive jealousy of Edgar, his virtuous half-brother. Three times Orlando spits out the word 'nothing' in the first scene of *As You Like It*, the same 'nothing' that thuds through *King Lear*, and echoes even in Arden. Sibling hatred is natural love perverted, love turned inside out, though deeply recognisable to many families. It's the oldest domestic story in the world.

Since their father's death, Oliver has barred Orlando from 'the place of a brother', denied him income and education, and housed him in a hovel that even horses would disdain. After their opening fight, Oliver hires Charles the wrestler to break Orlando's neck in public combat. Later, in the play's most redemptive moment, it is from Oliver's neck that Orlando will untwist a venomous 'green and gilded snake'. In the de Boys family, Orlando, the younger brother, occupies the moral high ground but in the ducal family, Senior, the elder brother, embodies virtue. His brother Frederick jeopardises his life as Oliver endangers Orlando's. These fraternal patterns are the opposite of the genuine sisterliness between cousins, Rosalind and Celia. Unlike the men locked in their power struggles, the women bond because they have no power. Rosalind is annihilated politically by her father's downfall, but Celia, too, is powerless in a man's world.

Orlando's indignation explodes as he pitches into Oliver, the first of four violent fights in which he features throughout the play. Seizing his brother by the throat, Orlando demands his rights,

> Orlando   You shall hear me. My father charged you in his will
> to give me good education. You have trained me like a
> peasant, obscuring and hiding from me all gentleman-like
> qualities. The spirit of my father grows strong in me, and I
> will no longer endure it! Therefore allow me such exercises
> as may become a gentleman, or give me the poor allottery
> my father left me by testament; with that I will go buy my
> fortunes.[2]

To the underlying Christian question, 'Am I my brother's keeper?' Oliver answers, No. To that same fraternal question, Orlando will later turn the other cheek and answer, Yes. By Act 4 Orlando will redeem potential fratricide in a life-saving rescue of his evil brother, out of pure love, and 'kindness, nobler ever than revenge.'

Orlando. Why did Shakespeare choose this name for his romantic male lead? It's almost a scrambled anagram of Rosalind. Orlando is the Italian, Spanish and French form of Roland, which echoes his father's name, Sir Rowland, meaning 'famous through the land'. *La Chanson de Roland*, a medieval Anglo-French epic poem, recounts Roland's deeds of heroism and derring-do. The poem is a shadowy ancestor of the Italian epic, *Orlando Furioso*, or *Orlando Maddened*, which Ariosto wrote between 1516–32 as a quasi-sequel to Boiardo's earlier *Orlando Inamorato*, or *Orlando in Love*. These various Rolands and Orlandos all underlie Shakespeare's, though his most direct model for Orlando was Rosader, the male lead in Thomas Lodge's *Rosalynde*, the prose romance of 1590 that was his immediate source for *As You Like It*. So closely linked are the names Orlando, Roland and Rosader to Rosalind's own name that they subliminally underpin her immediate connection with Orlando de Boys. Names such as Rosader, Roland and Orlando seem to slip between gender, their very ambiguity suggesting the wide spectrum of human sexuality in this play.

Sir John Harington's 1591 translation of Ariosto's *Orlando Furioso*, just a year after Lodge's *Rosalynde*, may have been a cue for Robert Greene's play, also called *Orlando Furioso*, which came out in 1592, imprinting the name 'Orlando' ever more modishly into literary fashion. Quarto versions of Greene's play were published after his death, including in 1599, the year of *As You Like It*. Greene's Orlando is driven mad by love for Angelica and has to undertake many tests of Herculean proportions to woo her. He sees himself as Hercules, picking up a thread from Ariosto who dedicated his *Orlando Furioso* to the patron he called the 'munificent offspring of Hercules'. The first time Rosalind catches sight of Orlando, she invests him with Herculean status, 'Now Hercules be thy speed, young man,' she urges him at the start of the wrestling match. From seeing him as Hercules, it's a short leap to falling in love. What Rosalind cannot know is that Oliver has secretly hired Charles the prizefighter to kill Orlando. But in his misery, resulting from Oliver's cruel treatment, death seems immaterial to Orlando,

> *Orlando* …if I be foiled there is but one shamed that was never gracious, if killed, but one dead that is willing to be so. I shall do my friends no wrong, for I have none to lament me; the world no injury, for in it I have nothing. Only in the world I fill up a place which may be better supplied when I have made it empty.[3]

These words immediately spark Rosalind's sense of kinship with Orlando. His despair and isolation feel like her own. She 'sees this man, understands his desolation, feels so much compassion, and recognises the feeling in herself', said Rebecca Hall who played Rosalind, directed by her father Peter Hall in 2004.[4]

Ignited by the physical thrill of the wrestling match, Orlando and Rosalind hurtle into a blaze of love at first sight. Shakespeare was interested in this phenomenon and had already treated it in the tragedy of *Romeo and Juliet*. In *As You Like It* he turns to comedy to examine the power of instant, overwhelming attraction. Recognising yourself in the other person can be a crucial element of falling in love. A mutual sense of oneness seems to imitate the rapport of twins, which a singleton has never experienced. For Rosalind and Orlando falling in love feels like finding their mirrored selves. They are well matched in status: she's the daughter of an exiled duke; he's the youngest son of a deceased knight. Both are living outside the golden circle of entitlement and come from fractured, dysfunctional and parentless families. Rosalind has already been demoted by her father's overthrow and will soon be banished by her uncle, while Orlando must flee his murderous brother. In Orlando's family history Rosalind's predicament is reflected. Their backstories mesh.

The audience accepts that Rosalind's heart has its reasons and we endorse her choice of Orlando. Lodge's Rosalynde loves her hero, Rosader, for many of the same chivalric virtues Shakespeare awards to Orlando. That previous Rosalynde 'felt herself grow passing passionate' thinking of her lover's perfection and 'his rare qualities…the comeliness of his person, the honour of his parents, and the virtues that, excelling both, made him so gracious in the eyes of every one'.[5] Falling in love is that involuntary physical response we call chemistry today. Rosalind's spontaneous attraction to Orlando is fired by meeting him in the heightened dramatic setting of what looks like a lost cause: a wrestling match, potentially to the death. Shakespeare understood the eroticism of violence. 'You know,' Janet Suzman told me, 'it's the physical nature of the meeting of Orlando and Rosalind – there's a spark. If he'd been lying down reading a poem under a tree, she probably wouldn't have fallen in love so irretrievably, but to see a modest young man, not boasting about himself, flattening the famous Charles the Wrestler – Bingo!'[6]

The body beautiful is a key factor in attraction and Rosalind sees Orlando as a stunningly handsome young man. Never before, perhaps, has she seen the naked male torso in such heroic action, and emotionally, she is ready for love. Being Rosalind, she perceives his soul through his body. This interplay between inner and outer man was clearly signposted in Lodge's earlier hero, Rosader. Lodge's Rosalynde loves Rosader equally 'for his inward life, as for his outward lineaments, able to content the eye with beauty, and the ear with the report of his virtue.' Orlando's total impact on Rosalind is immense for being unspecified. Shakespeare gives us only one oblique detail about his physical appearance. Later in the play, when she's furious with Orlando for his unpunctuality, Rosalind/Ganymede complains 'His very hair is of the dissembling colour.' Celia agrees. It is 'something browner than Judas,' meaning it's less red than the betrayer of Christ. But Celia concedes, Orlando's hair is 'An excellent colour – your chestnut was ever the only colour.'[7] So Rosalind's lover has hair like autumn conkers.

When I try to conjure up what Orlando looks like, I always think of the finest verbal portrait Shakespeare never wrote. It's Virginia Woolf's evocation of another imaginary Elizabethan young man, the hero of her maverick biography *Orlando*, who will eventually morph into a woman, the opposite direction of Rosalind's transgender adventure. Setting him down in the reign of Queen Elizabeth I, Woolf gave her Orlando a rhapsodic male beauty. 'The red of the cheeks was covered with peach down; the down on the lips was only a little thicker than the down on the cheeks. The lips themselves were short and slightly drawn back over teeth of an exquisite and almond whiteness. Nothing disturbed the arrowy nose in its short, tense flight…he had eyes like drenched violets, so large that the water seemed to have brimmed in them and widened them.'[8] When Woolf's ageing Queen Elizabeth gazed into the eyes of Orlando, she saw 'a pair of the finest legs that a young nobleman has ever stood upright upon…and a heart of gold; and loyalty and manly charm.'[9] It's a version of Orlando to fall in love with: an uncanny, if completely anachronistic glimmer of what Shakespeare's Rosalind sees.

Orlando's personality is more dynamic and certainly more honourable than many other romantic male leads in Shakespeare's comedies. Only Berowne, Petruchio and Benedick run him close but they are all men with compromising past histories, unlike innocent Orlando, new to love. Valentine is pallid, Proteus unfaithful, Lysander and Demetrius fickle and giddy, Bassanio unsatisfactory, Orsino shallow. It's not only Rosalind who calls Orlando, 'excellent young man!'[10] Even Oliver, his jealous elder brother, admits Orlando is,

> Oliver   …gentle, never schooled and yet learned, full of noble
> device, of all sorts enchantingly beloved, and indeed so
> much in the heart of the world, and especially of my
> own people, who best know him, that I am altogether
> misprized.[11]

Adam, the de Boys old family servant, heaps Orlando with epithets of praise drawn from tales of courtly love. He's a sweet master, kind, virtuous, gentle, strong, valiant, comely, and above all else, the image of his dead father, 'O you memory/Of old Sir Rowland!'[12] As the fairy story youngest son of a late medieval knight, Orlando exemplifies the perfect balance of chivalric virtues: extreme physical courage with soft-hearted gentleness. This gentleness stems from his noble birth and his manner, but he also exhibits the highest standards of moral behaviour. Orlando embraces the ideal values, 'trouthe and honour, fredom and curtesie,' of Chaucer's own medieval 'verray, parfit gentil' Knight.

Shakespeare wrote Orlando to match up to Rosalind's great-hearted love. But he's got some growing up to do and a testing journey to make. 'Orlando is a fascinating character. He's been brought up like a peasant, he starts in anger, he can channel the rage. He makes a very quiet journey,' considers Blanche McIntyre who directed *As You Like It* for Shakespeare's Globe in 2015. 'He has to learn, it's OK to make a joke, it's OK to be vulnerable. It happens very quietly and very subtly but he's gaining a sense of himself in the same way that Rosalind is. It's just that her journey is more obvious.'[13] She's the firework while Orlando is the glowing ember.

At the moment of his unexpected win over Charles the wrestler, Orlando and Rosalind lock glances. It's love at first sight for both of them. Janet Suzman says, 'Orlando has got to prove himself to be as fine a man as he was a wrestler. Rosalind knows that he's physically fine but now she's got to find out if he's morally fine.'[14] Duke Frederick's grudging response to Orlando's victory, 'I would thou hadst been son to some man else,' incites Rosalind's opposing reaction, 'My father loved Sir Rowland as his soul'. Orlando is not only a David who has defeated Goliath in Rosalind's eyes, but he's also a wronged 'gentleman'. Like Orlando, Rosalind is 'out of suits with fortune,' and galvanised by the parallels in their situations. She offers him all that she has to give, a chain from round her neck. 'Wear this for me,' she says in an erotically charged moment. Orlando doesn't even know her name and has to ask an attendant courtier, Le Beau. Christian Camargo's Orlando at the Old Vic in 2010, only discovered the name of the mystery gift-bearer by finding it engraved inside the locket she'd given him.

Out of breath after his win, Orlando is also out of words, literally rendered voiceless. He's upended emotionally in a way champion Charles couldn't manage physically. 'Can I not say, I thank you?' he berates himself. Why is he bereft of words? Because it's his first super-charged experience of love, as well as love at first sight. It's doubly world changing for him. Rosalind is racing ahead. She's already devising strategies to re-engage with this enthralling young man. 'He calls us back,' she persuades Celia shamelessly. 'My pride fell with my fortunes./I'll ask him what he would. – Did you call, sir?' Then in a rush, both impetuous and tender, she offers him something far finer than jewellery.

> Rosalind   Sir, you have wrestled well and overthrown
> More than your enemies.[15]

Orlando's amazement strikes him dumb while Celia drags Rosalind away.

> Orlando   What passion hangs these weights upon my tongue?
> I cannot speak to her, yet she urged conference.
> O poor Orlando, thou art overthrown![16]

Alex Waldmann's Orlando, in the RSC production at Stratford in 2013, sidled on to stage in a hoodie, a real teenager. In spite of, or perhaps because of the difference in their dress and status, Pippa Nixon's Rosalind was magnetically drawn to Orlando's friendless, solitary plight. It was an immediate bond. After Orlando's victory and Rosalind's reward of her locket, they came within inches of exchanging a panting kiss. Exhaling a throaty, sensuous giggle, it was obvious how much this Rosalind was in touch with her sexual desires. She couldn't wait to tell Celia that she'd found the father of her future children. Rosalind's physical directness spools back to Juliet's longing for consummation and forward to Perdita's desire for Florizel 'quick and in mine arms' in *The Winter's Tale*. Shakespeare's young women openly celebrate desire and attraction. Michael Boyd directed Katy Stephens as Rosalind in 2009/10 for the RSC. He said Rosalind 'has found a man whom she desires on sight, who shares her moral strength, and who surpasses her in potency and sense of wonder.'[17] So emotionally intuitive is Orlando that even George Bernard Shaw, the notorious debunker of Shakespeare who found Jaques' Seven Ages of Man speech too 'silly' for anyone over the age of seven, conceded that 'Orlando's intelligence is the intelligence of the heart'.[18]

Orlando's 'sanctified' virtues are fully reflected in the love he inspires in Adam, his old family retainer. Adam not only endures Oliver's insults, 'you old dog,' for Orlando's sake, but also warns him of Oliver's plan to burn him alive. Adam begs to accompany Orlando in flight, offering him his life savings of 500 crowns, the entire contents of his hard-earned pension pot. Even though Orlando has no parents and Adam apparently no children, an alternative sense of family is endorsed in their loving father-son relationship. Orlando now has a companion who would give his whole life, 'to the last gasp' for him. This tribute alone is a measure of Orlando's moral worth.

Orlando's emotional intelligence, that Adam responds to, and even Shaw noticed, is a direct outcome of the harmonious balance between his masculine and feminine qualities. He's as macho as Hercules in a fight but as compassionate as a mother to old Adam. Chaucer's Knight who was 'of his port as meeke as is a mayde,' possessed the same instinctive femininity. We say today that such men are 'in touch with their feminine side'. This equilibrium in his nature makes Orlando the ideal complement to Rosalind who learns she really likes the masculine in her personality. Machismo and the maternal coalesce in Orlando when he bursts upon Duke Senior's feast in Arden, demanding food with menaces on behalf of starving Adam.

It was a desperate time for outcasts such as Orlando and Adam during the last decade of the sixteenth century when *As You Like It* appeared. Harvests had repeatedly failed leaving many people whose only recourse was to beg 'a thievish living on the common road,' starving and homeless. Enclosures meant people could no longer live on the common land, and new laws against vagrancy made poor relief unreliable. There were no food banks and no welfare system. Orlando and Adam's situation on the open road was a familiar one but not every old Adam had an Orlando to support him. 'Why, how now, Adam? No greater heart in thee? Live a little, comfort a little, cheer thyself a little. If this uncouth forest yield anything savage I will either be food for it or bring it for food to thee,' Orlando heartens Adam in his bantering, colloquial prose.

Orlando	For my sake, be comfortable; hold death awhile at the arm's end. I will here be with thee presently, and if I bring thee not something to eat I will give thee leave to die. But if thou diest before I come, thou art a mocker of my labour. Well said, thou look'st cheerly, and I'll be with thee quickly. Yet thou liest in the bleak air. Come, I will bear thee to some shelter and thou shalt not die for lack of a dinner if there live anything in this desert. Cheerly, good Adam.[19]

Though a grown-up orphan, Orlando scrupulously obeys the Old Testament commandment, 'Honour thy father and mother,' in his tenderness for old Adam. He rejects the social differences between them. His chivalric nobility is instinctive, and not merely the result of birth. So when Duke Senior deflects Orlando's violent demands for food with generosity, Orlando quickly reverts from terrorism to his natural state of grace. Just as he'd been at home before in everyday prose, now he expresses himself in the formality of harmonious blank verse, perfectly attuned to the reception the Duke has offered him.

Orlando	Speak you so gently? Pardon me, I pray you. I thought that all things had been savage here And therefore put I on the countenance Of stern commandment. But whate'er you are, That in this desert inaccessible, Under the shade of melancholy boughs, Lose and neglect the creeping hours of time - If ever you have looked on better days, If ever been where bells have knolled to church, If ever sat at any good man's feast, If ever from your eyelids wiped a tear, And know what 'tis to pity and be pitied - Let gentleness my strong enforcement be, In the which hope, I blush and hide my sword.[20]

Gentleness with its derivatives and compounds, gentle, gently and gentleman, occur more often in *As You Like It* than in any of Shakespeare's other plays. Gentle virtues are constantly attributed to, or shown by Orlando. Gentleness is the keynote to Orlando who is handsome, brave, open-hearted and kind to the elderly. 'Like a doe, I go to find my fawn,' he tells Duke Senior, as he leaves on his mercy mission to collect Adam for his life-saving meal.

Orlando's nurturing capacity, his maternal, feminine side is one major reason for Rosalind to love him, while his blend of masculine and feminine makes him irresistible to women. Actresses have played not only transvestite Rosalind but they've also cross-dressed to inhabit Orlando. In a famous open-air production of 1884/85 at Coombe, a country house at Kingston-upon-Thames, tall, ruffled-haired Lady Archie Campbell confounded male criticism of the New Woman phenomenon of her times. Gender became simply irrelevant to her performance. Royalty attended and brought their children and the *Illustrated London News* devoted one of its broadsheet pages to more than a dozen romantic engravings of scenes from the show.[21]

'Lady Archibald Campbell's Orlando was a really remarkable performance. Too melancholy some seemed to think it. Yet is not Orlando lovesick? Too dreamy, I heard it said. Yet Orlando is a poet. And even admitting that the vigour of the lad who tripped up the Duke's wrestler was hardly sufficiently emphasised, still in the low music of Lady Archibald Campbell's voice, and in the strange beauty of her movements and gestures, there was a wonderful fascination,' wrote Oscar Wilde in his review.[22] Many theatregoers on their way back to town agreed with Wilde that 'few things are so pleasurable as to be able by an hour's drive to exchange Piccadilly for Parnassus.' It wasn't a complete novelty to see Lady Archie in thigh high boots and velvet jerkin. Other women had been cross-dressing for over a century to play male roles in Shakespeare. Though Sarah Siddons felt uncomfortable as Rosalind, she played Hamlet nine times from 1775 to 1805. She swirled on stage in a flowing black cape to disguise her womanly shape, and to free herself from expectations of gender in order to inhabit the complex inner life of the Danish prince. Since Siddons, many actresses including Sarah Bernhardt in 1899, Frances de la Tour in 1979, and Maxine Peake in 2014 have crossed gender boundaries to play Hamlet successfully. Bernhardt even claimed that the 'things Hamlet says, his impulses, his actions, all indicate to me that he was a woman.'[23]

If Lady Archie Campbell put the accent on Orlando's feminine qualities, it's an insight that many male Orlandos have since explored. In 1950, Hollywood film star Katherine Hepburn played Rosalind – or mostly Ganymede – on Broadway but one sixteen-year-old boy 'kept

LADY ARCHIBALD CAMPBELL AS

· O R L A N D O ·

Lady Archibald as Orlando, taken from The Illustrated London News 1884

coming back for Orlando', played by William Prince. It 'was a profound experience for me, and I can still see him in the role with complete clarity,' recalls Shakespearean scholar, Stephen Orgel. 'Orlando dazzled me the moment he appeared; when he turned his back he smote me to the heart...Such moments come as revelations.' Orgel confirms Michael Billington and Janet Suzman's view that there is an undeniable sexual component to all theatre. 'Why else are stars attractive?' asks Orgel.[24]

By the time Orlando re-meets Rosalind, now disguised as Ganymede in Arden, he's become an intense if laughable poet. 'His lyric verses are imperfect, but that's a manly failing', says director Michael Boyd. 'He has the open heart, the wit and the playfulness to spar as an equal with Rosalind on fire as Ganymede.'[25] There is an essential innocence and inexperience to both Orlando and Rosalind, what Ronald Pickup calls their 'chasteness – without being boring or safe.'[26] Unschooled in love, Orlando learns 'love is so many different things: it's painful, it's amazing, it's obsessive, it's dark, it's extreme. Love can be incredibly painful. It can make you sick and you don't know what's going on,' as Alex Waldmann said when he played the part for the RSC in 2013.[27]

Becoming a lover is one of the human rites of passage Jaques identifies in his Seven Ages of Man speech. He holds up the lover for our inspection, 'Sighing like furnace, with a woeful ballad/Made to his mistress' eyebrow.' It could be a portrait of Orlando himself in the first throes of love, turning poet, like so many young lovers then and since. He recovers from his temporary aphasia to spill out a cascade of love poems in Arden and impale them on trees. Orlando's first attempt is not the 'woeful ballad' scorned by Jaques but his own mini-version of a sonnet, in homage to its more usual fourteen-lined form.

> *Orlando*   Hang there, my verse, in witness of my love.
> And thou, thrice-crowned queen of night, survey
> With thy chaste eye, from thy pale sphere above,
> Thy huntress' name that my full life doth sway.
> O Rosalind! These trees shall be my books,
> And in their barks my thoughts I'll character,
> That every eye which in this forest looks
> Shall see thy virtue witnessed everywhere.
> Run, run, Orlando, carve on every tree
> The fair, the chaste and unexpressive she.[28]

Though only ten lines long, Orlando's would-be-sonnet ends on the typical rhyming couplet format of a Shakespearean sonnet, whose core meaning culminates in its final lines. Elizabethans used the word 'sonnet' to refer to any form of love lyric, not necessarily confined to its usual fourteen-lined, intricately rhyming structure. Sir Philip Sidney's 1591 sonnet sequence, *Astrophil and Stella*, set the standard in love poems and made sonnets the literary fashion to follow from Lodge to Shakespeare. Not all sonneteers were as skilful as Shakespeare, and the linguistic demands on a novice of stylish conceits, puns and wordplay were challenging. Even the great wordsmith Hamlet is mocked for his poetic effusions to Ophelia.

> *Doubt thou the stars are fire,*
> *Doubt that the sun doth move,*
> *Doubt truth to be a liar,*
> *But never doubt I love.*[29]

Orlando's efforts are ridiculed in Arden by Celia, Jaques and Touchstone, as well as by Rosalind. But his hackneyed similes do not express a hackneyed heart. Instead they come from a self-taught boy whose brother denied him the academic education Shakespeare himself received at Stratford Grammar School.

Orlando is seeking to express the urgency of his feelings through his poems. Epic comparison is one device he has in his poetic arsenal to convey his overwhelming vision of Rosalind:

> *Celia* (reading) *Therefore heaven Nature charged*
> *That one body should be filled*
> *With all graces wide-enlarged.*
> *Nature presently distilled*
> *Helen's cheek but not her heart,*
> *Cleopatra's majesty,*
> *Atalanta's better part,*
> *Sad Lucretia's modesty.*
> *Thus Rosalind of many parts*
> *By heavenly synod was devised,*
> *Of many faces, eyes and hearts*
> *To have the touches dearest prized.*
> *Heaven would that she these gifts should have,*
> *And I to live and die her slave.*[30]

Orlando's idealisation of this once glimpsed Rosalind doesn't sound like a real woman at all, even though, or perhaps because his rapture is so intense. Though artless and from his heart, the words simply can't match his feelings. They sound ludicrous and contrived in Celia's mocking recitation. When Dante Gabriel Rossetti revitalised the sonnet for the Victorians, he understood 'a Sonnet is a moment's monument.' Orlando is writing his ersatz sonnets to express that piercing moment of falling in love, at first sight, and for the first time. The fact that he's not a very good poet is endearing, and even makes his experience more universal.

However, he will have to be argued down from the trees, out of his overblown hyperbole, and into the reality of what love means. Rosalind lectures him that their instant attraction 'is merely a madness'. Orlando who has denounced his brother for denying him an education must enter Rosalind's University of Love, on the basis of her one-to-one tutorial system. Pippa Nixon who was Rosalind in 2013 reflects, 'Love is not about setting people up on a pedestal and deifying them as goddesses, which is what he does to her, and so she has to smash that down.'[31] During their courtship of conversations, Rosalind teaches Orlando to reject his fantasy in favour of true love expressed between equal individuals. Luckily, with his feminine sensibility and his emotional intelligence, Orlando is open to instruction. He has the capacity to learn and to make a parallel journey to Rosalind's.

Rosalind finds it thrilling and reassuring to feel her own love returned 100%. But it's still not equal enough. Rosalind runs ahead of Orlando. She's an adult while he's still an adolescent. So she plans a syllabus to teach Orlando what really 'tis to love'. She must liberate him from his poetic clichés, as well as from his conventional thinking about women. The audience watches Orlando mature during the play into a fit partner for Rosalind. It's the exam he has to pass, as knights had to pass tests to be worthy of their ladies, according to the rubric of courtly love. Rosalind will teach him to love a real woman, not a fantasy. Excitingly for them both, she can only do it when she's dressed as a man. Her male disguise frees her from conventional norms of womanhood. And her male disguise frees Orlando to articulate his true feelings, which had been unutterable when he'd met her first at court, as a woman. Their conversations will be seminars in growing up, about learning to love and to live, finally, without masks or disguise.

There are many facets to Orlando's personality. He's not all hunky fighter or moral seriousness. Nor can he be reduced to Celia's caricature of the 'wounded knight' she finds lying like a dropped acorn under a tree in Arden, pole-axed by love. Like Rosalind, he has the vitality of youth. And like her, he's witty and humorous with a turn of spoken phrase far more robust than his stilted written verse would suggest, as he shows in this skirmish with Jaques.

Jaques	God b'wi' you, let's meet as little as we can.
Orlando	I do desire we may be better strangers.
Jaques	I pray you, mar no more trees with writing love-songs in their barks.
Orlando	I pray you, mar no more of my verses with reading them ill-favouredly.
Jaques	Rosalind is your love's name?
Orlando	Yes, just.
Jaques	I do not like her name.
Orlando	There was no thought of pleasing you when she was christened.[32]

Even Jaques, the prince of language, has to acknowledge that Orlando has 'a nimble wit; I think 'twas made of Atalanta's heels,' the goddess with a legendary turn of speed. Orlando is quick enough with teenage repartee, telling Jaques to look for a fool in the brook where the sour critic will see his own reflection, but as a lover he needs time to grow. Time is the motif that opens his first forest encounter with Ganymede/Rosalind, and to which they both recur throughout their courtship. To her joshing opener asking him what hour of day it is, Orlando bowls back a whole series of questions about the 'swift foot of Time' so Ganymede can return play in a spate of improvisations. Captivated, Orlando enquires, 'Where dwell you, pretty youth?' Revealing her address, 'here in the skirts of the forest, like a fringe upon a petticoat,' is the equivalent of giving out your phone number. Even riskier than mentioning skirts and petticoats, Ganymede/Rosalind dares to 'thank God I am not a woman,' in the face of Orlando. Light as wind, s/he launches a zany plan to 'cure' a man who 'would not be cured' of his love. Intrigued, Orlando does agree to drop round 'to my cote' every day to play a dating game with this disarming young man who will simulate his 'very, very' Rosalind.

Does Orlando realise that Ganymede is Rosalind? He is only briefly suspicious that the boy's 'accent is something finer than you could purchase in so removed a dwelling,' and seems satisfied with Ganymede's diversionary answer about an unlikely education from 'an old religious uncle.' I asked Juliet Rylance about how she and Christian Camargo unravelled the essential puzzle of Orlando for today's playgoers? 'This is a question Christian and I have been over since day one of rehearsals. There is a moment when we're standing quite close to each other, and he notices my eyes and he has a split second of thinking, it's Rosalind, I mean, she's got the same eyes.'[33] For Rylance and Camargo it was just a tiny flicker in Orlando's mind. It's comedy and we can suspend our disbelief. Every production makes its own choice about when it dawns on Orlando that Ganymede is Rosalind. Director Michael Boyd says, 'I don't for one moment buy the idea that Orlando rumbles Rosalind before the wedding.'[34] When I asked Ronald Pickup if there'd been a moment when Orlando recognized Ganymede as Rosalind before the end of the play, he told me, 'No, not a moment.' However, when Rosalind asked Orlando, 'Did your brother tell you how I counterfeited to swoon when he showed me your [bloodstained] handkerchief?' and her lover answered 'Ay, and greater wonders than that,' it was a line that 'always got a great laugh in our production.'[35]

In her father's 2004 version, Rebecca Hall's Rosalind returned to the stage at the denouement, 'still wearing the coat and hat to reveal myself to Orlando, and indicated "Yes, look, it's been me all along. Sorry. How do you feel about that?" Even then it wasn't "Oh, great, let's hug, I love you." He played a moment of "You mean you've been having me on all this time? I don't know how I feel about that." And I played a moment of "Please, please, I'm sorry." And it was resolved silently.'[36] Hall's Orlando was her contemporary, Dan Stevens, 'whose initial rage mellows endearingly into that of a love-struck lad who writes terrible poems. Who but a poet as sure of himself as Shakespeare would have the guts to stick really bad poems in the middle of his plays?' asked one reviewer when the play arrived in Los Angeles. Orlando is 'a perfectly normal kid who is late for dates and stubbornly obsessed in his passion for a girl he's seen once. Stevens captures all those qualities.'[37]

Shakespeare's exploration of the subversive boy/girl/boy courtship between Orlando and Rosalind/Ganymede gripped Théophile Gautier who put it at the heart of his novel *Mademoiselle de Maupin*. Published in 1835 when Gautier was only twenty-four, it examines complex sexuality and desire with startling frankness. In the novel's staging of an amateur production of *As You Like It*, Gautier's hero, d'Albert, is allowed to play Orlando and confront his dream, 'to have both sexes in turn, to satisfy this dual nature. Man today, woman tomorrow.' D'Albert can't help feeling jealous of Orlando. 'You may be banished, but at least it is after you have striven and won through. Your wicked brother may take away all your rightful inheritance, but Rosalind gives you the necklace from off her neck. You may be poor, but you are loved.' The Forest of Arden welcomes Orlando 'in its great leafy arms,' and its trees 'yield to the point of your stylus when you wish to engrave the initials of Rosalind upon them.' Playing Orlando, D'Albert can avow the depth of his love for Rosalind, to Ganymede. 'Fair youth, I would I could make thee believe I love,' and 'Neither rhyme nor reason can express how much.' D'Albert wishes all lovers could hide away in a forest like Arden, and then 'suddenly, at the end of the path, come across the person we have been searching for and recognize her even though she might be wearing different clothes!'[38]

The most notable actor never to have played Orlando in the professional theatre was Henry Irving. When he produced *As You Like It* at the Lyceum in 1890/91 he was already over fifty and more likely to triumph as King Lear or Cardinal Wolsey. Too old for dashing Orlando, he denied Rosalind to Ellen Terry, ten years his junior, and the greatest actress of her day. Instead, Ada Rehan and Lily Langtry starred in Irving's productions but they never embodied Rosalind as Terry could have done in her prime.

Adjectives usually attached to the actor playing Orlando are: virile, dreamy, romantic, and handsome. Laurence Olivier was twenty-nine when he played Orlando in Paul Czinner's 1936 film. It was his first appearance in a Shakespeare role on screen and he didn't get on with his Rosalind, Elisabeth Bergner, ten years his senior, who almost sang the lines in her beguiling Middle European accent. By contrast, Olivier's very English enunciation of the period stood out in its cut-glass beauty, as did his capacity for stillness. His Orlando was grave and thoughtful. But maybe he was just seething.

In the same year, 1936, Michael Redgrave played Orlando to Edith Evans' transformative Rosalind. Their performances were electrified by their passionate off-stage affair. Again there was an age difference. Redgrave was twenty years junior to his Rosalind. If not the first Orlando to be bisexual, Redgrave was certainly the most outrageous. When his daughter Vanessa prepared to be Rosalind a generation later, she listened to an old recording of the production. She felt Dame Edith 'had recorded an Ordnance Survey of the Forest of Arden…Her tempo, her phrasing, her through line on the dialogue, were superb.'[39] In her turn, Vanessa's Rosalind became the benchmark performance of the early 1960s. Ian Bannen was her Orlando looking like a character 'from a contemporary novel who has lost his way in the forest.'[40] It could have been code for the way Bannen suggested Orlando's potential bisexuality, as he responded 'much more eagerly to the apparent boy than to the dream of the lost girl.'[41] Vanessa Redgrave whose Rosalind was 'a breathless ecstasy and a heady physical rapture, suggestive of the night before rather than the morning after,'[42] said she was, 'as every Rosalind becomes with her Orlando, in love with him.'[43] When the production transferred to London she fell tumultuously in love with film director Tony Richardson, as bisexual as her father, and married him during the run.

'Warm-hearted, tousle-haired' Michael Williams was an altogether more regular Orlando to Janet Suzman's Rosalind at Stratford in 1968.[44] She recalls, 'he was a delightful, lovely Orlando, very solid you know, dependable chap, decent, the kind of thing [Rosalind] sees in Silvius which is why she says to Phebe, "just stop your dramatizing!"'[45] At almost exactly the same time, 1967-69, Clifford Williams directed the play for the National Theatre, then at the Old Vic, in a bold, experimental, all-male production. 'These were not high-voiced boys – as used in Shakespeare's time – but grown men. Williams said his aim was to investigate love in an atmosphere of spiritual purity that transcends sexuality.'[46] Critics, perhaps surprisingly, found the result poetic rather than provocative. Jeremy Brett made a powerful Orlando to Ronald Pickup's subtle intersexual Rosalind. What emerged, thought Hilary Spurling, was 'a sense of the sobriety and intellectual strength of Shakespeare's discussion of love in the play.'[47]

David Suchet stepped up to play Orlando to Eileen Atkins' Rosalind in 1973. Both wore unisex jeans which visually collapsed gender differences for the modern world. In what was beginning to look like a tradition of older Rosalinds, Atkins was senior to Suchet by a dozen years. Peter McEnery played another boyish Orlando to Kate Nelligan's 'disgracefully, shamelessly smitten' Rosalind in 1977.[48] He looked 'still young enough to have no beard…and to play silly games with the teenage kid Ganymede that he meets in the forest.'[49] 'Scruffy, humorous, brave and enormously likeable, if in need of a bath,' Hilton McRae made a sympathetic Orlando to Juliet Stevenson's Rosalind directed by Adrian Noble for the RSC in 1985. He warmed 'the cerebral chill' of the first half of the play.[50]

When Juliet Rylance played Rosalind in 2010 with new husband, Christian Camargo as Orlando, there was an age gap in the opposite direction as Camargo is eight years older than Rylance. He concentrated on the dreamy, thoughtful, nurturing side of Orlando whose greatest love before Rosalind was for his surrogate parent, old Adam. I asked Rylance whether Rosalind sees some of her femininity reflected back to her in Orlando? 'Absolutely…I am quite masculine in my energy…and Christian is very emotional.' Rosalind and Orlando 'feed off each other. He knows that this crazy young boy [Ganymede] can give him a fire in his belly to actually court his Rosalind. And Rosalind is searching for that tender, soft, gentle love that she's never had and that he provides. It's what keeps drawing her in.'[51] We discussed how the relationship between Orlando and Rosalind contains a very modern message, that none of us is purely female or purely male. As a species, we're more complicated. As sexual beings we're more complex: we are all female and male in varying proportions.

Orlando's alliance of physical strength with emotional tenderness makes him irresistible to Rosalind. His compassion for old Adam becomes transcendent when he chooses to save the life of Oliver, the brother who has tried, twice, to have him murdered. In risking his own life to rescue Oliver from snake and lioness, we as well as Rosalind realise Orlando's true merit. Even more significant than his physical courage is Orlando's moral capacity to forgive Oliver. His wisdom makes him Rosalind's perfect match. Turning aside from revenge to embrace the finer action of chivalric, Christian forgiveness lifts Orlando from the realms of a typical romantic hero to the highest ideals of human behaviour. Michael

Boyd, Artistic Director of the RSC 2002–12, observes, 'it is Orlando's love, courage and physical strength when faced with the lion and Oliver that turns the fortunes of the play and even mystically disarms the troops of Frederick. Orlando in the theatre depends heavily on his Oliver to return the favour as he recounts the tale of Orlando's Christ-like sacrifice of his own blood to cleanse the sins of the world.'[52]

Drawn with the finest of knightly virtues, Orlando also anticipates future more equal relations between men and women. He's a new man for Rosalind, a new woman. Challenged and taught by Rosalind, this adolescent boy grows to full manhood to become her worthy partner and true contemporary. Yet in spite of Orlando's depth and complexity, his moral achievement and his authentic passion, why do some people feel that he's not quite 'up' to Rosalind? Perhaps it's just because he's pants as a poet? To convince us, he has to be played by an actor who is both powerful and sensitive. Orlando wrestles, falls in love, committedly, at first sight, is good at receiving as well as offering gifts, sustains and supports Old Adam, spars wittily with Ganymede, rescues and forgives his appalling elder brother – and Rosalind thinks he's worth it! It's been suggested that *As You Like It* could be called *The Education of Orlando*[53] – but I prefer *Orlando's Progress*.

Rof. It is not the fashion to see the Ladie the Epilogue: but it is no more vnhandsome, then to see the
Lord the Prologue. If it be true, that good wine needs
no bush, 'tis true, that a good play needes no Epilogue.
Yet to good wine they do vse good bushes : and good
playes proue the better by the helpe of good Epilogues:
What a case am I in then, that am neither a good Epilogue, nor cannot insinuate with you in the behalfe of a
good play? I am not furnish'd like a Begger, therefore
to begge will not become mee. My way is to coniure
you, and Ile begin with the Women. I charge you (O
women) for the loue you beare to men, to like as much
of this Play, as please you: And I charge you (O men)
for the loue you beare to women (as I perceiue by your
simpring, none of you hates them) that betweene you,
and the women, the play may please. If I were a Woman, I would kisse as many of you as had beards that
pleas'd me, complexions that lik'd me, and breaths that
I defi'de not : And I am sure, as many as haue good
beards, or good faces, or sweet breaths, will for my kind
offer, when I make curt'sie, bid me farewell.   _Exit._

From the First Folio edition of _The Workes of William Shakespeare_,
1623

EPILOGUE

Rosalind

It is not the fashion to see the lady the Epilogue, but it is no more unhandsome than to see the lord the Prologue. If it be true that good wine needs no bush, 'tis true that a good play needs no epilogue. Yet to good wine they do use good bushes, and good plays prove the better by the help of good epilogues. What a case am I in then, that am neither a good epilogue, nor can insinuate with you in the behalf of a good play. I am not furnished like a beggar, therefore to beg will not become me. My way is to conjure you, and I'll begin with the women. I charge you, O women, for the love you bear to men, to like as much of this play as please you. And I charge you, O men, for the love you bear to women (as I perceive by your simpering, none of you hates them), that between you and the women the play may please. If I were a woman I would kiss as many of you as had beards that pleased me, complexions that liked me and breaths that I defied not. And I am sure as many as have good beards, or good faces, or sweet breaths will for my kind offer, when I make curtsy, bid me farewell.

EPILOGUE

As You Like It
CURTAIN DOWN – LIGHTS UP – FINIS – EXIT – CUT!

Rosalind steps forward, alone, the focus of all eyes, to deliver her epilogue, the only heroine Shakespeare entrusted with this task. As well as star actor, she's been director and dramaturge, like David Garrick, Henry Irving or Kenneth Branagh, organising people and events from the moment she fell in love with Orlando, until this finale. But her mood isn't elegiac. Instead, it's insouciant, loving, mischievous, embracing, as she invites our applause for her play. The epilogue marks the transfiguration and the enduring appeal of Rosalind. She's not the same green girl at the end of the play that she was at the beginning. She's authoritative and confident. Actors and audience together have tracked Rosalind's progress through the play's five Acts. With eternal youth intact, she now breaks out of her chrysalis to advance to full maturity in the epilogue.

Rosalind says goodbye with a kiss, as if each one of us were Orlando. To both sexes s/he offers whatever we desire, as we like it. 'I would kiss as many of you as had beards that pleased me, complexions that liked me and breaths that I defied not. And I am sure as many as have good beards, or good faces, or sweet breaths will for my kind offer, when I make curtsy, bid me farewell' – by putting our hands together in ovation. The clapping breaks the spell and we leave the theatre elated and transformed before returning to the 'real' world, the rolling stream of life, and the business of living.

When Sophie Thompson (Emma's younger sister) played Rosalind in John Caird's production for the RSC in 1989/90, Orlando moved downstage first, as if he was about to deliver the final words, symmetrically balancing the fact that he'd opened the play five Acts earlier. But then he dried up, just as tongue-tied as he'd been when he first caught sight of Rosalind at the wrestling match in Act I. In this production, she watched him struggle, then pushed past to rescue him, launching into, 'It is not the fashion to see the lady the epilogue; but it is no more unhandsome than to see the lord the prologue,' before finishing the rest of the epilogue herself. It was comic and convincing.[1] The 2014 Southwark Playhouse production also used physical movement to indicate how far Rosalind had closed the gender gap. Sally Scott, who played Rosalind, told me, 'I felt it was very important for Rosalind to have the last word.' The Duke made to step forward, but 'I just pushed him aside. It felt a bit like those wedding speeches when the father of the bride gets up to do the speech, and you think, well, actually I'll talk about myself.'[2]

The epilogue, like all of Rosalind's part, was written for a boy actor to perform: a boy who first plays a woman, who then plays a man, and finally reveals himself as the female Rosalind in order to marry Orlando. Except that there's a further sex change still to come, for as Rosalind points out in the epilogue, 'she' was a boy acting the role all along. All that quick-change layering reaches a giddying climax in the epilogue. When Rosalind asks us to 'like as much of this play as please you,' to take it or leave it, exactly 'as you like it,' we hear not just the actor but Shakespeare breathing his own words into her mouth. His invisible presence pulses through Rosalind's epilogue. It feels like one of those rare occasions when we may be hearing the voice of Shakespeare himself.[3]

Rosalind breaks the first convention of epilogues by speaking as a woman. She also breaks the second convention by speaking in prose, at a time when epilogues were usually delivered in verse. However, another cross-dressing heroine, John Lyly's Galatea, had delivered a prose epilogue, a decade before Rosalind.

Galatea   Go all, 'tis I only that conclude all. You ladies [not *'women'* as Rosalind says] may see that Venus can make constancy fickleness, courage cowardice, modesty lightness, working things impossible in your sex, and tempering hardest hearts like softest wool. Yield, ladies, yield to love, ladies, which lurketh under your eyelids whilst you sleep, and playeth with your heartstrings whilst you wake; whose sweetness never breedeth satiety, labour weariness, nor grief bitterness. Cupid was begotten in a mist, nursed in clouds, and sucking only upon conceits. Confess him a conqueror, whom ye ought to regard, sith it is unpossible to resist; for this is infallible, that love conquereth all things but itself, and ladies all hearts but their own.[4]

Galatea's epilogue doesn't attempt Rosalind's risky strategy of dismantling the usual binary division between the sexes. She focuses on the comforting but predictable message that love conquers all. Unlike Galatea, Rosalind embraces complexity to unpeel yet a further layer of identity. Opening with characteristic attack, she seems to speak in the half-broken voice of a liberated teenage boy actor. 'It is not the fashion to see the lady the Epilogue,' s/he swaggers in the same voice that Ganymede used to court Orlando. I wonder if the youth who first played the part in 1599 came out of role in the epilogue, revealing his true masculine persona, or did he stay in character as Rosalind? We can never know. And what does the actress playing Rosalind today make of the great 'IF' of the play, '*If* I were a woman'? She may dip a curtsey, offer a bow, and speak both as male and female. Rosalind is not a-gender, she's gender fluid. 'Let's be done with gender stereotyping,' as Juliet Stevenson says.[5] The epilogue is where Rosalind makes her inclusive great leap into the future.

Today film can make combi-gender and every gradation visual in new ways. If we could put Shakespeare into a time machine, how he would have revelled in the freedom of the movies. At the end of Paul Czinner's 1936 film of *As You Like It*, the word EPILOGUE is engraved across a pair of wrought iron gates as they swing shut. Materialising before them, Elisabeth Bergner effortlessly sloughs skins from Ganymede into Rosalind, fading into and out of gender in a way that couldn't happen on stage. She made the epilogue magical, touching and erotic.

Seventy years later in 2006, Kenneth Branagh explored how film can interpret Shakespeare afresh. He set *As You Like It* in the dreamtime location of nineteenth-century Japan, actually shot among the trees of Wakehurst Place garden in West Sussex, Southern England. Branagh visually exploited the curious challenge he'd set himself.[6] He realised he could offset the imagery of Japanese prayer flags with the green shades of an English springtime. So he put all his bridegrooms against the flags awaiting their brides. In the finale, the cast whirled and danced back to the indoor Japanese court with its geometrically patterned floors and screens. From nineteenth-century Japan we cut seamlessly to the here and now, among all the paraphernalia of film making, cameras and caravans. Bryce Dallas Howard as Rosalind reappeared in her Ganymede outfit while the production team bustled around her. Suddenly we were back in our own western times with cars and movie trailers moving about as the off-camera staff started clearing the set. Watching the behind the scenes business of film made a neat parallel with the meta-theatrical way Rosalind's epilogue refers to acting and the playhouse to spin us through gender. The set was being broken up before our eyes as she gave the epilogue, speaking it as though the most natural thing in the world. It made modern sense of words and theatrical conventions more than four centuries old. Rosalind straddled the film's three time zones, said goodbye to her viewers, then firmly shut her trailer door. CUT!

After Rosalind has resolved her play, made 'these doubts all even,' restored paternity to her father, and given herself in marriage to Orlando, she does even stranger things in the epilogue. She becomes the playwright, writes the script for her own ending, and so breaks through the unseen fourth wall of theatre, between the world of the play and the world outside. Here she's at her most agile, slithering from gender to gender, both baffling and releasing the audience. By this stage of the play she's been through at least half a dozen illusory changes of sex. Her merging of gender and identity reaches apotheosis in the epilogue, where she speaks as an actor but transcends the role. Rosalind becomes man and woman. Everyperson. Past, present and future.

In Shakespeare's day, a male actor played a woman, Rosalind. The boy dressed as a girl then disguised himself as Ganymede who pretended to be Rosalind in order to play a dating game with Orlando with whom 'she' was in love, and who was in love with her. In the play's final Act, the boy actor impersonated Rosalind in order to marry Orlando. But in the epilogue Rosalind could change back into the boy player 'she' had always been. When the actor says today, 'If I were a woman,' how can we unravel this conundrum? In 1599 a male actor in his female persona suggested a mirage of potential. The Elizabethan audience was used to boy actors playing girls. They could accept the topsy-turvy convention, however pantomime or bizarre it seems to us. Perhaps they didn't see Rosalind as a woman or a man but as an all-encompassing human figure.

The 2015 production at Shakespeare's Globe hurtled us back to the way Rosalind might have performed the epilogue in 1599. Garlanded in her golden farthingale and airy cream ruff, Michelle Terry embodied a sumptuous vision of femininity, even recalling the young Elizabeth. But with the words, 'If I were a woman,' she ripped off her wide skirt to reveal a Ganymede suit of golden breeches and white hose. The audience gasped as she held the pose looking like an image of Virginia Woolf's dual-sex Orlando. We were racing back and forth through time. It was a startling moment even in 2015, and an entirely plausible suggestion of how a boy actor might have delivered the epilogue in Shakespeare's day.

After the Restoration when the first female actress appeared on stage to say, 'If I were a woman,' she could make sense of it by implying, 'If I were a real woman like one of you in the audience instead of a fictional character like Rosalind…' because in the epilogue, we see the actor beneath the role. At one performance the actor was tragically unmasked. In 1757, Peg Woffington, notorious for her 'breeches' parts and scandalous love life, collapsed in the middle of speaking the epilogue. 'O God! O God!' she screamed as she lurched into the wings where stagehands caught her. Even though Woffington was cut down by a stroke, the impact of her vivacious Rosalind would never die.[7] Rosalind's epilogue marks our liberation. She sends us back to the world with our minds and hearts open to a more humane view of relations between the sexes. Her work is done. She is free to dissolve, disappear, and leave us. Her character has always been a fiction, however real she's seemed. But the liberating ideas she leaves us with are material to our lives.

Shakespeare later risked a similar effect in the epilogue to *All's Well that Ends Well.* Its rhyming couplets make it sound far less innovative than Rosalind's wiry prose. The actor playing the King of France sheds his royal identity, although not his gender, to crave indulgence for the play we've just watched and applause for the company's efforts. We watch the man beneath the skin as the actor steps out of role in a way that far pre-dates Brecht.

The king's a beggar, now the play is done;
All is well ended if this suit be won,
That you express content; which we will pay
With strife to please you, day exceeding day.
Ours be your patience then and yours our parts;
Your gentle hands lend us and take our hearts.[8]

These metaphors of theatre and performance run throughout Shakespeare's plays. They are especially resonant in *As You Like It* and *Hamlet*, both written in 1599. Duke Senior's image of 'this wide and universal theatre'[9] prompts Jaques to remind us we strut life's stage only for our brief allotted span.

Jaques   All the world's a stage,
And all the men and women merely players.
They have their exits and their entrances,
And one man in his time plays many parts,
His acts being seven ages.[10]

Life as theatre was a familiar comparison during an age whose chief communal entertainments, apart from the church and the gallows, were in the playhouse. Sir Walter Raleigh explored the same metaphor in a poignant late poem, perhaps written while imprisoned in the Tower during the reign of James I.

What is our life? A play of passion,
Our mirth the music of division.
Our mothers' wombs the tiring-houses be,
Where we are dressed for this short comedy.
Heaven the judicious sharp spectator is,
That sits and marks still who doth act amiss.
Our graves that hide us from the searching sun
Are like drawn curtains when the play is done.
Thus march we, playing, to our latest rest,
Only we die in earnest, that's no jest.[11]

Life, like acting, is the performance art we all take part in, and Rosalind, more than anyone, understands the intimate connection between the two. In the Forest of Arden she discovers herself as a true thespian and gives the performance of her life as Ganymede. Her final colloquy with her audience is shot through with theatrical references to epilogue, prologue, good plays and good epilogues.

By her epilogue, Rosalind has broken all conventions of costume and gender. As she unpeels herself, we see the various Rosalinds. We're all acting; actors are all characters; characters do, and do not exist. Rosalind encapsulates the idea that these apparent opposites can be simultaneously true. She's boy and girl. She marches out of her uncle's French court, marches into England, Arden, Eden and everywhere. She's individual and everywoman, in a fictitious drama and yet alive, threatened by death but never dying, a heroine who breaks the bounds of her play and lives on long after it's over. Falstaff and Hamlet share an afterlife with her and inhabit our collective imaginations. The favourite fantasy of literary scholar Harold Bloom 'is that Falstaff did not allow himself to be done in by his murderous adopted son, the dreadful Prince Hal, and instead Shakespeare let him wander off to the Forest of Arden. There he sat on one end of a log, with the beautiful Rosalind on the other, and the two matched wits.'[12]

In *Twelfth Night*, the comedy thought to follow shortly after *As You Like It* in 1600, Feste the Clown sings the epilogue. He's an observer or commentator on human frailty. In just five stanzas, each with its poignant refrain, *For the rain it raineth every day*, he recalls the inexorable procession of Jaques' Seven Ages of Man speech, though Feste truncates them to just four.

> *Clown sings* When that I was and a little tiny boy,
>   With hey, ho, the wind and the rain,
> A foolish thing was but a toy,
>   For the rain it raineth every day.
>
> But when I came to man's estate,
>   With hey, ho, the wind and the rain,
> 'Gainst knaves and thieves men shut their gate,
>   For the rain it raineth every day.
>
> But when I came, alas, to wive,
>   With hey, ho, the wind and the rain,
> By swaggering could I never thrive,
>   For the rain it raineth every day.
>
> But when I came unto my beds,
>   With hey, ho, the wind and the rain,
> With toss-pots still 'had drunken heads,
>   For the rain it raineth every day.

> A great while ago the world begun,
>   With hey, ho, the wind and the rain,
> But that's all one, our play is done,
>   And we'll strive to please you every day.[13]

After all, it's only theatre. Having spent the play in his own particular disguise as a Fool, Feste dispels the world of the play with music, and copies the actor's usual ploy, and Rosalind's, by inviting us to break the magic with applause.

A decade after Rosalind brought *As You Like It* to its audacious conclusion, Dekker and Middleton gave an epilogue to their heroine Moll Cutpurse, the Roaring Girl, played, of course, by a boy actor.

> *Moll*   ...we with the painter shall
> In striving to please all please none at all.
> Yet for such faults as either the writers' wit
> Or negligence of the actors do commit,
> Both crave your pardons; if what both have done
> Cannot full pay your expectation,
> The Roaring Girl here herself shall hence
> Upon this stage give larger recompense,
> Whose mirth that you may share, in herself does woo you,
> And craves this sign: your hands to beckon her to you.[14]

Shakespeare had his epilogue imitators but they didn't expand, as he did, the range and potential of human development. However much brio Moll attempts, her epilogue is far less daring than Rosalind's. The Roaring Girl's purpose is to ingratiate her play, invite applause, advertise the next performance of the boy actor playing her, or perhaps the sensational appearance of Mary Frith, the real life model for Moll, at the Fortune Theatre. Where Rosalind strips back gender in the brisk colloquial prose of everyday, Moll's voice is constrained by clumsy rhyming couplets and doesn't challenge the identity of the boy actor taking the role. Yet both heroines confront our preconceptions about exactly what is a woman, what is a man. Moll, however, unlike Rosalind, reaches her epilogue fundamentally unchanged. She remains exactly what she is, a cross-dressing woman, like the real-life Mary Frith. But in her epilogue Rosalind weaves in and out of gender, intimately connecting with every member of her audience, inviting us to reassess the teasing nature of sexual desire. A satirist of society's preconceptions about gender, Rosalind anticipates the twenty-first century's dissolving norms of human relationships.

Since *As You Like It* was revived in 1740, Rosalind has usually, though not always, been played by a woman. This makes the epilogue doubly challenging for actresses who can find the line, 'If I were a woman,' either perplexing or even fatally embarrassing. Helen Faucit who played an acclaimed Rosalind many times during the Victorian era found the epilogue filled her with 'shrinking distaste.' It's not clear whether she retained the line, 'If I were a woman,' as she confessed she omitted some words and altered others. 'Speaking the Epilogue remained the one drawback to my pleasure. In it one addresses the audience neither as Ganymede nor as Rosalind, but as one's own very self. Anything of this kind was repugnant to me, my desire always being to lose myself in the character I was representing. When taken thus perforce out of my ideal, I felt stranded and altogether unhappy. Except when obliged, as in this instance, I never addressed an audience, having neither the wish nor the courage to do so. Therefore, as I advanced to speak the Epilogue, a painful shyness came over me, a kind of nervous fear, too, lest I should forget what I had to say, – a fear I never had at other times, – and thus the closing words always brought to me a sense of inexpressible relief.'[15]

In her self-conscious presentation of femininity, Helen Faucit felt exposed by the gender-teasing epilogue Shakespeare had written nearly three hundred years before for a boy to deliver. Had she become a professional actress as a way to conceal or protect her inner self? Would Faucit have felt less exposed if she'd been a man playing the part? Ronald Pickup, Rosalind in 1967, simply loved giving the epilogue, in some ways his favourite speech of the play. 'It was wonderful and extraordinary. I just spoke it as me, speaking to the audience in my own voice. We had embraced an audience and they were ready to respond.'[16] Yet even today, an actress can feel her soul laid bare in the epilogue, as Sally Scott did in 2014. 'It's not really Rosalind, it's not really Ganymede, it's sort of Sally, and I'm coming forward, and it's the actor and that's what's scary about it.'[17]

There's a clip on YouTube of Peggy Ashcroft performing the epilogue in 1957. Her RP diction is of its time, clipped, very British, and initially distancing. But then Ashcroft's energy and laugh break through, so you hear Rosalind, the authentic iconoclast. If the play has worked, the epilogue should move us, as well as make us laugh. Those who saw Maggie Smith's Rosalind at Stratford, Ontario in 1978/9, have never forgotten her epilogue. She reminded critic Ronald Bryden of Hans Christian Andersen's mermaid, 'walking on knives to be near her prince'. For Bernard Levin, Maggie Smith's Rosalind was one of the definitive performances of his lifetime. 'She spoke the epilogue like a chime of golden bells. But what she looked like as she did so I cannot tell you; for I saw it through eyes curtained with tears of joy.'[18]

Actresses today, like Juliet Stevenson, acknowledge the challenge of delivering the epilogue as a woman. They can only experiment and re-imagine a Rosalind for our times. In the epilogue Rosalind holds her arms wide open to embrace a modern new world where distinctions of hetero or homo, character and self are blurred. When it was written, *As You Like It* celebrated the loves that were then permitted – and more – but new Rosalinds can include every kind of love. Juliet Stevenson found, 'the epilogue is very problematic, because it's quite clearly written for a boy, and all the wit in it concerns the fact that it's a boy saying, 'If I were…' But we found a way through that. The audience doesn't leave the theatre necessarily united. There may be some conversations in the car on the way home that are challenging.'[19] As challenging perhaps as when Ibsen's shocking new play, *A Doll's House*, opened in Copenhagen in 1879 before reaching Broadway and London ten years later. Nora was said to have incited women to demand divorce as they were driven home in their carriages after the play.

Rosalind's epilogue can feel so problematic that some productions cut it altogether, as Christine Edzard decided to in her 1992 film of *As You Like It*. The setting in a contemporary urban wasteland made the epilogue seem unplayable, perhaps because there was no live audience to connect with. In the same year Adrian Lester played Rosalind in Cheek by Jowl's stage production. During the opening scenes as Rosalind at court, Lester used a slightly higher tone than his usual male voice. Then he lowered its timbre a little when in disguise as Ganymede. But this, as he told me, is how he approached Rosalind's epilogue. 'I tried to deliver it as honestly as I could. She/he thanks the audience for watching the play, flirts with both sexes in the audience a little, then for the line 'If I were a woman' I removed my head tie, earrings, and adjusted my voice so that I was no longer pretending to be female and wished them a good night. The moment I changed my voice, in some performances, got a huge intake of breath from the audience. The epilogue is a grateful acknowledgement that they have stayed and listened to the story. It can also be a plea for forgiveness if you have offended. But it always reminds you that you have been watching people pretend. And pretence is one of the core themes of the play.'[20] At the end it came as a shock to 'see' a male actor standing there. Adrian Lester could achieve this effect because he was an adult man, he wasn't a boy actor with an unbroken voice in 1599, nor even a woman of today. He could embody Everyperson.

Actresses adjust the way they perform the epilogue to fit their own interpretation of Rosalind. For Juliet Rylance in 2010, the epilogue was 'as much about Rosalind trying to figure out what the play has been about, as what the story means to the audience. I feel that she gets to the point where she realises that it's just about love conquering all. There's nothing else, there's nothing more than that.' In Sam Mendes' modern dress production at the Old Vic, Rylance knew she had to deliver the epilogue for her own times, not try to recreate the way a boy actor might have done it in 1599. The house lights went up and for the first time Rosalind could see us as clearly as we could see her. She who had been asking so many questions throughout the play looked for the answer in the audience. Rylance told me, 'they have it, they're just parts of you, they are the thirteenth character in the play. And you have to engage with them – so find the answers from them. I thought the epilogue is such a direct conversation. I can see everybody and we can really converse, breaking the spell, saying we're all together now and I'm talking to you, and you, and you.'[21] In giving us Rosalind's epilogue, Rylance returned us all to the real world.

Rosalind masterminds the denouement of *As You Like It* as Prospero unravels the plot at the end of *The Tempest*. Like Prospero, she's interested in magic. Since childhood, she claims, she's been taking lessons in the paranormal from a wise old magician. She may not brandish Prospero's magic staff, but she too can conjure visions and work enchantments like a modern movie director. Derek Jarman's innovative 1979 film of *The*

Tempest presented viewers with one of Prospero's earlier elegiac speeches instead of his usual epilogue. Prospero's poetic, airy verse seems at first far removed from the ludic, questing prose of Rosalind's epilogue with its 'ifs' of possibility, but like her, he plays on the illusory nature of theatre.

> Prospero   Our revels now are ended. These our *actors*,
> As I foretold you, were all spirits and
> Are melted into air, into thin air;
> And – like the *baseless fabric* of this vision -
> The cloud-capped towers, the gorgeous palaces,
> The solemn temples, the *great globe* itself,
> Yea, all which it inherit, shall dissolve,
> And like this *insubstantial pageant* faded,
> Leave not a rack behind. We are such stuff
> As dreams are made on, and our little life
> Is rounded with a sleep.[22]   [my italics]

As Prospero, played by Heathcote Williams in Jarman's film, lay in reverie, his voiceover floated into our ears, so we felt we were entering his inner consciousness. Giving this as Prospero's epilogue, with its foreshadowing of Raleigh's poem, revived in my head Jaques' earlier 'All the world's a stage' speech that compares theatrical entrances and exits with the ages, acts, scenes, and brevity of human life.

In *The Tempest* everyone learns something but the person who learns most, perhaps, is Prospero himself. Like Rosalind before him, though with darker magic arts at his disposal, Prospero has been the actor-manager of his play, and brought more than lovers to a satisfactory conclusion. He has learnt to turn aside from fraternal revenge, just as Duke Senior and Orlando have forgiven their erring brothers. In the comedy of *As You Like It*, Duke Frederick and Oliver are enabled to be re-made and converted. However, by 1611 when the *Tempest* had its first performance, it's questionable whether Prospero's forgiven brother, the usurping Duke of Milan, really learns anything. Prospero himself, though angry and wronged, has the strength to pardon his enemies and break his magic wand. He keeps his promise to Ariel. He forgives Caliban for plotting to overthrow him and turns aside from vengeance. Divested of his magic, the incantatory rhyming couplets of his epilogue, so different from Rosalind's playful, colloquial prose, undress him to become just another human being, whose power to forgive has set him free. Like Rosalind, he's one of us, he's become an Everyman.

> Prospero Now my charms are all o'erthrown,
> And what strength I have's mine own,
> Which is most faint. Now, 'tis true
> I must be here confined by you,
> Or sent to Naples. Let me not,
> Since I have my dukedom got
> And pardoned the deceiver, dwell
> In this bare island by your spell;
> But release me from my bands
> With the help of your good hands.
> Gentle breath of yours my sails
> Must fill, or else my project fails,
> Which was to please. Now I want
> Spirits to enforce, art to enchant;
> And my ending is despair,
> Unless I be relieved by prayer,
> Which pierces so that it assaults
> Mercy itself, and frees all faults.
> As you from crimes would pardoned be,
> Let your indulgence set me free.[23]

The epilogues of Rosalind and Prospero strip their impersonators, respectively, of gender confusion, and magic, allowing them to vanish into the wings, or back into everyday life. But they both retain the richness of their discoveries. We can be man and woman in every gradation of sexuality, and an inclusive Everyperson. The house lights may go up as Prospero speaks or dreams his epilogue, asking us to liberate him from the island by our prayer. In prayer we put our hands together as we do for applause, exactly as Rosalind asks us – to 'bid me farewell.'

Sharing three hours of the play together creates an intimate connection between actor and audience, and Rosalind's epilogue performs the final bonding alchemy. The spirit of the play may leave us changed, as well as Rosalind. As Pippa Nixon, who played the role for the RSC in 2013, observes, 'Rosalind is one of life's great teachers and you find that rather than simply playing the part, "giving your

Rosalind," she has indeed given and transformed you.'[24] If the play has worked, the epilogue leaves me uplifted and released in comedy's parallel to tragic catharsis. Rosalind is forever young but she speaks to people of all ages, not just to those in love, or to those in love unrequitedly, but to those who 'have loved ere now,' either with memories of first love, or with long lives of enduring love.

Rosalind is universal, she partakes of both sexes, she opens up opportunities for all of us to dare, to organise and to direct our own life stories. During the play she has extended the frontiers of our so-called 'male' and 'female' human natures to embrace a larger humanity. By the epilogue she encapsulates all possibilities. She is you and me. We are all Rosalind now.

A Woman For All Time – Rosalind's Daughters

Rosalind's daughters both fictional and real have been a core element in my reading life. Jo March was an early heroine and my first proto-Rosalind when I was seven; *Little Women* the first book I bought with my own saved-up pocket money. The small volume cost five shillings (25 pence today) from our local, suburban W.H. Smith and its pocket size snugly fitted my hands. The dark blue leatherette binding with gold-tooled title on the spine is now shabby with re-readings. I lay flat out on the grass beside our equally shabby old house and read it in the sunshine. As soon as I finished, I turned back to the first page, and read the book all over again. And again. I had no historical sense (how could I have?) that its American setting, and the Civil War where her father was away fighting, were worlds and years away from my mid-century British childhood, but I knew Jo was the sort of girl I wanted to be. Especially when she cut off her hair. I always had short hair. Once Jo cut her hair, my identification with her was complete. Unselfishness like Jo's was one of the female virtues my mother tried to inculcate in me when I was a child. Many years later, in Dublin, she heard Betty Friedan give a lecture which opened her eyes on to a new world of feminism. Inspired by Friedan, my mother applauded the fact that Rosalind's daughters, like Jo March herself, can achieve their ambitions and independence.

When Rosalind first crosses the stage as Ganymede today, there's a small intake of breath from the audience. Her long hair of Act 1 is usually shorn to indicate that she's crossed the border between the sexes.[1] Cutting your hair short was a seriously shocking act in the past. Women's hair was thought to be their crowning glory and a visual sign of sexual allure, especially during the Victorian era when elaborate hairpieces were often added to the wearer's own. Nowhere was the effect of masses of hair more provocative than in the intense portraits of women by Dante Gabriel Rossetti whom Mrs Gaskell called, 'not mad as a March hare, but hair-mad'. This fixation with women's hair persisted until the First World War when women entered the forces and munitions factories. While male farmhands were away at the Front during both World Wars, land girls took over their jobs and tied up their hair in headscarves for practical reasons. Women's hair wasn't scissored for style until the 1920s when the bobs and shingles of the Jazz Age came in. Even today, female celebrity hair is often big hair. Those 1980s sculptured helmets, symbols of wealth and power in the TV series, *Dynasty* and *Dallas*, are constantly reinvented. Twiggy's cool crop challenged the 1960s fashion for lavish hair, and it's still an assertive look for modern role models, such as Lena Dunham and Annie Lennox, who influence women today. Other public stars such as Kate Middleton, and Kim Sears, wife of tennis champion Andy Murray, sport long flowing manes of hair.

When Louisa May Alcott published *Little Women* in 1868/9, hair frenzy was at its height. Jo March was always a tomboy but she took pride in 'her long, thick hair' which 'was her one beauty', often wet, dishevelled, or flying through the novel – until Jo crosses the border and takes action on hair, 'with a very queer expression of countenance, for there was a mixture of fun and fear, satisfaction and regret in it, which puzzled the family as much as did the roll of bills she laid before her mother.' Secretly she'd had her wild tresses chopped and sold to contribute $25 to the straightened family finances. Under her new cap of Ganymede hair, Jo feels liberated. 'My head feels deliciously light and cool, and the barber said I will soon have a curly crop, which will be boyish, becoming, and easy to keep in order.' Her new hair was an outward badge not only of her altruism but, more importantly, of the independent way she will choose to make a professional career in journalism and writing. Katharine Hepburn played Jo March in the 1933 film of *Little Women*. She went on to play Rosalind on Broadway in 1950.

Rosalind is an enduring example of female empowerment. But does she have implications for men, too? Actor Sally Scott thinks Rosalind and Orlando have plenty to show young people of her generation. 'I do think their relationship is held up as an example, and rightly so, because they've taken the time to be authentic with each other.' Rosalind's insights about love are inclusive and directed equally to men and women. Scott loves 'the fact that Rosalind is the protagonist, that she initiates everything. She's an example to men of a woman who is standing on her own two feet. Men must feel that they're allowed to connect with their more sensitive side. Orlando is not your typical alpha hero and I feel she celebrates that.'[2]

Blanche McIntyre, director of *As You Like It* at Shakespeare's Globe during summer 2015, corroborates Scott, adding, 'Rosalind is confident in herself, she feels she has a right to be heard; she has a right to boss Orlando around if she feels he's messing it up, to cry if she feels unhappy. She can change her identity and it will be fine and can be even sexier. Rosalind is a wonderful message for young women. She does the talking.' But she's not all virtuous. Her tongue can be cruel. She can turn her back on Celia and be sharp with Phebe. 'Orlando loves that she shows off, but he anchors her. Orlando is an emotional man and his nurturing side makes him much more interesting. His feminine side is empowering for Rosalind. I think they're a lovely couple because neither of them fits into easily recognisable gender patterns.' So there is a message for young men, too, I asked Blanche. 'Yes, I think so.'[3]

Juliet Stevenson takes a feminist view. 'Rosalind knows that she needs to negotiate this love with Orlando from her newly realised self. And I would say, that in itself has an awful lot to teach young women. Love from the centre of who you are, be loved from the centre of who you are. Don't turn yourself into a shape that you think he wants, or she wants.' Stevenson probes the modern conundrum of gender relations. 'Young women are endlessly being asked to watch plays in which a man is the protagonist, in which it's his passion, his dynamic. So I would hope young men could watch a play with a young woman at its centre. We don't always learn through identification with our own gender. We must hear what Rosalind says about men and women because she's very, very equal in her witty, mocking dissection of male and female stereotypes. She's speaking to both genders very much. So I would say, both to young men and to young women, be true to yourselves when you love. Be true to yourselves and not to some idea of what femininity is, or should be in its prescribed form.' Stevenson says, 'Rosalind is iconoclastic, she challenges so many givens about gender: about men and women; how people should love; how to love; and how not to love; and all the clichés – and she pulls them all apart. This was central to my relationship to the play.'[4]

❧

Rosalind's daughters began to emerge almost immediately after *As You Like It* was posted on the Stationers' Register in 1600.[5] Moll Cutpurse, though brimming with verbal and physical vitality as the eponymous *Roaring Girl* in Middleton and Dekker's comedy of 1611, is a coarser successor to Rosalind. The play is sometimes revived, and Moll has been notably played by Helen Mirren in 1983, and by Lisa Dillon in 2014 for the RSC.

Notorious fixer, pickpocket, petty criminal, and disruptive force in the city underworld, Moll Cutpurse dresses as a drag king, without wanting to disguise her female gender. Most of the cast and all the audience know she is a woman. Her purpose is to outrage society, defy the biblical veto on cross-dressing, and to live an independent life. Like Rosalind, Moll is an outlaw from society. But where Moll is low down the social pile, Rosalind is an aristocrat. Earthy and humorous, Moll is 'such a kissing wench,' and like Rosalind enjoys quips and badinage, declaring herself, 'like Kent, unconquered!' But whereas Rosalind's driving purpose is enlightened marriage to the man of her choice, Moll explicitly rejects marriage. 'I have no humour to marry. I love to lie on both sides of the bed myself.' She's worked out a way to live on her own.

Rosalind, on the other hand, dresses as a man in Arden in order to conceal her sex and stay safe. Only her cousin Celia, their accomplice Touchstone, and we the audience know she's a woman. The first half of Moll's boast, 'I please myself and care not who else loves me,' proves an unexpected outcome for Rosalind. Living in her uncle's patriarchal court, female independence has never occurred to her before. Transfigured by doublet and hose, Rosalind as Ganymede can operate in the real world and even earn a living for herself and 'sister' Aliena. She and Celia could never have done this as two women under the control of Duke Frederick.

Apart from Moll, another woman gets into male disguise, though only temporarily, in *The Roaring Girl*. Mary Fitzallard does so with the single aim of achieving marriage with her true lover, Sebastian Wengrave. Once she's in drag, her kisses have a special thrill for Sebastian. 'Mary; I think a woman's lip tastes good in trousers.'[6] Then as now, the liminal area where male and female boundaries are blurred, seems specially erotic.

> *Sebastian*   I think every kiss she gives me now
> In this strange form is worth a pair of two.[7]

Kissing his boy-girlfriend is as exciting for Sebastian as it is for Orlando to kiss Ganymede.

Rosalind is a fictional character but *The Roaring Girl* had a real life model, Mary Frith, a celebrity who sauntered through Jacobean London in drag, smoking, drinking and roistering with the roaring boys. She made a sensational personal appearance in 1611 at the Fortune Theatre, flaunting her trademark costume of boots, breeches and a sword. Mary Frith, alias Moll Cutpurse, was a big draw on the London stage whether in her own person or fictionalised. The character escaped *The Roaring Girl* to thrill audiences again with a cameo appearance in a new play by Nathan Field, *Amends for Ladies* which probably premiered in 1615. (Field had to make amends to the ladies for his earlier play, *A Woman is a Weathercock*). Among a fresh crowd of roaring boys, Whorebang, Bots, Tearchaps and Spillblood, Nathan Field's Moll shows lesbian sensibilities to flirt with Grace, a housewife, who considers her, bizarrely, both 'man and horse.' Reprinted in 1639, *Amends* was boldly advertised 'with the merry pranks of Moll Cutpurse.'

Amends for Ladies focuses on a provocative debate about which state of life is best for women. Single, married or widowed? Three women, all played by boys, state their case: Lady Honour, an unmarried virgin, Lady Perfect, a virtuous wife, and Lady Bright, a widow. Only the last, Lady Bright, can operate independently in Jacobean society. Only she can say, 'I am mine own commander', the state Rosalind discovers for herself once she's in drag.

Rosalind's true daughter in *Amends* is Lady Honour who cross-dresses as a jaunty Irish pageboy, a disguise that frees her to speak her mind about love. Nathan Field the playwright, had been a boy actor in the Children of the Blackfriars Company from at least 1600. After his voice broke he joined Shakespeare's company, The King's Men. He would have been well aware of the special frisson of boy/girl/boy roles from his own experience as a teenage actor.

Before Lady Honour chooses, like Rosalind, to join her life with her lover's, she aspires to personal autonomy, unattainable for her at that time.

> *Lady Honour* Nay, all the freedom that a virgin hath
> Is much to be preferred. Who would endure
> The humours of so insolent a Thing
> As is a husband? Which of all the Herd
> Runs not possessed with some notorious vice,
> Drinking or whoring, fighting, jealousy…
> Is it not daily seen,
> Men take wives, but to dress their meat, to wash
> And starch their linen: for the other matter
> Of lying with them, that's but when they please…[8]

A woman living her own life, independent of a man, was an impossible challenge for most Jacobethans. But it fascinated them and was clearly up for discussion in 1615. Such public debate on stage was soon shut down with the playhouses in 1642 during the English Civil War and later under the Commonwealth.

With the Restoration of the monarchy under Charles II in 1660, English women were at last released to appear on the professional stage, and audiences were quick to applaud the new stars who vied to show a shapely leg in the popular breeches roles. Daring new actresses could exploit their feminine charms as Sylvia, who cross-dressed as Jack Wilful in George Farquhar's 1706 comedy, *The Recruiting Officer*, and at the same time they could embrace the thrill of androgyny. Peg Woffington who played Sylvia said after one of her shows, 'in my conscience! I believe Half the Men in the House take me for one of their own Sex'. Another actress sniped, 'It may be so; but, in my Conscience! the other Half can convince them to the contrary'.[9] Eighteenth-century actresses were expected to lead scandalous private lives and Woffington enjoyed many lovers, including the great David Garrick.

To my mind, Elizabeth Bennet, Jane Austen's fast talking heroine of *Pride and Prejudice*, is a real daughter of Rosalind, even though, in 1813, she doesn't cross-dress. Instead she tramps the fields six inches deep in mud like Ganymede, 'at a quick pace, jumping over stiles, and springing over puddles,' without any ladylike regard for petticoats. She's on a mission to visit her beloved sister Jane, a cousin Celia figure, who is marooned with 'flu at Mr Bingley's Netherfield. Here Elizabeth encounters Mr Darcy. Far from falling in love with each other at first sight they enjoy a mutual antipathy, the other side of the coin of mutual attraction. 'She is tolerable; but not handsome enough to tempt *me*,' says Darcy. Elizabeth told the story 'with great spirit among her friends; for she had a lively, playful disposition, which delighted in any thing ridiculous.' These are the exact qualities that Anna Jameson, one of the first female Shakespearean critics, noticed in Rosalind in 1832. 'The wit of Rosalind bubbles up and sparkles like the living fountain, refreshing all around. Her volubility is like the bird's song.'[10] Elizabeth Bennet exhibits the same delight in witty observation as Rosalind. 'Follies and nonsense, whims and inconsistencies *do* divert me, I own, and I laugh at them whenever I can.'

Elizabeth also shares Rosalind's capacity to teach, and to learn from the man who will become her life's partner. 'I hope I never ridicule what is wise or good.' Although apparently powerless as the second daughter of five in an only moderately comfortable family, Elizabeth is assertive in her dealings with Mr Darcy, with priggish clergyman Mr Collins, and with high and mighty Lady Catherine de Burgh. She believes she has the right to address men and women as her social equals even if they don't think they are hers. Rosalind, too, exercises social fluidity in the Forest of Arden, at ease with every class of person from dukes to goatherds. Elizabeth achieves emotional maturity like Rosalind, and combines reason with passion in her choice of a good man's love and final acceptance of Mr Darcy.[11] Jane Austen lets us know that Elizabeth will go on talking in her lively and 'sportive' manner with Mr Darcy long after their wedding. 'I am the happiest creature in the world,' she wrote to her aunt Gardiner, 'I am happier even than Jane; she only smiles, I laugh.' Her wit is not going to be dampened by marriage and nor is Rosalind's.

A generation later during the 1840s on the Yorkshire moors, the Brontë sisters, Charlotte, Emily and Anne, were writing impassioned novels, *Jane Eyre, Wuthering Heights* and *The Tenant of Wildfell Hall*. The Brontë sisters called themselves the Bell brothers in order to gain attention inside the masculine world of London publishers. As Charlotte's heroine Jane Eyre said, 'Women feel just as men feel; they need exercise for their faculties, and a field for their efforts as much as their brothers do.'[12] There was no alternative for the Brontës but going Ganymede, and styling themselves the brothers Currer, Ellis and Acton Bell.

The most famous and prolific author of the mid-nineteenth century, Amantine-Lucile-Aurore Dupin, known internationally as George Sand, didn't simply write under a male pseudonym, she also costumed herself as a cavalier. Her image excited both sexes, and herself, as she strode through Paris society in her severe English riding habit, dark hair spilling under her veiled top hat, a soft cravat at her throat, and a lighted cigar between her fingers. 'I can't convey how much my boots delighted me: I'd have gladly slept in them as my brother did when he was a lad and had just got his first pair. With those steel-tipped heels I was solid on the sidewalk at last. I dashed back and forth across Paris and felt I was going around the world,' wrote Sand in her autobiography.[13] (Quelle femme n'a jamais eu le fantasme de se retrouver dans la peau d'un homme?) She felt she was slipping hither and thither across gender, a state which fascinated her. A natural daughter of Rosalind, Sand paid homage to her Shakespearean heroine in 1856 when she freely translated *As You Like It* for the Comédie Française.

Thinking about the movement towards female emancipation was not confined to women writers in the nineteenth century. Thomas Hardy, too, was interested in independent women, as innovative in their Victorian way as Elizabethan Rosalind was in hers. His novel *Under the Greenwood Tree* published in 1872, taking its title from one of the songs in *As You Like It*, tacitly imagines a Victorian daughter of Rosalind. Although Fancy Day comes from a lower social class than the Duke's daughter, and doesn't cross-dress like Rosalind, she experiments, nevertheless, with dawning new freedoms for women, revolves a number of boyfriends, and makes sure she gets an education. Fancy is just as realistic and anti-romantic in her pastoral novel as Rosalind is in her pastoral play. *Under the Greenwood Tree* is the only one of Hardy's novels to have a happy ending like Shakespeare's comedy. His later novel in 1895, *Jude the Obscure*, examined another New Woman, Sue Bridehead, but her sacrifices were of tragic dimensions.

Hardy's *Under the Greenwood Tree* was published in the same year, 1872, as George Eliot's *Middlemarch*. Eliot's given name was Mary Anne Evans. She wrote under a male pseudonym, even though in the Victorian era she was brave enough to live openly with a married man, George Henry Lewes. Her pen name was a coded tribute to George, 'To L – I owe it.'[14] Eliot herself represents a latter-day daughter of Rosalind, prepared to live the truth about love. In her beguiling personal study of Eliot's novel, *The Road to Middlemarch*, Rebecca Mead identifies brainy but 'homely' Mary Garth as a daughter of 'clever, irresistible Rosalind.'[15] But for me, as I graduated from *Little Women* with its implicitly patronising title and began to make wider choices in my reading as a teenager, it was Gwendolen Harleth, George Eliot's risk-taking heroine in *Daniel Deronda*, who felt like a flawed but true descendant of Rosalind. Eliot even casts Gwendolen to play Rosalind.

The novel's opening question about Gwendolen is the question that intrigues most teenagers: 'Was she beautiful or not beautiful?'[16] When I was seventeen, I imagined I was Gwendolen, just as I'd thought I was Jane Austen's Emma when I was fourteen. It was Emma's penchant for matchmaking I loved, even though most of her efforts ended in disaster. My own efforts resulted in one or two successes years later, although I'd attempted many more. Rosalind herself is a proto-Emma, if you consider all the weddings she brokers by Act 5. Departing from Jane Austen's English canvas, drawn on her 'little bit of ivory', I went abroad on holiday with my family to the liberated Denmark of the late 1960s. Here I re-imagined the resort of Helsingør (coincidentally Hamlet's Elsinore) as George Eliot's middle European town of Leubronn. I found a casino and furtively replayed Gwendolen's reckless roulette with myself in the starring role. 'With a face which might possibly be looked at without admiration, but could hardly be passed with indifference',[17] Gwendolen was utterly riveting to me. Selfish, egotistical, but yearning to exercise her powers, she learns, bitterly, from experience.

'Lovely and vigorous as a tall, newly-opened lily,' Gwendolen is far too self-conscious ever to be wholly innocent, but while she's still in a state of semi-innocence, she enjoys being Rosalind. Queen of the archery contest in a forest of Arden setting, 'from roofed grove to open glade', Gwendolen takes the lead in an extempore *As You Like It*. 'When a pretty compliment had been turned to Gwendolen about her having the part of Rosalind, she felt the more compelled to be surpassing in liveliness. This was not very difficult to her, for the effect of what had happened to-day was an excitement which needed a vent, a sense of adventure rather than alarm.'

Gwendolen instantly identifies with Rosalind who had fallen in love with Orlando and then almost immediately been banished from court. Rosalind's escape to the Forest of Arden was an exciting and adventurous template. Receiving a problematical proposal from Grandcourt, a man she is not in love with, fills Gwendolen with that parallel 'excitement which needed a vent.'[18] Acting Rosalind puts her in touch with the idea of feminine empowerment. And above all else, imperious but penniless Gwendolen longs to be in command. However, as a result of her subsequent actions, Gwendolen Harleth turns out to be one of Rosalind's unusual tragic daughters.

Nora Helmer was a subliminal daughter of Rosalind's when she first broke out of her Norwegian doll's house in Ibsen's wildly controversial play, first staged in 1879, and constantly revived ever since. Actors today notice the connection between the two roles, even though Rosalind comes from the world of comedy and Nora belongs to the tragedy of modern life. Actor Cush Jumbo who has played an award-winning Rosalind, calls Nora, 'Ibsen's Rosalind. You never leave the stage and the journey she goes on is epic.'[19] Nora shocked Victorian society by leaving her three children in order to explore a life of her own, outside her infantilising marriage. From Nora onwards, women increasingly asserted their independence, sought to retain control over their earnings, to hold property, and to sign contracts in their own names. The Married Women's Property Act became law in 1882 in England. Rosalind and Nora make opposite but equally life-changing choices, choices that New Women began to make ever more decisively by the 1890s.

Rosalind was an inspirational prototype for the New Woman, a suffragette on a bicycle wearing the controversial vogue of rational dress, divided skirts or culottes. She was instantly recognised both as a role model for modern women, and as a slayer of hearts, by feminist writer, Ella Hepworth Dixon. Celebrating knickerbockers, an androgynous new trend in women's fashion, Ella noticed how 'those tweed-covered legs breathe defiance against the hydra-headed prejudices and conventions which perpetually harass womankind.' Ella was quite sure that 'Shakespeare knew this. He was aware that by donning masculine attire a woman…at once altered her manners and her attitude towards the world at large. Rosalind in petticoats is a conventional, slightly hysterical schoolgirl; Rosalind in doublet and hose is an impish wight; a merry, full-blooded, impudent youngster, who plagues Orlando, and steals feminine hearts without remorse. And it is to be remarked that, once she has worn breeches, her character is altered for good.'[20] More than a century later, actor Sally Scott still confirms Ella's observation. 'A literal transformation like that makes your physicality entirely different.' Once dressed as Ganymede, Scott told me, 'I've got those stomping walking boots with two pairs of socks in and they made this noise as I walked, this slopping noise. I think it's this idea about taking up space and I could be heard coming!'

Almost three hundred years after *As You Like It*, 'new woman' Ella Hepworth Dixon, an 'advanced female' in her own estimation, saw herself as a daughter of Rosalind whom she called her 'immortal prototype'.[21] Ella seized a whole array of opportunities for clever, entrepreneurial women. She became a journalist, magazine editor, novelist, playwright, critic, cultural commentator, and autobiographer. In carving a new career for a woman in the predominantly male workplace of late Victorian England, she looked to many of Shakespeare's women, but to Rosalind above all, for inspiration. Aligning their era with her own, she claimed they would have been her true contemporaries, and 'branded with the epithet "New Women."'[22]

Oscar Wilde promoted the writing of Ella Hepworth Dixon in *The Woman's World*, the magazine he edited for two years between 1887-1889. The following year his only novel, *The Picture of Dorian Gray*, appeared in *Lippincott's Monthly Magazine*. If Dorian was going to fall in love with any woman, it could be only with Sybil Vane, as she played the delicious role of Rosalind. 'You should have seen her!' Dorian exclaimed to his artist friend, Basil Hallward. 'When she came on in her boy's clothes, she was perfectly wonderful. She wore a moss-coloured velvet jerkin with cinnamon sleeves, slim brown cross-gartered hose, a dainty little green cap, and a hawk's feather caught in a jewel, and a hooded cloak lined with dull red. She had never seemed to me more exquisite. She had all the delicate grace of that Tanagra figurine that you have in your studio, Basil. Her hair clustered round her face like dark leaves round a pale rose...I forgot that I was in London and in the nineteenth century. I was away with my love in a forest that no man had ever seen.'[23] Sybil Vane as transvestite Rosalind represented an ideal sexual fusion for Dorian, if only briefly. She crossed both gender and time in his Arden of the mind.

Henry James did something daring with Rosalind in 1902 when he re-worked *As You Like It* in his long short story, 'The Papers', the same year he wrote about Shakespeare in his other, better-known tale, 'The Birthplace'. The papers of James's title are the newspapers, the world of the popular press, hacks and journalism. James explicitly compares his modern girl reporter, Maud Blandy, with Rosalind. James's critical re-write concerns Orlando, who is excised from the story. This is the first Rosalind to choose Jaques, a fellow hack, for her boyfriend, an even more radical re-imagining than George Sand's 1856 version of *As You Like It* which awarded him with Celia. James's male lead, Howard 'turned a little, to rest on his elbow, and, cycling suburban young man as he was, he might have been, outstretched under his tree, melancholy Jacques looking off into a forest glade, even as sailor-hatted Maud, in – for elegance – a new cotton blouse and a long-limbed angular attitude, might have prosefully suggested the mannish Rosalind.' James gives us an assertive Rosalind, at home in her own 'young bachelor' skin, quite different from Sybil Vane, Wilde's creature of artifice. By contrast, Maud Blandy 'might as easily have been christened John.' James weaves references and counter-references from *As You Like It* into 'The Papers.' When Maud sighs, 'I ain't a woman...I wish I were!' we hear Shakespeare's Rosalind speaking to us in her epilogue, 'If I were a woman...'

Maud and Howard bicycle out to Richmond Park, their Forest of Arden, to consider the outcome of a dangerous professional experiment they've conducted. Their direction is into the forest, not back to the city where Rosalind and Orlando are destined to go. Maud as Rosalind discovers a future with a new partner, Howard, who represents Jaques, but they make essentially the same decision as Rosalind and Orlando. '"We must love each other," said Howard Bight. "But can we live by that?" He thought again; then he decided. "Yes"... But it all came to something else. "Whom will *you* marry?"' Howard asks Maud. 'She only, at first, for answer, kept her eyes on him. Then she turned them about the place and saw no hindrance, and then, further, bending with a tenderness in which she felt so transformed, so won to something she had never been before, that she might even, to other eyes, well have looked so, she gravely kissed him. After which, as he took her arm, they walked on together' – as professional comrades into the twentieth century.[24]

Ford Madox Ford took up the discussion of the 'new woman' and the whole mystery of sexual attraction in his great series of novels, *Parade's End*. Here Valentine Wannop, a direct descendant of Rosalind, goes a step further into modern sexual relations. Valentine is an advanced suffragette and a young woman of complete integrity, prepared to commit herself to loving Christopher Tietjens, a married man and semi-autobiographical version of Ford himself. *Parade's End* was published between 1924-8, and written, in a sense, lest Ford forget his experience as an officer during the First World War. The war was the forest that Christopher Tietjens and Valentine must negotiate and emerge from; its armistice the catalyst for the decision to consummate their long restrained love. Valentine and Christopher's bond is built on 'the intimate conversation that means the final communion' of souls that 'in effect was love.'[25] This love based upon talk, though in a more melancholy key, is another incarnation of Rosalind and Orlando's courtship by conversation, which culminates in marriage. Three centuries after *As You Like It*, Ford can allow us into Valentine and Christopher's dialogue beyond consummation, and into the daily reality of their lives together. There's a tragic dimension to this. As

Rosalind pointed out: 'Maids are May when they are maids, but the sky changes when they are wives.'[26]

Brooding on the relationship between love and marriage, Virginia Woolf invented another daughter for Rosalind. She's Katharine Hilbery, a conflicted, independent minded woman in Woolf's second novel, *Night and Day*, which came out in 1919 although it was set before the outbreak of the Great War. William observes that his one-time fiancée, Katharine, 'pretends that she's never read Shakespeare. And why should she read Shakespeare, since she IS Shakespeare – Rosalind, you know.' Katharine's mother also sees her daughter as Rosalind and tells her, 'The best of life is built on what we say when we're in love. It isn't nonsense, Katharine,' she urged, 'it's the truth, it's the only truth.' Katharine finds this hard to reconcile with her quest for autonomy. But it's the same truth Rosalind discovers when she makes her free choice to say to Orlando, 'To you I give myself, for I am yours.' When Naomi Frederick played Rosalind at Shakespeare's Globe in 2009, she echoed Mrs Hilbery: 'I love this play! It's about love, living, and the things that count in life.'[27]

The title of Woolf's innovative 'biography,' *Orlando*, makes an elegant link with Shakespeare's Rosalind. Published in 1928, the hero-heroine, Orlando, is a modernist version of what Shakespeare's Rosalind stood for when she crossed the border between the sexes, and showed that women and men experience love with matching intensity and self-doubt. Woolf delivers *Orlando* in subtle homage to Shakespeare's Rosalind, even bearing the same name as her lover. In her effervescent concoction, Woolf not only undermined society's preconceived notions about what exactly is a man, what exactly is a woman, she also challenged the literary world about what exactly is a biography. 'It sprung upon me how I could revolutionise biography in a night', she told her lover, Vita Sackville-West, whose character inspired Orlando.[28]

Woolf's father, Leslie Stephen, was the first editor of the monumental and ground-breaking *Dictionary of National Biography*. His daughter's fantastic froth of a biography was a challenge to his world of masculine Victorian life writing that echoed the way Rosalind defied the male structures of court life, exemplified by her father and uncle. Woolf's Orlando goes on a parallel but contrary journey to

Shakespeare's Rosalind who is first girl, then boy, then girl. Or first, boy actor playing a girl, then girl playing a boy, then boy playing a girl, then boy actor again by the epilogue. Woolf's Orlando begins as a lad in the late sixteenth century, only to morph into a woman by the eighteenth century.

In Sally Potter's 1992 film, Tilda Swinton was the dazzling embodiment of Woolf's amorphous Orlando. For Swinton the book 'has always been a practical manual. A tourist guide to human experience, the best of wise companions…Where I once assumed it was a book about eternal youth, I now see it as a book about growing up, about learning to live.'[29] The universal process of growing up is part of Rosalind's perennial relevance. As she leaves us at the end of the play, she is filled with potential. Rosalind and Orlando have both expanded their emotional landscape in the Forest of Arden. Here they've learned to navigate the painful insecurities of adolescence, accepted they can feel all emotions in one day, and found out how to love and live.

After *Orlando*, Woolf continued to refer to Rosalind, and even to personify her. On 12 April 1937, the front cover of *Time* magazine carried a silvery, androgynous photograph of Virginia Woolf by Man Ray. The caption read, 'It is fatal to be a man or woman pure and simple.'[30] The quote was from Woolf's *A Room of One's Own*, the book based on a series of lectures Woolf had delivered to women students at Cambridge ten years earlier. Never an undergraduate herself, Woolf's agenda was to inspire young women and to see them educated. And she looked to Shakespeare's heroines, as well as to classical literature, to find role models for them. 'Women have burnt like beacons in all the works of all the poets from the beginning of time,' she told them, naming Rosalind among a roll call that included Antigone, Cleopatra, Lady Macbeth, Phèdre, Cressida, Desdemona and Webster's Duchess of Malfi. Woolf wanted young women not just to feature in literature, but also to make literature themselves, of whatever kind, in whatever genre, 'travel and adventure, and research and scholarship, and history and biography, and criticism and philosophy and science.'[31] 'So long as you write what you wish to write, that is all that matters…It is much more important to be oneself than anything else.'[32]

It must have been inspirational for young women to sit in that audience, listening to Virginia Woolf. She urged them to take their place side by side with men, for to her the mind was beyond sexual difference. 'It is fatal for anyone who writes to think of their sex.'[33] 'Perhaps to think, as I had been thinking these two days, of one sex as distinct from the other, is an effort. It interferes with the unity of the mind.'[34] She reminded them of Coleridge's view 'that a great mind is androgynous'[35] 'He meant, perhaps, that the androgynous mind is resonant and porous; that it transmits emotion without impediment; that it is naturally creative, incandescent and undivided.'[36] Shakespeare, too, she told them, 'was androgynous.'[37] In effect, she wanted them all to think like Rosalinds.

Virginia Woolf, though notoriously anti-Semitic, sustained an odd but successful marriage with Jewish writer Leonard Woolf. This made me wonder if there had been a Jewish Rosalind?

> "Yentl – you have the soul of a man."
> "So why was I born a woman?"
> "Even Heaven makes mistakes."

In the early 1960s, Isaac Bashevis Singer wrote *Yentl the Yeshiva Boy*, a fairy tale short story, in seven sections, faintly echoing Jaques' Seven Ages of Man speech. Yentl looks like a handsome young man. Hovering between the sexes, 'there was even a slight down on her upper lip,' she longs for an intellectual life. Her father teaches her the Torah, the Pentateuch, the Mishnah, the Gemara, and the Commentaries, in secret, behind locked doors and draped windows. After his death, Yentl cuts her hair and dresses as a boy called Anshel in order to study in the all-male Yeshiva where she is fulfilled, leading the life of the mind. Here she meets Avigdor, a masculine Orlando figure, and falls in love with him. Her new male identity gives Yentl freedom to speak her mind, and to dare. Intellect is what is important to Yentl but she also has the emotional strength to unmask herself eventually, with a flash of nudity, to Avigdor the man she secretly loves.

Unlike Rosalind, there's no happy ending for Yentl. But like Rosalind, she stage-manages her story. Yentl renounces her love for Avigdor, and after undertaking a potentially lesbian marriage to his girlfriend, Hadass, she arranges for Avigdor to marry Hadass, before she herself disappears. Avigdor collapses, only to appear at his wedding to Hadass as 'a figure of desolation.' He'd got what he wanted but seemed to be yearning for Yentl, or the boy Anshel with whom he'd enjoyed such friendship in the Yeshiva. The reader is left to imagine that Yentl will resume her male identity as Anshel and continue to study in some faraway place. Yentl's character and story are in a different key from the *joie de vivre* of Shakespeare's Rosalind, but her powerful drive, her feminist message and the complexity of Singer's narrative are resonant reminders. 'Truth itself is often concealed in such a way that the harder you look for it, the harder it is to find.' Soon after the wedding, Hadass became pregnant. 'The child was a boy and those assembled at the circumcision could scarcely believe their ears when they heard the father [Avigdor] name his son Anshel.'[38]

Rosalind is re-imagined again in the adventures of Villanelle, the transvestite, titian haired heroine of Jeanette Winterson's 1987 Venetian novel, *The Passion*. Villanelle recalls those pictures of Venetian courtesans in Rosalind's era. They wore 'braghessi' under their skirts which flew up to reveal the trousered legs beneath. Working in the Venice casino, Villanelle explains why 'I dressed as a boy because that's what the visitors liked to see. It was part of the game, trying to decide which sex was hidden behind tight breeches and extravagant face-paste.' It's 'the doom of paradox' that thrilled the onlookers.[39] In Winterson's novel, Venice a city of many masks, functions like the Forest of Arden. 'What you are one day will not constrain you on the next. You may explore yourself freely and, if you have wit …no one will stand in your way.'[40] Like Rosalind in drag, like Villanelle in disguise masked for *carnevale*, you can be whatever you want to be. And once you've found that freedom in being 'the other' you will never hand it back.

Through Villanelle's odyssey Winterson tries to untangle the mystery of love. 'Is this the explanation then when we meet someone we do not know and feel straight away that we have always known them?'[41] Perhaps as we've known ourselves? It's this same sense of identification that fires love at first sight between Rosalind and Orlando. As if they are 'family', as if they've always known each other, and can pick up a conversation that has been ongoing, in some mysterious way, since the beginning of their lives.

Rosalind's future life after the end of the play lies in government, ruling her father's dukedom with Orlando. Her daughters can be shape shifters in any era, professional women with a wide range of careers. Pat Barker set her 2007 novel, *Life Class*, at the Slade School of Fine Art before the First World War. Her heroine Elinor Brooke (whose surname may allude to Dorothea Brooke in George Eliot's *Middlemarch*) is a new Rosalind. 'She was trudging along thinking of Kit and what she was going to say to him, but then suddenly she straightened her back and she was Rosalind in the Forest of Arden, swaggering about in her doublet and hose. Really, she ought to stop going on like this. Any sane adult female ought to be able to walk through a wood without turning into Rosalind, but she never managed it. It was a sign of immaturity, this constant trying on of other identities. Fun, though.'

Elinor makes modern choices for the early twentieth century. She sleeps with her lover, Paul Tarrant, but she doesn't marry him. In 1599 Rosalind doesn't sleep with her lover but she does marry him. Different choices for different times. But both Rosalind and Elinor enjoy the trying on of various identities. It's an essential part of being young. In the wood, her Arden, 'She'd been Rosalind then, and it hadn't been an escape, she'd been happy.' Elinor 'did everything men did and generally better.' No surprise that men who desired her found it 'was more like being in love with a brilliant, egotistical boy than a girl.' Elinor is Ganymede and Ganymede is Rosalind and both sexes can contain these contradictions at the same time. Pat Barker gives us a modern Rosalind who straddles the last hundred years.[42]

In her spectacular film of *The Tempest* in 2010, Julie Taymor cast Helen Mirren as a female Prospera. Such bold transgender casting is in direct line of descent from cross-dressing Rosalind. Taymor revealed special rewards in seeing Prospero as a woman. She gave us something Shakespeare doesn't give us anywhere else: a strong, tender, tough, realistic, loving relationship between a mother and daughter. In her alchemist's robe of iridescent metallics, Prospera watches the wreck she's conjured up, and assures her daughter that by her magic she's done 'No harm!/I have done nothing but in care of thee,/Of thee, my dear one, thee my daughter.'[43] Felicity Jones's Miranda could be convincingly this Prospera's daughter, both physically and emotionally. Like a true daughter of Rosalind, she shows tenacity to eventually marry the man of her choice.

Love is love wherever you find it and in whatever pairings that weren't legally possible in Shakespeare's day. Rosalind continues to be a paradigm of love for our own times, as actor Alan Cumming affirms: 'I made my husband read a speech from *As You Like It* at our wedding. It's when Rosalind says to Celia: "O coz, coz, coz, my pretty little coz, that thou didst know how many fathom deep I am in love. But it cannot be sounded. My affection hath an unknown bottom, like the Bay of Portugal." I used to say it to him.'[44]

But there's still a journey to go on after the wedding's over and long after curtain down for Rosalind and Orlando, Shakespeare's contemporary couple. By the end of their play, we know marriage is only the beginning of the conversation and re-negotiation. It has been an education in love for both of them. 'But there's something about *As You Like It* you can't control,' says Michelle Terry. It has its wild and anarchic dimensions. Exploding the genres of tragedy and comedy – which he might have written as a Sondheim musical in the twenty-first century – makes this one of Shakespeare's most experimental plays. Once arrived in Arden, the liberating, discursive form lets plot atomise in favour of scenarios, duets and conversations. Playing Rosalind, Terry found, 'I just have to step on the stage, keep testing myself, keep running away to the woods, resisting being pinned down, labelled or reduced.' The message as well as the form is avant-garde, for as Terry notes, 'we all have masculine and feminine energies within us.' Over four centuries ago, Shakespeare was already probing and resisting a too literal binary explanation of human sexuality. 'What Rosalind is exploring is how to be, and that will never stop. You could talk about her forever. Keep asking the questions because we may never know the answers. The answer is: As You Like It.'[45]

WILLIAM SHAKESPEARE'S

AS YOU LIKE IT

PROGRAMME

FAMILY TREES

The de Boys family
Sir Rowland de Boys m. wife unknown, both deceased
|

1) Oliver   2) Jaques   3) Orlando

The ducal family
father and mother unknown
|

1) Duke Senior   2) Duke Frederick
m. wife unknown,   m. wife unknown
| |
Rosalind   Celia

CAST

On Oliver's estate

Oliver
Orlando
Adam

At the Palace

Duke Frederick
Celia
Rosalind
Le Beau, courtier
Charles, champion wrestler
Orlando
Touchstone, court fool
Lords and attendants

In the Forest of Arden

Duke Senior
Amiens, attendant lord
Jaques, attendant lord
Lords, pages, foresters

Rosalind as Ganymede
Celia as Aliena
Touchstone, court fool
Orlando
Adam
Corin, older shepherd
Silvius, young shepherd
Phebe, shepherdess
Audrey, goatherd
William, country fellow
Sir Oliver Mar-text, vicar
Oliver, Orlando's elder brother
Jaques, their middle brother

Wedding Celebrant

Hymen

TIME – any and all

As You Like It will always be a play for today. Prescient in Shakespeare's own times, it continues to spark discussion about what it means to be a woman, and what it means to be a man. Spring-boarding from a potential human tragedy, the play transforms into one of Shakespeare's most genial and sparkling comedies.

SYNOPSIS

Sir Rowland de Boys has died leaving his estate in a mess. He has three sons: Oliver, Jaques, and Orlando. The eldest, Oliver, has denied his youngest brother, Orlando, a fair share of the inheritance or even a decent education. The two fight viciously in the orchard. Oliver hires Charles, a professional wrestler, to put an end to Orlando who has challenged the champion to a public contest at Duke Frederick's court.

Two cousins come to watch the wrestling: Rosalind, daughter of Duke Senior, and Celia, daughter of Duke Frederick, who has deposed his elder brother, the legitimate duke, and banished him to the Forest of Arden. Orlando wins the wrestling match and locks glances with Rosalind who awards him a necklace from around her neck. They are both struck by love at first sight.

Having exiled the father, Duke Frederick turns on Rosalind and banishes her, too, on sentence of death. Celia refuses to be left behind. The two girls with the court entertainer, Touchstone, set off for Arden in search of Duke Senior, with Rosalind disguised as a boy called Ganymede, and Celia as his sister, Aliena.

Thwarted of his murderous intention to have his brother dispatched at the wrestling, Oliver plans to burn him to death but Adam, their family servant, warns Orlando in time, so that the young man and the old flee together to Arden.

In Arden, Duke Senior and his lords have set up a rural alternative to city life, with the sardonic philosopher, Jaques, a member of their entourage. As wit and commentator, he fulfills a similar function in Duke Senior's country court to that performed by Touchstone, back in Duke Frederick's urban court.

Rosalind/Ganymede and Celia/Aliena, together with Touchstone, now reach Arden where they hear a young shepherd, Silvius, proclaiming his passionate unrequited love for Phebe, a shepherdess, to Corin, an older shepherd. Rosalind understands Silvius's feeling as they reflect her own for Orlando. Rosalind and Celia employ Corin as agent to buy them a cottage, pasture, and a flock of sheep so they can live independently in Arden.

Orlando has also arrived in Arden, desperate about old Adam who is on the point of starvation. He attacks Duke Senior's party as they begin their forest meal and threatens them with violence. To his amazement, Duke Senior offers him only generosity, kindness and food, so Orlando's aggression immediately dissolves.

Back at the illegal court, Duke Frederick is furious about the loss of his daughter Celia, believed to have fled with

Rosalind. He seizes Oliver's estate and throws him out, on orders to find Orlando dead or alive.

Orlando's love for Rosalind turns him into a poet who nails his lyrics on Arden's tree trunks. Rosalind in her boy's disguise as Ganymede conceives an ingenious scheme to keep Orlando in her orbit. S/he promises to cure him of love if he'll take part in a play courtship. He must woo Ganymede who will stand in for the 'real' Rosalind.

Meanwhile Touchstone is in lust with Audrey, an earthy goatherd, and tries to get a second-rate country parson to marry them shabbily in the forest.

Still rejecting Silvius, Phebe falls madly in love with Ganymede at first sight, and in spite of his blatant rejection, she pursues him with an adoring love letter.

Ganymede/Rosalind invites Orlando to enter into an impromptu wedding in the forest, officiated reluctantly by Aliena/Celia.

Oliver arrives in Arden on his mission from Duke Frederick only to be saved from a hungry lioness by Orlando who turns aside from revenge to forgiveness. During the rescue Orlando is injured by the wild beast, and sends Oliver as substitute to explain to Ganymede why he's missed their date. When Oliver shows him the napkin streaked with Orlando's blood, Ganymede faints, and Oliver is the first person to suspect he might not be male.

Just as precipitately as Rosalind and Orlando had fallen in love at first sight, so Oliver falls in love with Celia, still disguised as Aliena. They plan to renounce court life, hand over their inheritance to Rosalind and Orlando, and remain in Arden, living the rural idyll as shepherds.

Ganymede recovers and becomes the impresario of events. S/he promises Orlando marriage with Rosalind, and Phebe and Silvius a satisfactory resolution. In front of Duke Senior, Ganymede unmasks himself as Rosalind to wed Orlando, Aliena unmasks to be Celia again and marry Oliver, and Phebe has to accept Silvius, at the same time as Touchstone marries Audrey.

The confusingly named Jaques de Boys, middle brother of Oliver and Orlando, brings news of how Duke Frederick set out to find his brother, Duke Senior, in Arden and put him to death. But on the journey he met an old religious man who converted him from his evil ways. Frederick has now renounced his throne, reinstated his banished brother and, in the company of Jaques the philosopher, has decided on a reformed life of spiritual retreat.

Duke Senior gifts his lands and 'potent dukedom' to his daughter Rosalind and new son-in-law Orlando who will return to court and rule humanely in his place.

Rosalind steps out of the play to address her own teasing Epilogue to the audience.

PROVERBS

from As You Like It

Phrases that have gone into the language or were already there, and still are...

laid on with a trowel

sweet are the uses of adversity

the weaker vessel

come hither

lack-lustre

how the world wags

all the world's a stage

seven ages

exits and entrances

second childishness

one man in his time plays many parts

neither rhyme nor reason

men have died from time to time, and worms have eaten them, but not for love

can one desire too much of a good thing?

a great reckoning in a little room

who ever loved that loved not at first sight?

men are April when they woo, December when they wed

stalking horse

the wise man knows himself to be a fool

Well, this is the Forest of Arden

When Charles Johnson revived *As You Like It* in his mangled version of 1723, the first production since Shakespeare's day, he called it *Love in a Forest*. Later in the century, in 1775, Walter Scott, as a child, was taken by his aunt Janet to see a restored *As You Like It*, where he may have seen the twenty-year-old Sarah Siddons play Rosalind.

What Arden meant to Shakespeare

For Shakespeare, the Forest of Arden in Warwickshire, once England's most extensive forest and still on the map today, was part of his native landscape as it was for any child who had been born and grown up in Stratford-upon-Avon. It was also an ancestral link with the maiden name of his mother, Mary Arden, born around 1535, at a time when 90% of the population worked on the land.

The man Rosalind loves has the surname de Boys which means literally 'of the woods'. As well as Rosalind and Orlando, Arden sheltered a variety of runaways, forced into its shade by court politics, dysfunctional families, or the harsh consequences of land enclosures. But its woods were also the backdrop for such traditional country pastimes as hunting, singing, dancing – and flirting.

Arden – earth, mind and body

Today when we think of Shakespeare's Forest of Arden we may imagine mistakenly the dense thickets of Grimm's fairy tales. But an Elizabethan audience knew its physical reality.

In Shakespeare's day, the contours of Arden looked like this: 'The Feldon lieth on this side Avon southward, a plain champagne country, and being rich in corn and green grass yieldeth a right goodly and pleasant prospect to them that look down upon it from an hill which they call Edgehill... Now let us enter into the woodland, which above the River Avon spreadeth itself northward much larger in compass than the Feldon, and so is for the most part thick set with woods, and yet not without pastures, cornfields, and sundry mines of iron.' (William Camden's *Britannia*, 1586.)

Arden was a place of contrasts: arable fields and open pastures where shepherds could watch their sheep grazing, and leafy glades studded with small villages and 'gospel oaks' to mark the way for country folk and travellers. Here under the greenwood tree when 'wedlock would be nibbling,' rural trysts could progress to lawful marriages, performed by shambling local vicars like Sir Oliver Mar-text. Shakespeare's Arden has the precision of a rambler's walk with an ordnance survey map in hand. How would you find Rosalind's sheepcote? Shakespeare provides exact directions,

West of this place, down in the neighbour bottom.
The rank of osiers by the murmuring stream
Left on your right hand brings you to the place.

At the same time, Arden also has the unspecified suggestiveness of Peter Pan's route to the Neverland, 'straight on till morning!' It can be any place, no place, all places.

Shakespeare's English Arden has roots in his immediate source for *As You Like It*, Thomas Lodge's story, *Rosalynde*, set in the French Ardennes. But the resonance of Arden transcends borders and whispers to us of classical Arcadia, Biblical Eden, Robin Hood's Sherwood Forest, or today's Cotswold dream of second homers from Birmingham and London. None of these – or all of these? For whoever heard of silvery olive trees in an English woodland? In Arden, indigenous deer and conies live alongside exotic snakes, lionesses and palm trees. The boundaries between geography and imagination are deliberately porous. It's a locus of the heart spun out of reality and fantasy.

Arden is a place of physical scenery, but it's also a spiritual and psychological location that couldn't be more different from Duke Frederick's court from which Duke Senior has been ejected, and Rosalind and Celia have fled. Outside the reach of the law, its overhanging canopy of boughs shelter new ways of justice. The virtues of forest life are constantly compared with Duke Frederick's illegitimate regime at court.

> *Duke Senior*   Now, my co-mates, and brothers in exile,
> Hath not old custom made this life more sweet
> Than that of painted pomp? Are not these woods
> More free from peril than the envious court?

However, Arden is no fairy tale for soft city men who now have to live out in the open air. Duke Senior and his newly democratic 'co-mates' are not adapted to 'the icy fang/And churlish chiding of the winter's wind' which 'bites and blows' upon their bodies.

To feed these bodies they have to hunt for deer, 'native burghers of this desert city.' Every habitat has both its inborn and incoming occupants. In their turn, the displaced courtiers invade the pastures of these 'poor dappled fools.'

Jaques accuses Duke Senior 'you do more usurp/Than doth your brother that hath banished you.' It's the same accusation of colonialism that will be levelled at Prospero for hijacking Caliban's island in *The Tempest*. Like Prospero, Duke Senior is no country-dabbling weekender. He feels the reality of Arden almost as much as shepherd Corin who leads a tough agricultural life, battling the season's cycle of snowdrifts, mud, rain and summer heat.

Arden is not Eden, at least physically, but it is a place where Corin's admirable principles can flourish. 'Sir, I am a true labourer; I earn that I eat, get that I wear, owe no man hate, envy no man's happiness, glad of other men's good, content with my harm; and the greatest of my pride is to see my ewes graze and my lambs suck.' But as Corin points out to Touchstone, forest lore couldn't be more different from court etiquette. 'Those that are good manners at the court are as ridiculous in the country as the behaviour of the country is most mockable at the court.'

Cross paths in the forest

As Dante knew, a life crisis can catapult you into the forest:

> In midway of the journey of our life,
> I found myself within a darkling wood,
> Because the rightful way had been lost.
> And ah! how hard a thing it is to say
> What this wood was, savage and rough, and strong.
>
> (Dante's *Divine Comedy*, transl. W.M. Rossetti.)

When Rosalind flees Duke Frederick's death sentence she finds two extremes under the forest roof of Arden: risk and refuge. Its bare branches or leafy groves are as contrary as winter and summer. The clown Touchstone who goes with Rosalind and Celia into the forest juggles nimbly with the contradictions of Arden. 'Truly, shepherd, in respect of itself, it is a good life; but in respect that it is a shepherd's life, it is nought. In respect that it is solitary, I like it very well; but in respect that it is private, it is a very vile life. Now in respect it is in the fields, it pleaseth me well; but in respect it is not in the court, it is tedious. As it is a spare life, look you, it fits my humour well; but as there is no more plenty in it, it goes much against my stomach.'

Pastoral and anti-pastoral

If forests were real, with both dense thickets and long sunlit clearings, they were also part of a literary fashion for pastoral themes, invented by Theocritus and Virgil, and revived during the Renaissance craze for classical literature. Edmund Spenser, Philip Sidney and Walter Raleigh all wrote popular pastoral works ahead of *As You Like It*. In 1579, Spenser's *Shepheardes Calender* even featured a heroine called Rosalind. Shakespeare incorporated significant pastoral scenes into his earlier play, *Two Gentlemen of Verona*, and into a later play, *The Winter's Tale*. Pastoral was an urban form for sophisticated city writers. They cunningly subverted the pastoral with the political. The appeal of pastoral for both writers and readers was that it allowed an author to address risqué or forbidden themes through the lives and loves of shepherds and shepherdesses.

Because the roots of pastoral lay far back in classical times, it linked subliminally with feelings about loss, nostalgia for a Golden World or Arcadia that spectators might glimpse between its glancing shadows. As the pastoral format lay, apparently safely, in the past, it could infuse the present, conveying serious social comment beneath a bucolic exterior. Pastoral settings provided a convenient code through which writers could project moral and political criticism of contemporary society. Arden's very existence is an implicit critique of the corrupt court that Rosalind and Orlando have left behind. It was an appraisal that the Elizabethan audience would have had no difficulty in de-coding.

In a further provocation, Arden offers another view on country life. This is the anti-pastoral, anti-social, misanthropic, pessimistic, death-infected world view held by Jaques, Monsieur Melancholy. His cynical and patriarchal Seven Ages of Man speech is wittily parodied by Touchstone. 'And so, from hour to hour, we ripe and ripe,/And then, from hour to hour, we rot and rot.'

The audience in Arden

Into the playhouse we go, into that Wooden O of the great Globe itself, bursting with potential for Shakespeare and the Lord Chamberlain's Men in 1599. In theatre we look not only for entertainment and time out, but also for uplift, insights, wisdom and clarification about how to live. In the forest of Arden, as in the playhouse, questions about how to love and how to live are more intense than in the workaday world outside.

When Rosalind enters Arden as Ganymede, she matches our own experience of watching the play. Like the fluidity of Rosalind's gender, the forest is a multiple location for us, in the mind and in the woods, real and unreal, literal and metaphorical, tangible and visionary, conscious and subconscious, replenishing and threatening, positive and negative all at the same time. Not either/or – but embracing and inclusive. Above all, Arden is a place for psyches to be restored. The forest with its lofty branches above, and its deep roots beneath the earth, is an emblem of the unconscious.

Entering Arden takes us with Rosalind and Orlando into the long Interval of questing possibilities between life in a corrupt society at the beginning of the play, and its moral renewal at the end. By keeping us in Arden for most of the play, Shakespeare takes us, not into a convoluted comic plot, but into the forest greenwood stippled with grassy dells where we can join Rosalind's absorbing discussion about human love. The conversational structure of *As You Like It* is expansive and avant-garde. Sauntering through four Acts in Arden gives Rosalind and us space to find our voices, our true selves, our freedom and autonomy. Arden is a safe place to explore both the dangerous and thrilling nature of grown-up sexuality. It's the place where we become aware.

Becoming a tree

Shakespeare's productions had none of the elaborate forest scenery so beloved of Victorian shows. The Elizabethan stage was bare. Rosalind simply tells us that this is the Forest of Arden and that's enough. Actors like Maggie Smith perform their 'due diligence' to evoke vast forests or one particular tree. 'During *As You Like It*, [at Stratford, Ontario, 1997-8] when she was off stage, Maggie used to walk through the park because Robin [Phillips, director] had suggested that it would be a good idea to remain in contact with the trees. People would sometimes stop and stare when they came across her in costume, apparently nowhere near the theatre. But she always was. And she walked, every Rosalind day, through the trees.'

Combining fieldwork with her inventive genius, Maggie Smith brought the trees into her performance as she rehearsed Rosalind's zany *tour de force* catalogue of torments awaiting Orlando after marriage. Smith was escalating into Rosalind's crescendo of taunts that a woman may turn jealous, clamorous, newfangled and giddy, worse than a Barbary cock-pigeon, a parrot, an ape or a monkey, when as an exercise to unlock the serious intention behind the speech, the director suggested to Maggie 'that she should first of all make it as funny as possible. She improvised an entire menagerie and monkey-house, squawking and swinging around the tree that was the single feature of the set [but didn't exist in the rehearsal room]. The entire company was laid out on the floor with laughter and Robin recalled how remarkable had been the evocation of the tree where no tree stood: "Everybody stopped and looked at an empty rehearsal room with a blank wall. They stared at a space where she had just been halfway up a tree and swinging in its branches. To this day, I cannot tell you how she did it, how she swung from those branches without leaving the ground. I don't understand it, but she did it. We all saw her in the tree. I called a coffee break and people dispersed in stunned silence."' (Michael Coveney's *Maggie Smith: A Biography*, 2015.)

Was Shakespeare in Arden, too?

According to time-honoured and possibly reliable tradition, Shakespeare himself played the role of faithful old Adam in *As You Like It*. In 1779 Edward Capell, the Shakespearean editor and scholar, reported a story that had been circulating around Stratford for many years. A very elderly man, perhaps a relation of Shakespeare's, remembered seeing him brought on stage on another actor's back. This was probably Adam supported by his young master Orlando when both were destitute outcasts in Arden. Coleridge is said to have believed the legend. 'Think of the scene between him and Orlando; and think again, that the actor of that part had to carry the author of that play in his arms! Think of having had Shakespeare in one's arms!'

But the play's early audiences may have enjoyed yet another in-joke after the character of old Adam vanished from the scene. Did Shakespeare slip into his native Warwickshire accent, and step out on stage again? How the crowd would have loved to see him play his own namesake William, the bashful country lover of raucous Audrey, seen off by Touchstone, the city wide-boy.

The forest will always be there

Arden is a place to grow up, a place of disturbing otherness, but it's also a place of eternal innocence, somewhere we can all have tucked away at the back of our minds. The forest provides dreamtime, a place of transition like adolescence, that rehearsal room before growing up. As Sondheim observed in his 1986 musical *Into the Woods*, you change, you're different in the woods. Here we understand things we've never understood before, and this ultimately frees us to leave the forest. However, Arden always remains in our imagination. It's the Wild Wood in Kenneth Grahame's *Wind in the Willows*, it's Alice's Wonderland, Peter Pan's Neverland. In our contemporary urban worlds, forests are more allusive and meaningful than ever, as escape routes and potent symbols. A.A. Milne described the forest as the place where we can 'have magic adventures, more wonderful than any I have told you about; but now, when we wake up in the morning, they are gone before we can catch hold of them… But, of course, it isn't really Good-bye, because the Forest will always be there.'

ACKNOWLEDGEMENTS

Rosalind is a consummate actress so it's only appropriate that my first thanks go to the great actors who have so generously talked to me about their experiences of playing Rosalind from the 1960s to the present day, both female and male, established stars and rising young names. They are Janet Suzman, Ronald Pickup, Juliet Stevenson, Juliet Rylance, Sally Scott, Adrian Lester and Michelle Terry. From an award winning director's perspective, Blanche McIntyre also gave me an invaluable interview.

Friends, scholars and thespians who discussed Rosalind with me, pointed me towards early theatrical performances, or to unknown images, or to examples of Rosalind's daughters in the modern world, include Kate Bassett, Valerie Fehlbaum, Charlotte Gray, Lavinia Greacen, Jean Hewison, Eva Hoffman, Rosalind Kaye, Linda Matlin, Pam Morris, Susannah Pearse, Virginia Surtees and John Wallace. From the sphere of my previous biographies, Pre-Raphaelite experts and friends on both sides of the Atlantic such as Judith Bronkhurst, Dennis Lanigan, Tim McGee, Len Roberts and Francis Sharp have offered vital insights and sleuthing about works of art inspired by Shakespeare.

Three libraries in particular have been key to my reading about Rosalind, and their librarians unfailingly helpful. These are The London Library, the British Library and the exceptional public library in the Barbican Centre. I am also very grateful to The Institute of Psychoanalysis whose unique programme, 'The Stuff of Dreams' in 2014/15 chaired by Andrea Sabbadini, gave me another perspective. Their inspired season combined showings of films of Shakespeare's plays with probing discussions between actors, critics, academics and psychoanalysts.

I am particularly indebted to my scrupulous first readers of *Rosalind*, the Shakespearean scholar, Professor Russ McDonald, and my son, the writer Adam Thirlwell. My daughter Zoë Thirlwell read the Interval chapter on Elizabeth I with her historian's eye.

This book could not have been written without the regular once a month, one-to-one writers' meetings I enjoy with my oldest friend, Patricia Potts (Tosh) who has consistently encouraged and challenged me. Her expertise and intellectual rigour, in different fields from my own, made me try to hone every sentence!

At Oberon I've been blessed with the most enthusiastic, supportive and meticulous editor in George Spender. His colleague James Illman provided the gorgeously decorative and allusive jacket design for which I'm hugely grateful. My thanks go to the Biographers' Club without whose annual dinner I would never have met James Hogan and Charles Glanville who run Oberon Books and liked my idea of a biography of Rosalind from the start. Thanks as ever go to my wise literary agent, Felicity Bryan, and her loyal assistant, Michele Topham, in Oxford.

My lifelong debts are to Shakespeare himself who gave me such a rich and creative subject in Rosalind, and to my two unforgettable teachers of his works, Laura Pettoello and Hugo Dyson.

SOURCES AND NOTES

All quotations from *As You Like It* are from Arden 3 edited by
Juliet Dusinberre (London: Bloomsbury, 2006)

PROLOGUE
Enter Rosalind

1   *AYLI*, 2.5.1-5.

2   *Dorothy Jordan as Rosalind in As You Like It* by Sir William Beechey, oil on canvas, 762 x 634 mm, Private Collection, shown in 'The First Actresses' exhibition at the National Portrait Gallery, London, October 2011 – January 2012.

3   *Diary and Letters of Madame d'Arblay*, (Fanny Burney) edited by her niece Charlotte Barrett, 7 vol. (London: Henry Colburn, 1842-6), 5, p. 40, Wednesday, July 29th, [1789].

4   *The Autobiography of Leigh Hunt: With Reminiscences of Friends and Contemporaries*, 3 vol. (London: Smith, Elder & Co., 1850), 1, pp. 148-9.

5   James Boaden, *The Life of Mrs Jordan*, 2 vol. (London: Edward Bull, 1831) 1, p. 46.

6   W. Fraser Rae, *Sheridan: a Biography*, 2 vol. (London: R. Bentley & Son, 1896), 2, pp. 12-13.

7   Weds 16th January 1839, www.queenvictoriasjournals.org

8   W. Fraser Rae, *Sheridan: a Biography*, 2 vol. (London: R. Bentley & Son, 1896) 2, pp. 12-13.

9   Adrian Lester talking to Mark Lawson on 'Front Row', Radio 4, 27 August 2012.

10 Interview by e-mail with Adrian Lester, 9 September 2015.

11 Jonathan Bate and Russell Jackson, eds, *Shakespeare: An Illustrated Stage History* (Oxford: Oxford University Press, 1996), p. 6.

12 Open University video to accompany A 210 *Approaching Literature*, 1995.

13 *AYLI*, 3.2.146-8.

14 His sources are *Standards of Living in the Later Middle Ages* by Christopher Dyer, (Cambridge: Cambridge University Press, revised ed. 1989) p. 316, and *The Tudor Tailor* by Ninya Mikhaila and Jane Malcolm-Davies, (London: Batsford, 2006) p. 9 – whose figures are for sixteenth-century Londoners. Interestingly, people were taller in Saxon times, and got shorter than the Tudors in Georgian and Victorian times, only becoming taller again towards the end of the twentieth century, according to the chart in *The Tudor Tailor*.

15 *AYLI*, 3.2.262.

16 Ibid., 3.5.119–124.

17 Ibid., 4.3.50. in the letter Phebe sends to Ganymede via Silvius.

18 Ibid., 3.5.47-8.

19 This suggestion from Lois Potter, *The Life of William Shakespeare: A Critical Biography* (Oxford: Wiley-Blackwell, 2012), p. 235.

20 Published in *The Twelve-Pound Look and other plays* by J.M. Barrie, (London: Hodder and Stoughton, 1921). Broadcast on BBC Radio 4, 3 June 2002.

21 Information from Eileen Page who took the part of Beatrice Page at a rehearsed reading of *Rosalind* at the Park Theatre, London, 11 October 2015. Eileen was taught at RADA by Irene Vanbrugh who first played Barrie's role and remembered Ellen Terry.

ACT ONE
In the Green Room – Rosalind's Ancestors

1 Ovid's *Metamorphoses*, this ed. (Oxford: Oxford University Press, 1990), trans. A.D. Melville, Book IX, final section.

2 Ibid., Book X.

3 *AYLI*, 2.4.1.

4 Ibid., 2.4.56-7.

5 Ibid., 3.2. 229-30. In the next scene, 3.3.8-9, Jaques also mentions Jove, commenting in an aside on Touchstone's reference to 'the most capricious poet, honest Ovid': 'O knowledge ill-inhabited, worse than Jove in a thatched house!'

6 All references to *The Tale of Gamelyn* are from the online edition of Chaucer's Works, Vol. V., ed. W.W. Skeat, and from *The Tale of Gamelyn*, eds. Stephen Knight and Thomas H. Ohlgren, available online from Robbins Library Digital Projects, University of Rochester, originally published in *Robin Hood and Other Outlaw Tales* (Kalamazoo, Michigan: Medieval Institute Publications, 1997).

7 All references to *Rosalynde* by Thomas Lodge, first printed 1590, this 2nd edition ed. W.W. Greg, (London: Humphrey Milford, O.U.P. 1931) 1ˢᵗ ed. 1907. There's a 1592 copy of *Rosalynde* in the British Library and two in the Bodleian Library, Oxford.

8 Ibid., pp. 7-8.

9 Ibid., pp. 13, 16-17.

10 Ibid., p. 19.

11 Ibid., p. 21.

12 Ibid., pp. 21-2.

13 Ibid., pp. 25-6.

14 Ibid., pp. 26-7.

15 Ibid., p. 48.

16 Ibid., pp. 66-73.

17 Ibid., pp. 77-85.

18 Ibid., pp. 85-92.

19 *AYLI*, 4.1.40-4.

20 Ibid., 5.4.26-7.

1 *Appreciations* by Walter Pater, first published 1889, this ed. (London: Macmillan, 1924), p. 169.

2 Ibid., p. 170.

3 *Love's Labour's Lost*, 2.1.114-17.

4 Ibid., 2.1.117-120.

5 Ibid., 5.2.380-4.

6 Ibid., 4.3.318–19, 324-7.

7 Ibid., 4.3.11-12.

8 Ibid., 3.1.184.

9 Ibid., 5.2.59-60.

10 Ibid., 5.2.260-61.

11 Ibid., 5.2.396-9, 412–13.

12 Ibid., 5.2.835-42.

13 Ibid., 5.2.862-6.

14 Ibid., 5.2.919.

15 *Romeo and Juliet*, 1.1.215-22.

16 Ibid., 2.1.17-20.

17 *Two Gentlemen of Verona*, 2.4.189-92.

18 Remarks by Simon Godwin, director of the RSC's 2014 production of *Two Gentlemen of Verona*, from his interview with Carol Chillington Rutter on the RSC App to accompany the play.

19 *Two Gents*, 2.7.49–56.

20 Ibid., 2.7.75-8.

21 Ibid., 4.4.88, 95-8.

22 Ibid., 4.4.130-5.

23 Ibid., 4.4.156-162, 171-7.

24 Simon Godwin, director of the RSC's 2014 production of *Two Gentlemen of Verona*, from his interview with Carol Chillington Rutter on the RSC App to accompany the play.

25 *Two Gents*, 4.4.182-4.

26 Holman Hunt, *Valentine rescuing Silvia from Proteus*, 1850-51, oil on canvas, Birmingham Museums and Art Gallery, Catalogue entry 71 in *William Holman Hunt: A Catalogue Raisonné* by Judith Bronkhurst (London and New Haven: Yale University Press for the Paul Mellon Centre, 2006).

27 Simon Godwin, director of the RSC production of *Two Gentlemen of Verona* 2014/15.

28 *The Merchant of Venice*, 3.2.149-174.

29 Helena Normanton was the first woman to practise at the English Bar. Eventually, in 1948, she became the first woman to prosecute in a murder trial, and together with Rose Heilbron,

was the first of two women appointed King's Counsel in 1949. From biographies of Ivy Williams and Helena Normanton posted by Kitty Piper, 27 June 2014 and 15 October 2014 on the *First100 Years* website, launched by Obelisk with the Law Society. Piper adds, 'as one scholar puts it, Normanton should be to women lawyers what Neil Armstrong is to astronauts.'

30 *Merchant*, 4.1.193-8.

31 Ibid., 4.1.253-8.

32 Ibid., 4.1.278-83.

33 Ibid., 4.1.302-308.

34 Ibid., 4.1.318, 320-328.

35 Ibid., 4.1.342-352.

36 Herbert Farjeon, *The Shakespearean Scene: Dramatic Criticisms* (London: Hutchinson, 1949), pp. 50-1.

37 John Peter's review in *The Sunday Times*, 4 June 1989.

ACT TWO SCENE TWO
Younger Sisters

1 *Liverpool Echo*, 13 June 2014, article on Jodie McNee by Catherine Jones.

2 *Twelfth Night*, 2.2.26-31.

3 Ibid., 2.4.23-28.

4 Ibid., 2.4.38-9.

5 Peter Hall, from his Foreword to *Twelfth Night*, (London: The Folio Society, 1960.)

6 *Twelfth Night*, 2.4.111-119.

7 William Hazlitt, *Characters of Shakespear's Plays*, 1817, 1818, this ed. (London: J.M. Dent & Sons Ltd., 1906), p. 199.

8 *Twelfth Night*, 1.4.31-4.

9 W.H. Auden, *The Dyer's Hand and other essays*, (London: Faber and Faber, 1963), p. 521.

10 *Twelfth Night*, 2.4.94-6.

11 *AYLI*, 3.5.42-4, 73-5.

12 *Twelfth Night*, 2.2.24-5, 32-8.

13 Ibid., 3.1.159-162.

14 William Hazlitt, *Characters of Shakespear's Plays*, 1817, 1818, this ed. (London: J.M. Dent & Sons Ltd., 1906), p. 3.

15 G.B. Shaw's *Cymbeline Refinished*, 1936, is a re-working of *Cymbeline* Act V, available on Project Gutenberg Australia.

16 *Cymbeline*, 2.2.14-16.

17 Ibid., 2.2.37-42.

18 Ibid., 2.4.171-5.

19 Ibid., 3.4.41-5.

20 *AYLI*, 1.3.58, 60.

21 *Cymbeline*, 3.4.168-9.

22 Ibid., 3.6.1-4.

23 Ibid., 3.6.14-17.

24 William Hazlitt, *Characters of Shakespear's Plays*, 1817, 1818, this ed. (London: J.M. Dent & Sons Ltd., 1906), p. 6.

25 *Cymbeline*, 4.2.258-63.

26 From Sir Ian McKellen's website homepage: *Acting Shakespeare 1947-86*.

27 *Cymbeline*, 5.5.261-4.

28 Harriet Walter on Imogen from *Players of Shakespeare* 3, eds. Russell Jackson and Robert Smallwood, (Cambridge: Cambridge University Press, 1993).

29 *Much Ado About Nothing*, 4.1.302, 305, 316.

30 Ibid., 2.1.16-17.

31 Ibid., 2.1.48-52.

32 Ibid., 1.1.225-28.

33 Ibid., 1.1.96-7.

34 Ibid., 2.1.230-31.

35 Ibid., 2.3.18-21.

36 Ibid., 2.3.212, 214-16, 239, 248-9.

37 Ibid., 3.1.107-111.

38 Ibid., 5.2. 35-6, 39-40.

39 Ibid., 4.1.266, 282-8.

40 Meera Syal in the programme for the RSC production of *Much Ado*, 2012.

41 *Much Ado*, 4.1.311, 316, 321-3.

42 Ibid., 4.2.327-9.

43 Ibid., 5.2.33-4.

44 Ibid., 5.4.74.

45 Ibid., 5.4.77.

46 *The Way of the World* by William Congreve, 1700, this ed. New Mermaids, ed. Brian Gibbons (London: Ernest Benn, 1971) IV.i.165-171; IV.i.278-9; V.i.536-540.

47 Ian Shuttleworth, *Financial Times*, 17 October 2014.

48 Susannah Clapp, *The Observer*, 24 May 2015.

1   *AYLI*, 1.3.111-122.

2   I am grateful to Professor Russ McDonald for pointing this out. See *The Bedford Shakespeare* ed. Russ McDonald and Lena Cowen Orlin (Boston, New York: Bedford/St. Martin's, 2015), p. 409.

3   Herbert Farjeon, *The Shakespearean Scene: Dramatic Criticisms* (London: Hutchinson, 1949), p. 190. Elizabeth is supposed to have said this to William Lambarde on the occasion of the rebellion by the Earl of Essex in 1601, and see TLS review of *Richard II* at Shakespeare's Globe by Lucy Munro, 31 July 2015, p. 17.

4   *AYLI*, 1.3.56-60.

5   Rebecca Hall on Rosalind in *Shakespeare on Stage* ed. Julian Curry (London: Nick Hern Books, 2010).

6   *AYLI*, 1.3.74-9.

7   Interview with Sally Scott, 10 October 2014.

8   *AYLI*, 1.3.108-111.

9   Deuteronomy, 22.5. in the Authorised Version of the Bible, 1611. The Geneva Bible version which Shakespeare may have known is slightly different: 'The woman shalt not wear that which pertaineth unto a man, neither shall a man put on a woman's raiment, for all that do so, are abomination unto the LORD thy God.'

10 John Rainolds in *Th'Overthrow of Stage Playes,* published by the puritan press of Richard Schilders, Middelburg, the Netherlands, 1599. I have modernised the spelling in the quotation.

11 During the visit of Elizabeth I to Oxford, at Christ Church, in a play by Richard Edwards. ODNB article on John Rainolds by Mordechai Feingold.

12 Jeanette Winterson, *The Passion* (London: Bloomsbury, 1987), this ed. Penguin 1988, p. 72.

13 Title page of Lyly's *Galathea* as printed 1592.

14 John Lyly, *Galatea*, ed. Leah Scragg (Manchester: Manchester University Press, 2012), I.2.95-8.

15 Ibid. 2.1.1-5.

16 Ibid. 2.5.1-4.

17 Female wrestling entered the Olympics in 2004 but is scheduled to disappear again from 2020.

18 *AYLI*, 2.4.90-92.

19 Ovid, *Ars Amatoria, The Art of Love*, Book 1, II, 89-92.

20 Michael Billington, *The Modern Actor* (London: Hamish Hamilton, 1973), pp. 219-222.

21 Interview with Janet Suzman, London, 1 October 2014.

22 *AYLI*, 3.2.85-8.

23 Ibid., 3.2.98-109.

24 Ibid., 3.2.132-4.

25 Ibid., 3.2.191-7.

26 Ibid., 3.2.212-17.

27 Russ McDonald, *The Bedford Companion to Shakespeare: An Introduction with Documents* 2nd ed. (Boston and New York: Bedford/St. Martin's, 2001), p. 299.

28 *Hero and Leander* from *The Works of Christopher Marlowe* ed. C.F. Tucker Brooke, (Oxford: Oxford University Press, 1966), 83-84, 147-48.

29 *The Tragedy of Dido, Queen of Carthage*, 1.1.1-2, 28, 42-5, as edition above.

30 For lists of boy actors about the right age to have played Rosalind in 1599, e.g. Alexander Cooke, Samuel Gilburne or even Nathan Field, see E.K. Chambers, *The Elizabethan Stage*, 4 vols, first published 1923, this ed. (Oxford: The Clarendon Press, 1951), II, pp. 316-7, and David Kathman, 'How old were Shakespeare's Boy Actors?' in Peter Holland, ed., *Shakespeare survey: an annual survey of Shakespearian study & production* (Cambridge: Cambridge University Press, 2005), vol. 58, pp. 220-246.

31 *The Taming of the Shrew*, Induction. 1. 130-31.

32 William Prynne, *Histriomastrix: The Player's Scourge, or Actor's Tragedy*, c. 1631-3, pp. 211-12, quoted by Stephen Orgel, *Impersonations: The Performance of gender in Shakespeare's England* (Cambridge: Cambridge University Press, 1996), p. 30.

33 Interview with Juliet Rylance, 11 August 2010.

34 For a theoretical discussion of gender as performance see Judith Butler, *Gender Trouble: Feminism and the Subversion of Identity* (Routledge: New York and London, 1990). 'In what senses, then, is gender an act? As in other ritual social dramas, the action of gender requires a performance that is *repeated*...Genders can be neither true nor false, neither real nor apparent, neither original nor derived. As credible bearers of those attributes, however, genders can also be rendered thoroughly and radically *incredible*.' pp. 140-1.

35 *AYLI*, 3.2.346-52.

36 Ibid., 2.4.31-40.

37 Ibid., 3.2.359-69.

38 Rebecca Hall on Rosalind in *Shakespeare on Stage* ed. Julian Curry (London: Nick Hern Books, 2010).

39 *AYLI*, 3.2.390-400, 403.

40 *Hamlet*, 2.2.420–24.

41 Over 100 years later in Bach's day, 'boys were still trebles at 16 or 17' says Stephen Cleobury, Choirmaster of King's College, Cambridge, *Observer*, 21 December 2014.

42 Portrait miniature of *A Young Man Leaning Against a Tree Amongst Roses* by Nicholas Hilliard, c. 1585-95, Victoria and Albert Museum. No: P.163-1910.

43 At the Donmar Warehouse London in 2013 and 2014, and in New York off-Broadway in 2015.

44 *AYLI*, 3.5.46-61.

45 Interview with Janet Suzman, 1 October 2014.

46 Brian Sewell, *Outsider: always almost: never quite – An Autobiography* (London: Quartet, 2011), p. 14.

47   Rebecca Hall on Rosalind in *Shakespeare on Stage* ed. Julian Curry (London: Nick Hern Books, 2010)

48   *Sunday Telegraph* 8 October 1967, quoted in *As You Like It from 1600 to the Present: Critical Essays*, ed. Edward Tomarken (Routledge, London and New York, 1997), p. 47.

49   Interview with Ronald Pickup, 16 October 2015.

50   'A princess and a saucy lackey' by Matt Trueman, the *Guardian*, 13 July 2015. Ronald Pickup and Michelle Terry who played Rosalind 40 years apart, explain how they approached the role.

51   Jonathan Bate and Russell Jackson (eds), *Shakespeare: An Illustrated Stage History* (Oxford: Oxford University Press, 1996), p. 6.

52   Interview by e-mail with Adrian Lester, 9 September 2015.

53   Michael Billington, *Guardian Weekly*, 23 June 1973, quoted by Penny Gay, *As She Likes It: Shakespeare's Unruly Women* (London and New York: Routledge, 1994), p. 67.

54   Gregory Doran on Shakespeare's Comedies interviewed by Bettany Hughes for 'The Ideas that Make us' broadcast on BBC Radio 4, 25 August 2014.

55   *Shakespeare's Montaigne: The Florio Translation of the Essays, A Selection* eds. Stephen Greenblatt and Peter G. Platt (New York: The New York Review of Books, 2014), 'Upon some verses of *Virgil*', p. 278.

56   'The Lives of Others' in *Royal Society of Literature Review*, Spring 2015, p. 9, Harriet Walter and Hilary Mantel in discussion with Timberlake Wertenbaker.

57   *AYLI*, 4.1.35-47.

58   Shakespeare's Sonnet 20.

59   Shakespeare's Sonnet 116.

60   *AYLI*, 4.1.84-99.

61   Camille Paglia, *Sexual Personae: Art and Decadence from Nefertiti to Emily Dickinson* (New Haven: Yale University Press, 1990).

62   John Lyly, *Galatea*, ed. Leah Scragg (Manchester: Manchester University Press, 2012), 3.2.15-16.

63   *AYLI*, 4.1.102-131.

64   Marriage service words from the Book of Common Prayer, 1552.

65   *AYLI*, 4.1.136-39.

66   Discussion between Pippa Nixon (Rosalind), Maria Aberg (Director), Alex Waldmann (Orlando) about the RSC production of AYLI in 2013, published on the RSC website 25 September 2013 and uploaded to YouTube.

67   *AYLI*, 4.1.139--146.

68   Ibid., 4.1.149-162.

69   Ibid., 4.1.165-186.

70   Ibid., 5.1.47-57.

71   Ibid., 5.2.31-38.

72   Ibid., 5.2.57-66.

73   Ibid., 5.2.69--71.

74 Ibid., 5.2.79-104.

75 Ibid., 5.2.106-116.

76 Ibid., 5.4.68-81, 95-101.

77 Ibid., 5.4.114-122.

78 Jan Kott, *The Gender of Rosalind* [reprinted from *New Theatre Quarterly*] (Evanston, Illinois: Northwestern University Press, 1992).

79 Lithographic portrait inscribed in the block: Ellen Tree October 21, 1836. Published 1838. Information from Paul Meredith, House Manager at Smallhythe Place, Kent, National Trust.

80 ODNB article on Ellen Tree by M. Glen Wilson.

81 *Shakespeare in America* ed. James Shapiro (The Library of America, 2014), pp. 56-7.

82 John Coleman, *Fifty Years of an Actor's Life* 2 vols. (London: Hutchinson, 1904), I, p. 306.

83 Ibid., II, p. 363.

84 Ibid., I, p. 306.

INTERVAL
Gloriana

1 *Elizabeth I, Collected Works*, eds. Leah S. Marcus, Janel Mueller, and Mary Beth Rose (Chicago and London: The University of Chicago Press, 2000), p. 97, Queen Elizabeth's speech to a joint delegation of Lords and Commons, November 5, 1566.

2 J.E. Neale, *Queen Elizabeth* (London: Cape, 1934), p. 215.

3 *The Pelican Portrait* by Nicholas Hilliard or his workshop, c. 1575, Walker Art Gallery, Liverpool.

4 *The Phoenix Portrait* by Nicholas Hilliard or his workshop, c. 1575, National Portrait Gallery, London.

5 Judi Dench played Titania in 2010 at the Rose Theatre, Kingston, dressed as Elizabeth I.

6 Queen Elizabeth I ('The Ditchley portrait') by Marcus Gheeraerts the Younger, c. 1592, National Portrait Gallery London, 2561.

7 Queen Elizabeth I by Nicholas Hilliard, 1572, National Portrait Gallery London, 108.

8 Elizabeth Jenkins, *Elizabeth and Leicester* (London: Victor Gollancz, 1961), p. 137.

9 The Holinshed Texts (1587, vol. 6, p. 1158) The Holinshed Project, Oxford University, available online.

10 *Elizabeth I, Collected Works*, p. 170, Queen Elizabeth's speech at the close of the Parliamentary Session, March 15, 1576.

11 Ibid., p. 188, Queen Elizabeth's first reply to the Parliamentary Petitions urging the execution of Mary, Queen of Scots, November 12, 1586.

12 Ibid., p. 193, Queen Elizabeth's first reply to the Parliamentary Petitions urging the execution of Mary, Queen of Scots, November 12, 1586.

13 Ibid., p.182, Queen Elizabeth's speech at the closing of Parliament, March 29, 1585.

14 Elizabeth Jenkins, *Elizabeth and Leicester* (London: Victor Gollancz, 1961), p. 153.

15 John Foxe, *Acts and Monuments*, vol. viii, p. 601, available online.

16 *Elizabeth I: Collected Works*, p. 326, Queen Elizabeth's Armada speech to the troops at Tilbury, August 9, 1588.

17 First published posthumously 1570.

18 Jenkins, Elizabeth, *Elizabeth and Leicester* (London: Victor Gollancz, 1961), p. 48.

19 Henry Harington, ed., *Nugæ Antiquæ*, 2 vol. (1769-75), 2, 216, quoted in 'Harington's Gossip' by Jason Scott-Warren in *The Myth of Elizabeth*, eds. Susan Doran and Thomas S. Freeman (Basingstoke: Palgrave Macmillan, 2003), p. 222.

20 *AYLI*, 4.1.24-6.

21 Interview with Juliet Stevenson, 26 March 2015.

22 Marc Norman and Tom Stoppard, *Shakespeare in Love* (London: Faber and Faber, 1999), p. 148.

23 *AYLI*, 1.3.114-117.

24 William Camden, *Annals of Elizabeth*, first printed in Latin 1615, first English edition 1627.

25 Elizabeth Jenkins, *Elizabeth and Leicester* (London: Victor Gollancz, 1961), p. 355.

26 *Elizabeth I: Collected Works*, pp. 325-6, Queen Elizabeth's Armada speech to the troops at Tilbury, August 9, 1588.

27 *Henry V*, 4.3.40-51.

28 *Elizabeth I: Collected Works*, p. 326, Queen Elizabeth's Armada speech to the troops at Tilbury, August 9, 1588.

29 Elizabeth Jenkins, *Elizabeth and Leicester* (London: Victor Gollancz, 1961), p. 48.

30 *Elizabeth I: Collected Works*, p. 342, Elizabeth's Golden speech to her last parliament, November 30, 1601.

31 Ben Jonson, 'Conversations with Drummond', 470, in *The Complete Poems*, ed. George Parfitt, rev. ed., (Harmondsworth: Penguin, 1988), pp. 459-80, and J.E. Neale, *Queen Elizabeth* (London: Cape, 1934), p. 393.

32 Modern audiences heard Ellen Terry's lectures, reincarnated by Eileen Atkins, first at Chichester, and then at the Sam Wanamaker Theatre in 2014/16.

33 Terry, Ellen, *Four Lectures on Shakespeare* (London: Martin Hopkinson Ltd.,1932), p. 81.

34 Ibid.

35 From the title page of *Love's Labour's Lost* printed in 1598.

36 *Elizabeth I: Collected Works*, p. 59, Queen Elizabeth's first speech before Parliament, February 10, 1559.

37 Ibid., p. 58.

38 *A Midsummer Night's Dream*, II, i, 155-164.

39 *Elizabeth I: Collected Works*, p. 72, Queen Elizabeth's answer to the Commons' Petition that she marry, January 28, 1563 (preferring the slightly alternative version.)

40 Elizabeth Jenkins, *Elizabeth and Leicester* (London: Victor Gollancz, 1961), p, 122.

41 Ibid., p. 90.

42 Ibid., p. 198.

43 Ibid., p. 141.

44 'The ashes and the phoenix' by Mark Bostridge, *TLS*, 8 January 2010, p. 13.

45 Susan Doran, *Elizabeth I and her Circle* (Oxford: Oxford University Press, 2015), p. 21.

46 Henry Harington, ed., *Nugæ Antiquæ*, 2 vols (1769-75), 2, 216, quoted in 'Harington's Gossip' by Jason Scott-Warren in *The Myth of Elizabeth*, eds. Susan Doran and Thomas S. Freeman (Basingstoke: Palgrave Macmillan, 2003), p. 222.

47 Elizabeth Jenkins, *Elizabeth and Leicester* (London: Victor Gollancz, 1961), p. 370.

48 'Popular Perceptions of Elizabeth' by Sara Mendelson in *Elizabeth I: Always Her Own Free Woman*, eds. Carole Levin, Jo Eldridge Carney and Debra Barrett-Graves (Aldershot: Ashgate, 2003), chapter 11, p. 193.

49 *Elizabeth I: Collected Works*, pp. 337, 340, Elizabeth's Golden Speech, November 30, 1601.

50 Ibid., p. 189, Queen Elizabeth's first reply to the Parliamentary Petitions urging the execution of Mary, Queen of Scots, November 12, 1586.

51 *The Robben Island Shakespeare* was displayed at the British Museum during the exhibition *Shakespeare: Staging the World* in 2012. The South African *Collected Works of Shakespeare* was sent by his wife Theresa to Sonny Venkatrathnam when he was imprisoned. Now known as the *Robben Island Shakespeare*, he called it 'the Bible by Shakespeare', disguised it as a Hindu holy book and passed it round the political prisoners, including Nelson Mandela. They underlined and dated specific quotations that spoke specially to each individual. Duke Senior's speech from *As You Like It* is signed and dated: Mobbs Gqirana 27/3/75.

52 *AYLI*, 2.1.20, 12-17.

53 *Elizabeth I: Collected Works*, pp. 337-9. Several versions of the Golden Speech survive. This one is from the Commons journal of Hayward Townshend, who was one of the 141 men present on 30 November 1601.

54 Ian Donaldson, *Ben Jonson: A Life* (Oxford: Oxford University Press, 2011), p. 466, n. 20, suggests *AYLI* may have been performed at court early in 1599, based on discussion in Appendix 3 of *AYLI*, The Arden Shakespeare, ed. Juliet Dusinberre, 2006. See also 'Pancakes and a Date for "As You Like It"' by Juliet Dusinberre, *Shakespeare Quarterly*, Vol. 54, No. 4 (Winter, 2003), pp. 371-405. Folger Shakespeare Library in association with George Washington University.

55 *King Henry VIII*, 5.4.17-19, 30-1, 33-7, 56-7, 60-2.

56 *AYLI*, 4.1.120-29.

57 From a poem by George Peele, 1595, quoted by Frances A. Yates, *Astraea* (London: Pimlico, 1993) p. 62. First published (London: Routledge & Kegan Paul, 1975).

58 Elizabeth's response to Philip of Spain's religious persecution in the Netherlands, 1586, via the Spanish Ambassador, 1586, Elizabeth Jenkins, *Elizabeth and Leicester* (London: Victor Gollancz, 1961) p. 311.

59 *Sayings of Queen Elizabeth* ed. Frederick Chamberlin (London: John Lane The Bodley Head; New York: Dodd, Mead and Company, 1923), p. 4. Letter to Edward VI, c. 1550.

60 *AYLI*, 2.7.121-27.

61 Elizabeth Jenkins, *Elizabeth and Leicester* (London: Victor Gollancz, 1961), p. 48.

62 Probably composed c. 1570.

63 *Antony and Cleopatra*, 3.7.16-18.

64 *Rosa Electa* (The Chosen Rose) by William Rogers probably after Isaac Oliver, c. 1590-95, Roy Strong, *Gloriana: The Portraits of Queen Elizabeth I* (London: Thames and Hudson, 1987), p. 145.

ACT FOUR
Like the Bay of Portugal – Rosalind's Love Life

1   Camille Paglia, *Sexual Personae: Art and Decadence from Nefertiti to Emily Dickinson* (New Haven: Yale University Press, 1990), Chapter 7, 'Shakespeare and Dionysus: *As You Like It* and *Antony and Cleopatra*'.

2   James Shapiro, *1599: A Year in the Life of William Shakespeare* (London: Faber and Faber, 2005).

3   *AYLI*, 3.5.82-3.

4   Pippa Nixon in discussion on RSC website 25 September 2013 and uploaded to YouTube.

5   *Romeo and Juliet*, 1.4.25-6.

6   Ibid., 1.5.43-6, 51-2.

7   Ibid. 2.2.142-8.

8   Interview with Juliet Rylance at the Old Vic, 11 August 2010.

9   *AYLI*, 2.4. 43-52.

10 Anna Jameson, *Shakespeare's Heroines* first published 1832, this ed. (London: George Bell & Sons, 1898), p. 10.

11 Rebecca West, *The Court and the Castle* (London: Macmillan, 1958), p. 135, originally delivered as the Terry Lectures at Yale University.

12 Anthony Trollope, *The Duke's Children* in a newly restored version from the original manuscript (London: The Folio Society, 2015).

13 Anthony Trollope, *The Duke's Children*, first published 1880, Chapter 5.

14 Interview with Jean Hewison, 11 January 2015.

15 Carole Woddis ed., *Sheer Bloody Magic: Conversations with Actresses* (London: Virago, 1991), p. 99.

16 Walter Pater, *Appreciations*, first published 1889, this ed. (London: Macmillan, 1924), p. 170.

17 Open University video 1995 to accompany A 210 'Approaching Literature'.

18 Harold Bloom, *Shakespeare: the invention of the human* (London: Fourth Estate, 1999), p. 204.

19 *AYLI*, 4.1.195-6.

20 Ibid., 3.2.191-2.

21 Carole Woddis ed., *Sheer Bloody Magic: Conversations with Actresses* (London: Virago, 1991), p. 136.

22 Interview with Juliet Rylance at the Old Vic, 11 August 2010.

23   *AYLI*, 2.7.136-9.

24   Ian Donaldson, *Ben Jonson: A Life* (Oxford: Oxford University Press, 2011), p. 155.

25   'Shine here to us, and thou art everywhere;/ This bed thy centre is, these walls, thy sphere.' From Donne's poem 'The Sunne Rising'.

26   *AYLI*, 3.2.384-8.

27   Rebecca Hall on Rosalind in *Shakespeare on Stage* ed. Julian Curry (London: Nick Hern Books, 2010), pp. 72-3.

28   W.H. Auden, *Lectures on Shakespeare*, ed. Arthur Kirsch (Princeton: Princeton University Press, 2000), pp. 138 and 144.

29   'Shakespeare's Women' presented by Joely Richardson, BBC 4, 19 June 2012.

30   Bernard Levin's review of *AYLI* in *Royal Shakespeare Theatre Company in Stratford-on-Avon and London 1960-63* ed. John Goodwin (London: Max Reinhardt, 1964)

31   *AYLI*, 3.4.19-29.

32   Ibid., 1.1.109-113.

33   Ibid., 1.3. 85-6.

34   Ibid., 1.3.130-34.

35   Ibid., 2.4.93-4.

36   From the dedication to Browning's last published work, *Asolando*, 1889. Robert Browning, *The Poems* ed. John Pettigrew, 2 vol. (Harmondsworth: Penguin, 1981), 2, p. 874.

37   *AYLI*, 2.7.22-8.

38   Ibid., 2.7.140-44.

39   Ibid., 3.2.291–322.

40   Unsigned reviews in the *Sunday Pictorial* (15 Nov. 1936), and in *The Times* (12 Feb. 1937) from the Casebook Series *Much Ado about Nothing* and *As You Like It* ed. John Russell Brown (London and Basingstoke: Macmillan, 1979), pp. 234-5.

41   *AYLI*, 3.2.404–6.

42   Ibid., 4.1.57-84.

43   *The Merchant of Venice*, 3.2.70-1.

44   *AYLI*, 4.1.128-139.

45   Interview with Juliet Stevenson, 26 March 2015.

46   Interview with Adrian Lester by e-mail, 9 September 2015.

47   *AYLI*, 2.5.1-5, 33-9.

48   Ibid., 2.7.175-191.

49   Ibid., 5.3.16-37.

50   ODNB article on Thomas Morley by Michael W. Foster.

51   David Lindley, *Shakespeare and Music* (London: Arden Shakespeare, 2006), p. 198.

52   *AYLI*, 5.4.18-25.

53   Thomas Lodge, *Rosalynde*, first published 1590, this edition ed. W.W. Greg, (London: Humphrey Milford, O.U.P., 1931), p. 158.

54 *AYLI*, 5.4.116-124.

55 George Bernard Shaw, *The Saturday Review*, 5 December 1896 in *Shaw on Shakespeare* ed. Edwin Wilson (London: Cassell, 1961), p. 27.

56 Interview with Michelle Terry at Shakespeare's Globe, 19 June 2015.

57 *AYLI*, 5.4.139–144.

ACT FIVE SCENE ONE
Celia – Juno's Swan

1   *AYLI*, 1.2.265.

2   Juliet Stevenson discussing playing Rosalind on Front Row, BBC Radio 4, 25 May 2015.

3   Juliet Stevenson in *Clamorous Voices* ed. Carol Rutter (London: The Women's Press, 1988) p. 97.

4   Though Shakespeare's lads, like his girls, sometimes enjoy perfect teenage amity. Before their friendship is shattered by sexual jealousy, Polixenes and Leontes look back on a golden youth spent together.

    We were as twinned lambs that did frisk i' th' sun,
    And bleat the one at th' other. What we changed
    Was innocence for innocence; we knew not
    The doctrine of ill-doing, nor dreamed
    That any did. *The Winter's Tale*, 1.2.66-70.

5   *The George Eliot Letters* ed. Gordon S. Haight 9 vol. (London: Oxford University Press, 1954-78), George Eliot to Maria Lewis, 2[8] May 1840, 1, p. 51.

6   *AYLI*, 1.1.102-107.

7   *A Midsummer Night's Dream*, 3.2.203-212.

8   *Much Ado*, 3.1.49-56.

9   *AYLI*, 1.2.2-7.

10 Ibid., 1.2.8-14.

11 Fiona Shaw and Adam Phillips in a discussion on 'Acting, Self-fashioning and the Formation of Identity' chaired by Lisa Appignanesi at the National Portrait Gallery, London, 21 July 2011.

12 Fiona Shaw quoted by Carol Rutter, *Clamorous Voices: Shakespeare's Women Today* (London: The Women's Press, 1988), p. 101.

13 *AYLI*, 1.2.17-23.

14 Ibid., 1.2.31-46.

15 Ibid., 1.2.102.

16 Ibid., 1.2.70-72.

17 Ibid., 1.2.165-6, 170-1.

18 Ibid., 1.2.202-3, 205-6.

19 Ibid., 1.2.228-234.

20 Ibid., 1.2.242, 244.

21 Ibid., 1.3.24-32.

22 Ibid., 1.3.68-73.

23 'The Silver Swan' was first published in 1612 in Gibbons' *First Set of Madrigals and Motets of 5 parts*. I suggest it could have been circulating before that.

24 *AYLI*, 1.3.77-9.

25 Ibid., 1.3.82-3.

26 Ibid., 1.3.86-107.

27 Ibid., 1.3.108-111.

28 Ibid., 1.3.111-113.

29 Ibid., 1.3.124-5.

30 Ibid., 1.3.129-135.

31 Interview with Janet Suzman, 1 October 2014.

32 *AYLI*, 3.2.186-88.

33 Ibid., 3.2.225-28, 234.

34 Ibid., 3.4.1-3.

35 Ibid., 3.4.25-27.

36 Ibid., 3.4.36-41.

37 Ibid., 4.1.189-92.

38 Ibid., 4.3.65-9.

39 Ibid., 5.2.28-31, 38-40.

40 John Forster, *The Life of Charles Dickens* 3 vol. (London: Chapman and Hall, 1874), 3. Chap. 5, p.109, 'Residence in Paris 1855-56.'

41 Michael Coveney, *Maggie Smith: A Biography* (London: Weidenfeld & Nicolson, 2015), pp. 55-6.

42 Mary Cowden Clarke, *The Girlhood of Shakespeare's Heroines: a series of fifteen tales*, 3 vol. first published 1850-52, this ed. (London: Bickers and Son, 1864), 'Rosalind and Celia; The Friends' in vol 2.

ACT FIVE SCENE TWO
Orlando — So Much in the Heart of the World

1 *Hamlet*, 3.3.37-8, 53-4.

2 *AYLI*, 1.1.62-70.

3 Ibid., 1.2.178-184.

4 Rebecca Hall on Rosalind, from *Shakespeare on Stage* ed. Julian Curry (London: Nick Hern Books, 2010).

5 Thomas Lodge, *Rosalynde*, first published 1590, this edition ed. W.W. Greg (London: Humphrey Milford, O.U.P., 1931, 2nd ed.), p. 24.

6 Interview with Janet Suzman, 1 October 2014.

7   *AYLI*, 3.4.4-10.

8   Virginia Woolf, *Orlando*, first published 1928, this ed. (Harmondsworth: Penguin Books, 1963), p. 10.

9   Ibid, p. 16.

10 *AYLI*, 1.2.204.

11 Ibid., 1.1.156–160.

12 Ibid., 2.3.3-4.

13 Interview with Blanche McIntyre at Shakespeare's Globe, 26 June 2015.

14 Interview with Janet Suzman, 1 October 2014.

15 *AYLI*, 1.2.243-4.

16 Ibid., 1.2.246-8.

17 Michael Boyd in conversation with Dominic Cooke in *The RSC Shakespeare: As You Like It* eds. Jonathan Bate and Eric Rasmussen (Basingstoke: Macmillan, 2010), p. 153.

18 *Shaw on Shakespeare*, ed. Edwin Wilson (London: Cassell, 1961), p. 32.

19 *AYLI*, 2.6.5-8, 9-18.

20 Ibid., 2.7.107-120.

21 *Illustrated London News*, 9 August 1884.

22 *Dramatic Review*, 6 June 1885.

23 Sarah Bernhardt, untitled article, January 21, 1923. Apparently Bernhardt made this comment after appearing as Hamlet on 20 May 1899. Bernhardt, Sarah. Unmarked clipping, stamped January 21, 1923. Harvard Theatre Collection: 'Hamlet—Productions—Women as Hamlet (1 of 2)." Cited by Woo, Celestine (2007) 'Sarah Siddons's Performances as Hamlet: Breaching the Breeches Part', European Romantic Review, 18: 5, 573-95, p. 582.

24 Stephen Orgel, 'Afterword' in *Shakespeare, Memory and Performance*, ed. Peter Holland (Cambridge: Cambridge University Press, 2006), pp. 347-8.

25 Michael Boyd in conversation with Dominic Cooke in *The RSC Shakespeare: As You Like It* eds. Jonathan Bate and Eric Rasmussen (Basingstoke: Macmillan, 2010), p. 153.

26 Interview with Ronald Pickup, 16 October 2015.

27 Alex Waldmann on Orlando for the RSC AYLI 2013, published on RSC website on 25 September 2013 and uploaded to YouTube.

28 *AYLI*, 3.2.1-10.

29 *Hamlet*, 2.2.115-18.

30 *AYLI*, 3.2.138-51.

31 Pippa Nixon on Rosalind for the RSC AYLI 2013, published on RSC website on 25 September 2013 and uploaded to YouTube.

32 *AYLI*, 3.2.250-60.

33 Interview with Juliet Rylance at the Old Vic, 11 August 2010.

34 Michael Boyd in conversation with Dominic Cooke in *The RSC Shakespeare: As You Like It* eds. Jonathan Bate and Eric Rasmussen (Basingstoke: Macmillan, 2010), p. 157.

35 Interview with Ronald Pickup, 16 October 2015 and *AYLI*, 5.2.25-7.

36 Rebecca Hall on Rosalind, *Shakespeare on Stage* ed. Julian Curry (London: Nick Hern Books, 2010).

37 Laura Hitchcock, *Curtain Up*, The Internet Theater Magazine, 13 February 2005.

38 Théophile Gautier, *Mademoiselle de Maupin*, transl. and ed. Helen Constantine, (London: Penguin Books, 2005), pp. 215-16.

39 Vanessa Redgrave, *An Autobiography* (London: Hutchinson, 1991), p. 93.

40 J.C. Trewin, *Birmingham Post*, 5 July 1961.

41 J.W. Lambert, *Sunday Times*, 9 July 1961.

42 Michael Billington, *The Modern Actor* (London: Hamish Hamilton, 1973), p. 235.

43 Vanessa Redgrave, *An Autobiography* (London: Hutchinson, 1991), p. 95.

44 Don Chapman, *Oxford Mail*, 22 May 1968.

45 Interview with Janet Suzman, 1 October 2014.

46 From the Jeremy Brett Archive online.

47 Hilary Spurling, *The Spectator*, 12 October 1967.

48 John Barber, *Daily Telegraph*, 9 September 1977.

49 B.A. Young, *Financial Times*, 8 September 1977.

50 Michael Ratcliffe, *Observer*, 24 April 1985.

51 Interview with Juliet Rylance at the Old Vic, 11 August 2010.

52 Michael Boyd in conversation with Dominic Cooke in *The RSC Shakespeare: As You Like It* eds. Jonathan Bate and Eric Rasmussen (Basingstoke: Macmillan, 2010), p. 153-4.

53 'The Education of Orlando' by Marjorie Garber in *Comedy from Shakespeare to Sheridan*, eds. A.R. Braunmuller and J.C. Bulman (Newark: University of Delaware Press, London and Toronto: Associated University Press, 1986), pp. 102-112.

EPILOGUE
As You Like It

1   *Players of Shakespeare 3: Further Essays in Shakespearian performance by players with the Royal Shakespeare Company*, eds. Russell Jackson and Robert Smallwood (Cambridge: Cambridge University Press, 1993), Sophie Thompson on 'Rosalind (and Celia) in *As You Like It*,' pp. 77–86, p. 85.

2   Interview with Sally Scott, 10 October 2014.

3   The other occasions may include Falstaff to Prince Hal, 'Play out the play! I have much to say in the behalf of that Falstaff' and Hamlet directing the Player King, 'Suit the action to the word, the word to the action.'

4   Galatea's Epilogue from *Galatea* by John Lyly, 1588, this ed. Leah Scragg (Manchester: Manchester University Press, 2012) p. 115.

5   Juliet Stevenson on 'Playing Rosalind', *Front Row*, BBC Radio 4, 25 May 2015.

6   Feature on Kenneth Branagh's film of *As You Like It* in the *Saturday Telegraph Magazine*, 18 February 2006.

7 Peg Woffington, 1720–1760, lived on for another 3 years but never acted again. This account from Tate Wilkinson, *Memoirs*, 1790, cited in Gamini Salgado, *Eyewitnesses of Shakespeare: First Hand Accounts of Performances 1590-1890* (Sussex University Press, 1975), p.162 and Edward Robins, *Twelve Great Actresses* (London: GP. Putnam's Sons, 1900), p. 112.

8 *All's Well That Ends Well*, 5.3. Epilogue, 1-6.

9 *AYLI*, 2.7.138.

10 Ibid., 2.7.140-44.

11 *The New Oxford Book of Sixteenth Century Verse* ed. Emrys Jones (Oxford: Oxford University Press, 1991), p. 390.

12 'Who else is there?' by Harold Bloom, Forward to *Shakespeare and Me: 38 Great Writers, Actors, and Directors on What the Bard means to them – and us*, ed. Susannah Carson (London: Oneworld, 2014).

13 *Twelfth Night*, 5.1.388-407.

14 Thomas Dekker and Thomas Middleton, *The Roaring Girl* c. 1607-10, first printed 1611, this text for the 2014 RSC production, eds. Jo Davies and Pippa Hall, (London: Nick Hern Books, 2014) pp. 122-3.

15 Helena Faucit, Lady Martin, *On Some of Shakespeare's Female Characters* (Edinburgh and London: William Blackwood and Sons, 1885), pp. 358-9.

16 Interview with Ronald Pickup, 16 October 2015.

17 Interview with Sally Scott, 10 October 2014.

18 Michael Coveney, *Maggie Smith: a bright particular star* (London: Gollancz, 1992) p. 181.

19 Interview with Juliet Stevenson, 26 March 2015.

20 Interview by e-mail with Adrian Lester, 9 September 2015.

21 Interview with Juliet Rylance, 11 August 2010.

22 *The Tempest*, 4.1.148-158.

23 *The Tempest*, 5.1. Epilogue, 1-20.

24 Pippa Nixon's introduction to BBC Radio 3's production of *As You Like It*, 1 March 2015, in which she played Rosalind.

A Woman For All Time – Rosalind's Daughters

1   Rosalind as Ganymede doesn't always have short hair. Katy Stephens played her with a long male ponytail in 2010 for the RSC.

2   Interview with Sally Scott, 10 October 2104.

3   Interview with Blanche McIntyre, 26 June 2015.

4   Interview with Juliet Stevenson, 26 March 2015.

5   Dorothea cross-dresses in Cervantes' *Don Quixote* in 1605.

6   Or 'Methinks a woman's lip tastes well in a doublet' quoted by Stephen Orgel, *Impersonations: The Performance of gender in Shakespeare's England* (Cambridge: Cambridge University Press, 1996), p. 70.

7   Thomas Dekker and Thomas Middleton, *The Roaring Girl*, 1611, from the Prompt Book version for the RSC production of 2014, eds. Jo Davies and Pippa Hill (London: Nick Hern Books, 2014), Act 2, Scene 2, p. 41; Act 5, Scene 1, p. 109; Act 4, Scene 1, p. 77, pp. 122-3.

8   *The Plays of Nathan Field* ed. William Peery, (Austin: University of Texas Press, 1950), Act 1, Scene1, p. 162, spelling updated.

9   Quoted by Michael Caines in 'By our squabbles' reviewing Felicity Nussbaum, *Rival Queens* (Philadelphia, Pa.; Oxford: University of Pennsylvania Press, 2010) in *The Times Literary Supplement*, 18 February 2011.

10 Anna Jameson, *Shakespeare's Heroines* first published 1832, this ed. (London: George Bell & Sons, 1898), on Rosalind pp. 74-80.

11 Jane Austen, *Pride and Prejudice* first published 1813, this ed. (London: Oxford University Press, 1959), p. 12, p. 57.

12 Charlotte Brontë, *Jane Eyre*, first published 1847, this edition (London: Vintage, 2007), p. 133.

13 George Sand, *Story of my life* transl. Dan Hofstadter (London: The Folio Society, 1984), p. 214. First published as *Histoire de ma vie*, Paris, 1854.

14 Rebecca Mead, *The Road to Middlemarch: My Life with George Eliot* (London: Granta Books, 2014), p. 178, quoting Blanche Colton Williams, *George Eliot: A Biography* (New York, Macmillan, 1936).

15 Ibid., pp. 90-1.

16 George Eliot, *Daniel Deronda*, first published 1876, this ed. (Harmondsworth: Penguin, 1995), p. 7.

17 Ibid. p. 9.

18 Ibid. pp. 150-1.

19 Cush Jumbo in 'All Dolled Up' by Susanna Rustin, *The Guardian*, 10 August 2013.

20 'Pensées de Femme', *Lady's Pictorial*, 11 January 1896, p. 53. Many thanks to Dr Valerie Fehlbaum, author of *Ella Hepworth Dixon: The Story of a Modern Woman* (Aldershot: Ashgate, 2005) for leading me to these quotations.

21 *The Idler* 6, August 1894, p. 209.

22 *Lady's Pictorial*, 5 October, 1895, p. 524.

23 Oscar Wilde, *The Picture of Dorian Gray* first published 1890, this edition (London: World's Classics, 1994), p. 75.

24 Henry James, 'The Papers' first published in *The Better Sort*, 1903, this edition Henry James: *Collected Stories* vol 2, (London, Everyman's Library, 1999), pp. 785-883.

25 Ford Madox Ford, *Parade's End* first published 1924-28, this ed. (London: Penguin, 1988), p. 629.

26 *AYLI*, 4.1.138-9.

27 Naomi Frederick from www.globe-education.org/Adoptanactor

28 *The Letters of Virginia Woolf*, ed. Nigel Nicolson and Joanne Trautmann, 6 vol. (London: The Hogarth Press, 1975-80) 3, *A Change of Perspective*, 9 October 1927, p. 429.

29 Tilda Swinton, *The Telegraph*, 9 January 2012, and from her Introduction to *Orlando* by Virginia Woolf, (Edinburgh: Canongate, 2012).

30 *Time* Vol XXIX No 15.

31 Virginia Woolf, *A Room of One's Own* first published 1929, this ed. (London: Grafton Books/Collins, 1988) p. 103.

32 Ibid., pp. 101, 105.

33 Ibid., p. 99.

34 Ibid., p. 92.

35 Coleridge: *Table Talk*, 1 September 1832

36 Virginia Woolf, *A Room of One's Own*, 1929, this ed. (London: Grafton Books/Collins, 1988) p. 94.

37 Ibid., p. 98

38 Isaac Bashevis Singer, 'Yentl the Yeshiva Boy' transl. Marion Magid and Elizabeth Pollet, *Collected Stories: Gimpel the Fool* to *The Letter Writer* ed. Ilan Stavans, (New York: The Library of America, 2004) pp. 439-463. Published in English in *Commentary*, September 1962, and in Yiddish as 'Yentl der yeshive-boher in *Di goldene keyt* 46 (1963). *Mayses fun hintern oyvn*. Tel Aviv: Farlag Y.L. Perets, 1971. (*Stories from Behind the Stove*).

39 Jeanette Winterson, *The Passion* (London: Bloomsbury, 1987) this edition Penguin 1988, p. 54, p. 61.

40 Ibid. p. 150.

41 Ibid. p. 144.

42 Pat Barker, *Life Class* (London: Hamish Hamilton, 2007) pp. 79, 88, 97, 99.

43 *The Tempest*, I. ii. 16-17.

44 Alan Cumming in *The Observer* Magazine, 1 July 2012.

45 Interview with Michelle Terry at Shakespeare's Globe, 19 June 2015.

FILMOGRAPHY

1908   The Kalem Company of New York produced the first silent film version of *As You Like It.*

1912   The Vitagraph Company of America made the next silent film of the play, starring Rose Coghlan, then aged sixty-one, as Rosalind.

1936   Though still in black and white, Paul Czinner made the first movie of *As You Like It* with sound, directing his wife Elisabeth Bergner as Rosalind. Advised by J.M. Barrie, edited by David Lean and with music by William Walton, the film also starred Laurence Olivier in his first on-screen Shakespearean role as Orlando.

1963   *As You Like It* was a BBC TV version of the Royal Shakespeare Company stage production of 1961-2, directed by Michael Elliott and starring Vanessa Redgrave as Rosalind.

1978   As part of the BBC TV series first conceived by Cedric Messina to film all Shakespeare's plays, Basil Coleman's film of *As You Like It* was shot on location at Glamis Castle in Scotland and cast Helen Mirren as Rosalind. It was first transmitted in the UK in 1978 and in the USA in 1979.

1992   Christine Edzard directed a colour video film of *As You Like It* released in the UK. Emma Croft played Rosalind in blue jeans and a bobble hat looking convincingly boyish.

1995   Videotape of the all-male Cheek by Jowl stage production of *As You Like It*, filmed at the Albery Theatre, 11 February 1995, lodged in the National Video Archive of Stage performances, Theatre Museum and Federation of Entertainment Unions.

2006   Kenneth Branagh directed his movie of *As You Like It* set in nineteenth-century Japan and filmed in the gardens of Wakehurst Place, Sussex, with an all-star cast. Alfred Molina was Touchstone, Janet McTeer Audrey, Brian Blessed played both Dukes, Richard Briers took the part of old Adam which Shakespeare himself may once have played, Kevin Kline was Jaques, Adrian Lester played Oliver de Boys, David Oyelowo his brother Orlando, and Romola Garai was Celia to the Rosalind of Bryce Dallas Howard.

2009   Shakespeare's Globe released a DVD of their Summer 2009 production, shot at the theatre on 6 and 8 October 2009, directed by Thea Sharrock with Naomi Frederick as Rosalind.

List of Illustrations

1. Vanessa Redgrave as Rosalind for the RSC, 1961-63. © Trinity Mirror / Mirrorpix / Alamy Stock Photo

2. *Mrs Siddons as Rosalind* by Joseph Wright of Derby, oil sketch on panel, 240 x 165 mm, c. 1778, Smallhythe Place, Kent, National Trust. © National Trust Images

3. *Ganymede with Zeus disguised as an eagle* by Bertel Thorvaldsen, marble, 93.3 x 118.3 cm, 1817, Thorvaldsen Museum, Copenhagen, A44.

4. *Valentine rescuing Silvia from Proteus* by William Holman Hunt, 1850-51, from Shakespeare's play *The Two Gentlemen of Verona*, oil on canvas, 100.2 x 133.4 cm, 1850-51, Birmingham Museums and Art Gallery. © Birmingham Museums Trust

5. Rebecca Hall as Rosalind at Theatre Royal Bath and in the USA, 2003. © Tristram Kenton/Lebrecht Music & Arts

6. Janet Suzman as Rosalind for the RSC, 1968. Reg Wilson © RSC

7. Sally Scott as Rosalind (left) with Kaisa Hammarlund as Celia/Aliena (right) at the Southwark Playhouse, 2014. © Robert Workman

8. Juliet Rylance as Rosalind with Christian Camargo as Orlando at The Old Vic, 2010. © Geraint Lewis

9. Adrian Lester (right) as Rosalind for Cheek by Jowl, 1991. © Haynes/Lebrecht Music & Arts

10. *The Mock Marriage of Orlando and Rosalind* (with Celia looking on) by Walter Deverell, from *As You Like It*, Act 4 Scene 1, oil on canvas, 608 x 506 mm, 1853, Birmingham Museums and Art Gallery. © Birmingham Museums Trust

11. Pippa Nixon as Rosalind for the RSC, 2013. Keith Pattison © RSC

12. Edith Evans as Rosalind at The Old Vic, 1936/7. © Lebrecht Music & Arts

13. Juliet Stevenson as Rosalind with Fiona Shaw as Celia for the RSC 1985. Joe Cocks Studio Collection © Shakespeare Birthplace Trust

14. Katharine Hepburn as Rosalind with William Prince as Orlando on Broadway 1950. © Archive Photos/Stringer / Moviepix / Getty Images

15. Laurence Olivier as Orlando in the 1936 film of *As You Like It.* © John Kobal Foundation / Moviepix / Getty Images

16. Ronald Pickup as Rosalind at The Old Vic, 1967. © Zoë Dominic

17. Helen Faucit (Lady Martin) in 1881, drawing by Annette Elias, from Sir Theodore Martin's Helena Faucit (Lady Martin) 1900. © University of Victoria Library

18. Dorothy Jordan as Rosalind by Sir William Beechey, oil on canvas, 762 x 634 mm, 1787, Private Collection.

19. Elisabeth Bergner as Rosalind in the 1936 film of *As You Like It.* © 'INTER-ALLIED / Ronald Grant Archive / Mary Evans'

20. Cush Jumbo as Rosalind at the Royal Exchange Theatre Manchester, 2012. © Jonathan Keenan Photography

21. *As You Like It* (triptych) by Arthur Hughes, oil on canvas, 71 x 99 cm, 1871-3, Walker Art Gallery, Liverpool, showing the right wing of the triptych, 71 x 46 cm, inscribed on the tree: 'Rosalind', and on a scroll on the left '[From the east to western] Ind, / [No] jewel is [like] Rosalind…'

Index

Note: Shakespearean characters (shown in **bold** type) are from *As You Like It* unless otherwise stated.

underlying fragility of
83
use of language by
20, 29, 49, 67–70,
82, 111–12, 93, 96,
165
'Rosalind', general use of
name 15–16
Rosalind (play by Barrie)
8–10
Rosaline (in *Love's Labour's
Lost*) 24–9, 58, 100
Rosaline (in *Romeo and
Juliet*) 24, 29, 112
roses, symbolism of 92,
109
Rossetti, Dante Gabriel
163, 186–7
Rossetti, William and
Lucy vii
Royal Shakespeare
Company (RSC)
28, 30, 51, 55, 58,
76–7, 81, 96, 112,
121, 129, 134, 156,
161, 168–9, 172,
184, 189
Rubens, Peter Paul 69
Rylance, Juliet 3, 69, 77,
113, 119, 165, 168,
182

Sackville-West, Vita 199
St Laurent, Yves 75
Sand, George 147–8, 197
Scott, Sally 60–1, 173,
180,   187–8,
196
Sears, Kim 187
(Duke) Senior 15–16,
22–4, 34, 59–60, 73,
86, 90, 94–5, 104,
107, 119, 122, 132,
145, 150–1, 158,
177, 183, 217–18
Sewell, Brian 75
sexual aspect of drama
65, 161
Shakespeare, Susanna 80
Shakespeare, William
as an actor 223
aspects of writing
viii, 57, 61,173, 177

life and times of 3,
67, 106
modern productions
of 41
studies of women
100
view of love 78,
152, 167
: *see also under
individual works and
characters*
Shakespeare in Love (film,
1998) 62, 97
Shaw, Fiona 118, 134,
137
Shaw, George Bernard
47, 131, 156–7
The Shepheardes Calender
15–16, 219
Siddons, Sarah 3, 52,
88, 159
Sidney, Mary 95
Sidney, Sir Philip 162,
219
Silverstone, Alicia 28
Silvius 13, 15–16, 21–2,
45–6, 52, 70–5, 83,
85, 89, 115, 122,
132, 144, 146, 167
Singer, Isaac Bashevis
201–2
Smith, Maggie 148, 181,
221–2
Sondheim, Stephen 204,
224
sonnets 162–3
Southampton, Earl of 72
Spanish Armada 95, 97
Spenser, Edmund 15,
90, 219
Spurling, Hilary 167
Stephen, Leslie 199
Stephens, Katy 156
Stevens, Dan 165
Stevenson, Juliet 96,
127, 134–5, 137,
143, 168, 174, 181,
188–9
Stoppard, Tom 62, 97
Stubbes, Philip 62
Stubbs, Imogen 44
Suchet, David 168
Sullivan, Arthur 25

sumptuary laws 61–2
Suzman, Janet 65, 70,
74, 117, 153, 155,
161, 167
Swinton, Tilda 105, 200
Syal, Meera 55–6

The Taming of the Shrew
53–4
Taymor, Julie 203
The Tempest 3, 13, 47,
119, 182–4, 203–4,
217–18
Tennyson, Lord 25
Terry, Ellen 3, 9, 52, 100,
166
Terry, Michelle 58,
131–2, 176,
204
theatre as a metaphor for
life   119, 177
Theocritus 16, 219
Thompson, Sophie 172
time, similes about 122–4
Touchstone 8, 16, 18,
66–7, 70, 80, 83–6,
115, 123, 130, 132,
138, 142–3, 148,
162, 189, 218–20,
223
Tree, Ellen 8, 88
Trollope, Anthony 116
Tudor rose 82, 109
Twelfth Night 29, 31,
42–7, 66, 112–13,
127, 178–9
Twelfth Night (film, 1996)
44
Twiggy 75, 187
Two Gentlemen of Verona
29–34,   44–5, 219

Under the Greenwood Tree
193–4

Viola (in *Twelfth Night*)
42–7, 66
Virgil 15–16, 219

Waldmann, Alex 81, 156,
161
Walter, Harriet 3, 51–2,
77